Boom and Bust Colorado

Boom and Bust Colorado
From the 1859 Gold Rush to the 2020 Pandemic

Thomas J. Noel and
William J. Hansen

TWODOT®

GUILFORD, CONNECTICUT
HELENA, MONTANA

TWODOT®

An imprint of Globe Pequot, the trade division of
The Rowman & Littlefield Publishing Group, Inc.
4501 Forbes Blvd., Ste. 200
Lanham, MD 20706
TwoDotBooks.com

Distributed by NATIONAL BOOK NETWORK

British Library Cataloguing in Publication Information available

Library of Congress Cataloging-in-Publication Data

Names: Noel, Thomas J. (Thomas Jacob) author. | Hansen, William J., author.
Title: Boom and bust Colorado : from the 1859 gold rush to the 2020
  pandemic / Thomas J. Noel and William J. Hansen.
Description: Guilford, Connecticut : TwoDot, 2021. | Includes
  bibliographical references and index. | Summary: "A history of Colorado
  through the lens of its uniquely mythic economy, from boom to boom and
  into the future"— Provided by publisher.
Identifiers: LCCN 2021017530 (print) | LCCN 2021017531 (ebook) | ISBN
  9781493040933 (paperback) | ISBN 9781493040940 (epub)
Subjects: LCSH: Colorado--Economic conditions. | Colorado—Social
  conditions. | Colorado—History.
Classification: LCC HC107.C7 N64 2021 (print) | LCC HC107.C7 (ebook) |
  DDC 330.9788—dc23
LC record available at https://lccn.loc.gov/2021017530
LC ebook record available at https://lccn.loc.gov/2021017531

♾™ The paper used in this publication meets the minimum requirements of American National
Standard for Information Sciences—Permanence of Paper for Printed Library Materials, ANSI/
NISO Z39.48-1992.

Contents

Acknowledgments vi
Introduction vii

CHAPTER ONE: Gold Rush 1
CHAPTER TWO: Silver Boom. 24
CHAPTER THREE: The Panic of 1893. 45
CHAPTER FOUR: Booming Populism, Suffrage, and Women's
    Achievements 55
CHAPTER FIVE: Economic Diversity: Ranching, Agriculture, and
    Manufacturing. 66
CHAPTER SIX: The Gilded Age Rush to Respectability
    and the 1918 Flu Pandemic 82
CHAPTER SEVEN: Boom and Bust Gambling 101
CHAPTER EIGHT: Transportation: From Stagecoaches
    to the Space Age. 119
CHAPTER NINE: Touring the Highest State 139
CHAPTER TEN: The Beeriest State 161
CHAPTER ELEVEN: Rocky Mountain High 182
CHAPTER TWELVE: Colorado's 2020 COVID-19 Bust:
    History Repeated 205

Sources 233
Index 235
About the Authors 251

ACKNOWLEDGMENTS

THE DENVER PUBLIC LIBRARY WESTERN HISTORY & GENEALOGY DEPART-ment is a researcher's heaven. At DPL Jim Kroll, Brian Trembath, James Rogers, Roger Dudley, and the staff have been wonderful resources, as has DPL's incredibly fast and knowledgeable photo librarian, Coi Drummond Gehrig. A tip of the hat as well to History Colorado's Hart Research Center for all they do. Thanks to Moya Hansen of the Black American West Museum, Dave Thomas of the Gilpin County Historical Society, and Lee Malloy, cofounder of Denver's International Church of Cannabis.

This project could also not have been completed without the assistance of the many people we encountered in the research libraries as well as brew-pubs, casinos, pot shops, and tourist destinations who willingly answered our often-naïve inquiries. Some of their stories can now be told and are included in the text. Mike and Deb Kupecz, Jeremiah Moore, Jay Homstad, Kaleigh Nitz, Neal Levin, T. J. Trump, Kathleen Barlow, Bill Bessessen, Steve Leonard, Vi Noel, David Sikora of Twenty-Twenty Design, and Amy Zimmer have been most helpful. At Globe Pequot Press, Katherine O'Dell, Erin Turner, Sarah Parke, and Meredith Dias have been patient and most helpful with their crackerjack editing.

Tom "Dr. Colorado" Noel and William J. Hansen, Esq.

INTRODUCTION

I wonder, sometimes, whether men and women in fact are capable of learning from history, . . . whether we progress from one stage to the next in an upward course or whether we just ride the cycles of boom and bust, . . . ascent and decline.

—FORMER PRESIDENT BARACK OBAMA

COLORADO HAS WITHSTOOD MANY BOOMS AND BUSTS, RISES AND FALLS, expansions and contractions but generally in an upward trajectory, fueled by Western optimism and resilience, innovation and diversification, and progressive and ever-evolving social values. The 2020 COVID-19 bust has tested that upward trajectory. As President Harry S. Truman noted, "The only thing new is the history we don't know." The 2020 bust was not unprecedented, just seldom remembered. The 1918 "Spanish Flu" pandemic hit Colorado badly and, in many ways, followed a similar pattern as the 2020 pandemic. Whether today's Colorado has truly learned from history is for future historians to evaluate.

The initial 1859 gold rush led to what would quickly become Colorado Territory in 1861, followed by statehood in 1876. The mineral bonanza began Colorado's roller-coaster ride of ups (booms) and downs (busts) in gold, silver, ranching, farming, manufacturing, tourism, culture, and, more recently, gambling, beer, and marijuana. The sudden social, cultural, and economic upheaval of the 2020 COVID-19 pandemic changed everything. The Colorado economy crashed, the worst collapse since the Great Depression. Boom times descended to doom and gloom. This book is a topical exploration of how those ups and downs continue to shape the state's history. A comprehensive history of Colorado is beyond this book. Many booms and busts overlap eras, requiring a retracing of their origins. The final chapter addresses how the 2020 COVID-19 pandemic affected many of Colorado's historic industries.

Colorado's vast plains, western canyonlands, and high, rugged Rocky Mountains have been the constant settings shaping the state's economic growth. Colorado's Rocky Mountains were initially an impenetrable barrier.

Civilization stacked up at the edge of the Front Range until trails turned to rails and the mountains' resources could be tapped. Colorado was constantly bypassed by Wyoming, where the early pioneer trails crossed its gentler passes. Railroads, interstate highways, and even aviation routes initially circumvented Colorado's Rockies, the highest on the continent. But the grandeur of the scenic Colorado Rockies also lured early tourists delighted to find the "Switzerland of America."

Many also came to Colorado "chasing the cure" for tuberculosis, which long ravaged the nation. Many stayed, feeling cured by the fresh air, sun, and high, dry Colorado climate. Colorado became the "World's Sanitarium," forming the foundation of a booming health industry. With improved transportation breaching the Rockies during the era of automobiles, tourism boomed. Thanks to the winter sports industry, tourism became a four-season moneymaker.

Colorado had long been rumored to hold vast riches of gold and silver. A few flakes of real gold discovered in 1858, fueled by both hype and unbridled hope, launched the Colorado gold rush of 1859. With the frenzied cry of "Pikes Peak or Bust," an estimated 100,000 argonauts trekked across the vast plains to the Colorado diggings at the confluence of Cherry Creek and the South Platte River, where Denver sprouted. When gold could not be scooped up by the panful in the river and creek bottoms, most returned home dejected and busted. It was all a hoax, they claimed. The more experienced and intrepid gold seekers scrambled over the tributaries of the South Platte and Arkansas Rivers to eventually discover the mother lodes in the rugged Rocky Mountains.

Soon after, silver was found hidden among the mountains and, as the initial gold boom waned in the late 1870s, a silver boom began. Silver soon transcended gold and became Colorado's leading industry. Unfortunately, the silver rush was largely buoyed by national politics and subsidies where gold and silver were both the bases of the national wealth standards. When money policy changed with the repeal of the Silver Purchase Act in 1893, the silver industry crashed. The resulting Panic of 1893 affected Colorado worse than any other state due to its overreliance on the single industry of silver mining.

But bust times brought a rise in Populist politics and sweeping social reactions, the most prominent being Colorado's adoption of women's suffrage. Colorado was the first state in the Union where men voting only on that issue approved women's right to vote. Women were empowered to enter the workforce, establish charities and social clubs, and take on some of the abuses wrought on the state during the wild and woolly era of mineral extraction. A boom in social reforms followed, including the rise of labor unions, improved living standards, and the adoption of Prohibition. Gambling and drug abuse were driven underground. The 1893 bust also led Coloradans to realize that economic diversification was essential for survival and growth. Ranching, farming, and industry grew.

Flush times and the newly rich and powerful elite had also created a Gilded Age in Colorado where status was everything. Big business flourished, fueled by the largest years of immigration in the nation. Class stratification created a gross disparity of wealth. While the rich reveled in their gilded monuments of prosperity, the masses largely lived in poverty. Some immigrants were welcomed, while others were marginalized. This period demonstrates that what can seem a boom for some was, at the same time, a bust for others. The Gilded Age also brought a rush to respectability as Colorado tried to emerge from its Wild West origins, and Denver sought to cast off its image as a western mining and smelting center and cow town to become the sophisticated and cultured hub of the Rocky Mountain West.

The progressive populism of the early twentieth century saw a period of recovery from the Panic of 1893. Colorado saw boom times in agriculture and industry leading up to the First World War, only to be busted by the 1918 "Spanish Flu" pandemic. A deep recession followed but boom times returned during the Roaring Twenties, only to go bust again during the Great Depression of the 1930s.

A number of Colorado's current boom times went through periods of boom, bust, and a resurgent boom as social values changed. Gambling, beer, and even marijuana emerged from such cycles. Initially viewed as sins of the Old West, beer, gambling, and pot were suppressed by periods of prohibition but eventually resurrected so long as some greater social good could be realized by taxing these vices for good causes.

Colorado's modern marijuana boom has dark origins tracing the course of racial discrimination and prejudice in the state. As Colorado's economy demanded more immigrant labor, marijuana came north with the Mexican migrants. The Depression-era backlash against Hispanics caused panic amid Colorado's white society, despite previous evidence of marijuana's healthful effects. Colorado was at the forefront of national prohibition of marijuana in the 1930s. Black people also became the focus of prosecution, followed by the threatening counterculture young whites of the Beat and hippie generations. As these whites aged, Colorado again became the epicenter of decriminalization and eventual legalization, first for medicinal use and then as the first state to allow recreational use.

This boom and bust cycle highlights and somewhat mirrors the previous periods of marginalization of racial and ethnic groups. Native Americans were first swept aside during the gold and silver rush eras. Colorado's earliest Euro-American settlers were the Spanish and Mexicans moving up from the south and then, together with other Hispanic immigrants, reduced to second-class citizens. African Americans fled the Jim Crow South for Colorado in the late 1800s and early 1900s but confronted discrimination as elsewhere.

Successful struggles to embrace and welcome all such diverse peoples in a booming diverse society have perhaps been the greatest achievement Colorado has attained in its roller-coaster history. But the 2020 bust largely quashed such perceived accomplishments. The pandemic hit the nonwhite populations the hardest in employment, housing, food, and medical insecurity. The rich again got richer, the poor got poorer, and the racial divide widened and broke into open strife as Colorado and the rest of the nation was once again confronted with a racial reawakening.

Few could have predicted a pandemic that could ravage a state or national economy in such "modern times." For Coloradans, the 2020 pandemic bust will be transformative and generation-altering. Reliance on the internet and e-commerce have, of necessity, been accelerated for working and shopping from home. Urban centers, and especially Denver, will somehow have to be reborn and resurrected in the face of residents and workers abandoning downtown areas as they become ghost towns. With deserted streets and boarded-up buildings, Denver has lost its pulse and cultural allure. Restaurants, bars, and entertainment venues have closed (at least temporarily), while small businesses and large office towers alike stand empty and silent. Few want to go where people used to gather. The devastation to the transportation industry and public health restrictions have dampened out-of-state tourism and recreation. Ranching and agriculture have been hurt. Colorado's longtime lucrative "sin" pastimes of gambling, beer, and marijuana have perhaps ironically survived the bust.

All of Colorado will have to pivot to some cliché-ridden "new normal." For most Coloradans, their lives will be defined as "before" and "after." On December 22, 2020, History Colorado posted a 1966 quotation from Robert F. Kennedy to perhaps reflect an optimistic note in such perilous periods: "Like it or not, we live in interesting times. They are times of danger and uncertainty; but they are also more open to the creative energy of [people] than any other time in history."

Only time will tell.

CHAPTER ONE

Gold Rush

BEFORE THE 1859 GOLD RUSH, COLORADO WAS A LARGELY UNEXPLORED expanse of what explorer Stephen A. Long had described as the "Great American Desert" in the east and the rugged impenetrable Rocky Mountains blocking further travel west. Only a few intrepid mountain men and trappers had hazarded the Rockies. They enjoyed a brief boom and bust period until silk hats replaced beaver hats in the 1840s. "Civilization" ended in the states along the Mississippi and Missouri Rivers. With no navigable rivers, sojourners trekking west skirted Colorado's Rockies by heading north over the gentler passes of Wyoming or southwest to Santa Fe. All of that would change with the gold rush of 1859.

When conjuring the image of a gold rush, most readers will probably imagine the California gold rush in 1849. After witnessing the earlier California rush firsthand, Mark Twain diagnosed it as "the California Sudden-Riches Disease." In the decade since the '49ers had succumbed to that illness, the California gold rush was waning, and the whole country had sunken into a deep financial depression. Businesses and farms failed, and many were out of work. It took little proof in the summer 1858 to spark another outbreak of the "Sudden-Riches Disease," followed by an 1859 epidemic of "Gold Fever." Much of modern Colorado was then part of Kansas Territory, which was already bleeding over the slavery question, and the regional differences were about to explode into the Civil War. Why struggle with poverty or toil on farms or in factories when you could head west to Colorado, strike it rich, and escape the troubles back east?

Colorado's story began with a boom during the 1859 gold rush as some 100,000 fortune seekers swarmed into the Rocky Mountain region. The number of argonauts who poured into the region far exceeded the

Ever-hopeful prospectors, young and old, including grizzled veterans of both the Georgia and California gold rushes, stampeded to Colorado to pan for gold. TOM NOEL COLLECTION

California gold rush a decade earlier. Those infected with "Gold Fever" literally rushed to lay claim to the riches that might be found in the mountainous region.

EARLY HISPANIC EXPLORATION

However, golden rumors had drifted out of the Rocky Mountains for three centuries before Colorado's 1859 gold rush. In his 1540 expedition, General Francisco Vázquez de Coronado followed the Rio Grande north from Mexico looking for the seven golden cities of Cibola. He saw Colorado's gold-laced mountains shimmering on the horizon but failed to explore them.

Spanish explorer Don Juan María de Rivera was the first to memorialize the mineral riches of the Colorado Rockies. In a report on his 1765 expedition, Rivera revealed that he found silver near the mountain range he called La Plata (*plata* is Spanish for "silver" or "fortune") and mentioned the possibility of gold in the area as well.

During that period, Spain concentrated on linking its New Mexico claims, including present-day Colorado south of the Arkansas River, with those lands it held in California. Two Franciscan priests, Fathers Francisco Atanasio Domínguez and Silvestre Vélez de Escalante, set out from Santa Fe in 1776 to find an overland route to Monterey, the capital of Spanish California. Yutas (Utes), whom Escalante described as "of good features and very friendly," guided the padres. The ten-man Domínguez-Escalante party included Captain Don Bernardo y Pacheco Miera, an engineer, artist, and cartographer, who drew the first known map of Colorado. Father Escalante's diary reported "rivers showing signs of precious metals," as well as ancient cliff dwellings of the ancestral Puebloans.

Spanish and then Mexican presence in the area increased over the next decades and, during the 1850s, Mexicans began settling in the San Luis Valley of what is now south-central Colorado. They established towns along the Rio Grande and its tributaries. Founded in 1851, seven years before the gold rush, the town of San Luis remains an agricultural hamlet. It and other valley towns would provide wheat, sheep, beef, and other products to feed the gold rushers.

Although William "Green" Russell is generally given credit for the find that gave birth to Colorado's 1859 gold rush, Jerome Smiley's 1901 *History of Denver* reveals another side of history. Smiley, who interviewed pioneers who were on the scene in the late 1850s, reported that in 1857, a year before Russell's strike, Spanish-speaking settlers found gold and established a settlement known as Mexican Diggings along the South Platte River about where Florida Avenue crosses the river near Overland Park in today's Denver. Except for this brief mention, all traces of the settlement of Mexican Diggings are gone.

The disappearance of Mexican Diggings typifies much of Colorado's documented history. English-speaking peoples and their historians tend to omit references to earlier Spanish or—after Mexico gained its independence in 1821—Mexican settlements in what is now Colorado. Instead, these historians emphasize the western expansion from the early English colonies and ignore the northern migration of the Spanish and Latin American settlers. New Mexico had been first settled by the Spanish in the late sixteenth century, and Santa Fe was already a colonial hamlet by 1607, before the English colonies at Jamestown and Plymouth had even been founded. The Spanish and their Mexican successors had then explored northward and slowly settled into southern Colorado. The name *Colorado*, Spanish for "red" or "colorful," is one reminder of those who were the first Euro-Americans to settle the highest state.

WILLIAM RUSSELL AND THE FIRST MAJOR DISCOVERY OF GOLD

In the 1830s, the nation's first major gold strike in the South led to the removal of the Cherokee from their native lands. William Greeneberry "Green" Russell took some of these experienced Cherokee friends with him from his native Georgia on an 1848 overland trek to the gold mines of California, passing along Colorado's Front Range over what would become known as the north–south Cherokee Trail. On the way, he noticed promising-looking geology in Colorado, which he and members of his party came back to successfully prospect ten years later. Russell, who had mined in north Georgia where he grew up and in California, knew where to look for gold. In the summer of 1858, he and his party found about $500 worth of surface gold in the streambeds of Cherry Creek and the South Platte River.

Reports of Russell's find in the South Platte and Cherry Creek, supported by a few samples of real gold, spread like wildfire. "GOLD!" shrieked the newspapers, often exaggerating the story in the supply towns of St. Louis, Kansas City, Leavenworth, and Topeka, all eager to cash in on provisioning the frenzied argonauts. Supposedly authoritative "guidebooks" proliferated, minimizing the risks and rigors of cross-prairie travel to the naïve and gullible. "Pikes Peak or Bust" was the rallying cry, as that 14,110-foot-high mountain was the region's best-known landmark.

Russell named the Colorado gold rush town he established in October of 1858 Auraria, from the Latin word for gold. This was also the name of a town where he had mined gold in Georgia.

William Greeneberry Russell and his party of Georgians found the gold that launched the Colorado gold rush. DENVER PUBLIC LIBRARY, WESTERN HISTORY DEPARTMENT

A Yankee from Pennsylvania, William H. Larimer Jr. joined the rush a few months later. He came not to mine but to mine the miners by setting up a supply town. He established Denver City on the northeast bank of Cherry Creek on November 22, 1858, a month after Russell founded Auraria on the southwest side. The towns consolidated in 1860 as Denver City.

The 1858 discovery of gold in the South Platte River and Cherry Creek turned into a deluge in 1859. Gold fever ignited high hopes of the gold seekers, which shone in the "Cherry Creek Emigrant's Song," published in Colorado's first newspaper, the *Rocky Mountain News*, on June 18, 1859:

> Then ho boys ho, to Cherry Creek we'll go.
> There's plenty of gold in the West, we are told,
> In the new Eldorado.
>
> We'll rock our cradles around Pike's Peak,
> In search of the dust, and for nuggets seek.
> If the Indians ask us why we are there,
> We'll tell them we're made as free as the air.
>
> The gold is there, 'most anywhere,
> You can take it out rich with an iron crowbar.
> And where it is thick, with a shovel and a pick,
> You can pick it out in humps as big as a brick.
>
> At Cherry Creek if the dirt don't pay,
> We can strike our tents most any day.
> We know we are bound to strike a streak
> Of very rich quartz among the mountain peaks.
>
> Oh dear girls, now don't you cry,
> We are coming back by and by.
> Don't you fret or shed a tear,
> Be patient and wait about one year.

But after completing the long overland trek, the reality soon dampened gold seekers' expectations, hopes, and dreams. Most of the easily accessible placer gold found in the Front Range streambeds was a mere flash in the

6

Of the more than 100,000 argonauts stampeding to the Colorado gold fields, over 60 percent failed or became "go-backers"—busted! DENVER PUBLIC LIBRARY, WESTERN HISTORY DEPARTMENT

pan and soon played out. Auraria and Denver were nothing more than a few tents and log cabins when most arrived in 1859. Huge gold nuggets could not be easily scooped out of the streams by the panful, as most assumed. Disillusioned and dejected by what they claimed was a "humbug" or hoax, most turned back—busted.

A year after their initial find, Russell's party ventured west up the streambeds into the mountains, seeking the source of the placer gold found in the Front Range creek and river bottoms. The more intrepid and experienced gold grubbers knew the "color" in the streambeds had to come from somewhere, and a mad scramble up the tributaries of the South Platte and Arkansas Rivers followed in a desperate attempt to find the "Mother Lode." Russell's former mining experience again paid off. They discovered a rich strike in Russell Gulch southwest of what would become Central City, revitalizing the gold rush for decades to come.

Russell wrote home to his family in Georgia on June 17, 1859: "The prospects in the veins or mountain diggings, as they call them here, are improving.

The First Coloradans

Before the gold rush, before the Spanish-speaking settlers, another people occupied much of what is now Colorado. The Ute Indians' domain included most of the Colorado Rockies. Being nomadic hunters and gatherers, they had no sense of landownership or permanent settlements. Living off the land, they revered the land and were careful to protect its natural resources. The Utes placed no value on gold or any other precious metals. In fact, the Utes reportedly called gold "the excrement of the gods," and the Great Spirit believed that it portended disaster. That fear proved prescient, and conflict was inevitable.

Archaeologists and anthropologists believe the Utes entered Colorado from the west around 1300 and, by 1600, occupied most of the state. Sometimes called the "Black Indians," the Utes initially fought their lighter-skinned cousins like the Arapaho and Cheyenne, being

The Ute Indians became a thriving horse culture with no concept of landownership or regard for the mineral wealth craved by the whites. TOM NOEL COLLECTION

swept west by advancing "civilization." The Utes eventually retreated to their ancestral mountain domains in central and western Colorado, just as the Great Spirit had foretold.

A seismic change in the Ute lifestyle and culture occurred in the late seventeenth and early eighteenth centuries, when the Spanish moving up from the south introduced the horse to the region. Through raids, warfare, strays, and trade, the Utes were among the first indigenous people of North America to acquire and master the horse. The mounted Utes became fierce warriors, skilled big-game hunters, and advanced traders and raiders as they roamed faster and farther over their vast domain. Horses became a symbol of power, wealth, and pride—far more so than the shiny metals over which they trod.

The invasion of white settlers seeking to dominate, own, and use the land and its resources caused tension with Native inhabitants. Warily, the Utes watched Euro-Americans swarm up golden streams. Words were spoken and promises were made. Treaties were reached and breached. The Utes were forced to retreat further into their ancestral mountain homelands—first west of the Continental Divide in 1863, acceding to "protected" reservations that they supposedly owned "in perpetuity." Perpetuity lasted ten years and then the Brunot Treaty forced the Utes to give up the gold- and silver-rich San Juan Mountains.

The Utes tried to remain peaceful during the invasion of miners and settlers. Finally revolting at attempts to make them good Christian farmers, the Utes massacred the White River reservation agent, Nathan Meeker, and his staff and captured and abused Meeker's wife and daughter, provoking Colorado's last Indian War. The ensuing outcry of "The Utes must go!" led to the Ute Removal Act of 1880. Most were herded into what is now Utah, the state named for them. A few remained in Colorado on two small reservations in the barren southwest corner of the state.

While Colorado boomed in the mining era, the Utes and other indigenous peoples were swept aside and their vibrant societies displaced over the course of a mere twenty years. Still, the reservations for the Southern Utes and for the Ute Mountain Utes survive to this day and keep alive their rich culture from a complete bust.

There are now about 75 sluices in operation, all washing the ore taken from the veins, which are paying variously from $5 to $50 per day."

Five to fifty dollars a day seemed like a fortune at a time when the average income hovered at around two hundred dollars a year. With the outbreak of the Civil War, Colorado became a Yankee bastion, and Russell returned home to his native Georgia to join the Confederacy and disappeared from Colorado history. Many of the upstream towns like Russell Gulch also went bust and disappeared, joining many of the other boom camps as a ghost town.

THE CLEAR CREEK MOTHER LODE

After the Russell party's find on Cherry Creek, the first major strike came on the north fork of Vasquez Creek, named for an early fur trader. As thousands of Anglo-American miners poured in to reap the gold, that creek's name was changed to Clear Creek.

Gregory Gulch produced Colorado's first pay dirt bonanza amid early environmental havoc. COURTESY OF LIBRARY OF CONGRESS

Thirty miles west of Denver, John H. Gregory, another experienced prospector from Georgia, beat Russell's strike in Russell Gulch by a few weeks and found the first major mother lode on May 6, 1859. The Gregory Lode was one of the first gold veins—other finds had been placer (surface) gold washed downstream from the richer embedded ores in the mountains.

Almost overnight, 10,000 gold seekers rushed to the Gregory site, and the town of Central City sprang up to support the influx. Within weeks of Gregory's 1859 strike, canvas, slab, and log shacks climbed the rocky hillsides like stairs. Locals joked that "a fella can't spit tobaccy juice out his front door without putting out the fire in his neighbor's chimney." Central City sparkled as the first hub of Colorado Territory's initial bonanza years. After a fire destroyed much of the wooden town in 1874, many downtown property owners quickly rebuilt brick and stone buildings, some of which still wear the date 1874. A true boom and bust town, Central City's population peaked in 1900 at 3,114 and hit a rock bottom of 226 in 1970 before bouncing back to 713 in 2019. Tourism and gambling would save Central City from near extinction.

FROM ORES TO METALS
In 1860, the town of Black Hawk sprang up a mile down Gregory Gulch from Central City, just where the gulch meets the north fork of Clear Creek. The early gold mills there were primitive and recovered only a small percentage of the gold, which was embedded in complex quartz ores. Because there was no way of doing the extraction on-site, some miners sent especially rich ore all the way to Swansea, Wales, where sophisticated smelters could extract more of the gold.

It took a chemistry professor from Brown University to reverse Colorado's declining gold production due to recalcitrant ores. Nathaniel P. Hill visited Wales to tour the advanced Swansea smelters and took copious notes. He returned to Black Hawk, where he built the Boston and Colorado Smelter using the knowledge he'd gained in Wales and an infusion of capital from Boston. Other smelters in the area would also adopt more-efficient ore processing, and by 1870, fifteen stamp mills were crushing ores to feed twenty-five smelters that darkened Black Hawk skies with sulphurous smoke. Twenty-four hours a day Back Hawk throbbed to the beat of its stamp mills, where huge steel- or iron-tipped lead weights pulverized the ores. To feed the

Aunt Clara Brown: Central City's Angel

Of all the people washed into Colorado by the gold rush, one of the most remarkable was Clara Brown. "Aunt" Clara, as everyone affectionately called her, was born an enslaved person in Tennessee in 1800. She was sold as a young woman to a Kentucky planter, George Brown, whose last name she borrowed. He recognized Clara as an extraordinary woman and encouraged her to learn to read and write and study the Bible. Impressed with her piety and character, he freed her to go to St. Louis, where enslaved people had a chance for a better life.

Aunt Clara Brown was celebrated as Colorado's "colored angel of charity." TOM NOEL COLLECTION

Before gaining her freedom, Clara had married and had children. When asked about her husband by a reporter for the *Denver Tribune Republican* on June 26, 1885, she rocked back slowly and said, "I don't remember just when he was sold nearly thirty years ago. I don't know where they took him. I had four children, too, darlin'. They sold them, too."

Clara's faith was rewarded in St. Louis when she joined a wagon train headed to Colorado. "I go always where Jesus calls me, honey," she explained. Having no money for passage, she earned her way by cooking and cleaning.

In June of 1859, she became the first African American woman to reach the Colorado gold fields. In Central City, she opened a shop as a laundress, washing the filthy clothes of miners. She also cooked, cleaned, served as a midwife, and nursed the many sick and injured in her home, often without pay if they could not afford it. She began prudently investing her savings in property and, by the end of the Civil War, had saved enough to help build the town's still-standing St. James Methodist Church.

Clara also used her substantial savings to go back south, looking for her children and other relatives and friends. She did find one daughter to bring back to Colorado, along with a substantial number of other formerly enslaved people.

Aunt Clara Brown passed away in her sleep in 1885. At her burial in Denver's Riverside Cemetery, Colorado governor James B. Grant, Denver mayor John L. Routt, and other dignitaries heard Aunt Clara praised as "the kind old friend whose heart always responded to the cry of distress, and who, rising from the humble position of slave to the angelic type of noble woman, won our sympathy and commanded our respect."

Today, Aunt Clara Brown is commemorated by a stained-glass window in the Colorado State Capitol, a chair in the Central City Opera House, and a new tombstone in Riverside Cemetery.

smelters, much of Gilpin County was deforested for charcoal and remains largely treeless to this day.

In 1879, Hill moved his smelter to Denver for better rail connections to mines throughout Colorado. He named it the Argo after the ship in classical Greek mythology that Jason sailed in during his search for the Golden Fleece. And Hill sailed into a fortune with his Argo. He used smelter profits to buy the *Denver Republican* newspaper and to get into politics. He made generous donations to state legislators who, at the time, selected each state's US senators, a post Hill held from 1879 to 1885. Thanks to Hill, and later to James B. Grant and the Guggenheim family, Denver became a major hub for smelting ores to extract not only gold but also silver, lead, and zinc.

Besides Hill's Argo Smelter, the even larger Globe and Grant smelters arose in the Swansea and Globeville neighborhoods in north-central Denver. Smelters emerged as Colorado's major employer in the 1880s and 1890s. Other Colorado towns, most notably Colorado City, Leadville, and Pueblo, also became smelting hubs. While gold and silver mining captured the glamour and attention, it was the grimy, fiery smelters where ores were cooked that ultimately made the fortunes of entrepreneurs such as the Guggenheims and their American Smelting and Refining Company, a worldwide ore processor to this day. ASARCO'S Globeville site is now a Superfund site, with ongoing efforts to cope with toxic wastes. Cleaning up after mining and smelting is in itself a gold mine for those doing environmental reclamation.

Boomtowns and Mining Districts

Boulder County originally boomed with strikes at Gold Hill, Nederland, Caribou, and lesser mining camps. Gold Hill, one of the first and most promising gold camps, attracted experienced argonauts who realized that the tiny grains of gold in Boulder City had washed down from veins up in the hills. These veteran prospectors headed for the hills and struck a mother lode January 16, 1859, on Gold Run Creek. Up sprang the town of Gold Hill, where David Horsfal, Matthew McCaslin, and others found their big bonanza—the Horsfal Lode.

Gold Hillers actually created Colorado's first mining district in the spring of 1859, although it was quickly surpassed and overwhelmed by the Central City–Black Hawk mining district. California gold rush veterans such as Anthony Arnett and Matthew McCaslin fathered "Mountain District No. 1" to impose some law and order and to regulate mining claims. The Gold Hill Mining District allowed each miner one mountain claim and one gulch claim with water rights. Favoring working miners over nonresident speculators, the Gold Hill laws of 1859 required miners to work their claim at least one day in ten or surrender it.

A stampede of argonauts swelled Gold Hill's population to 1,500 in the summer of 1860, according to the *Rocky Mountain News*. However, the 1860 US Census taker counted only 487 official residents who produced more than $100,000 by 1861.

As the heavy metal flowed out of Gold Hill, the town sought a mill to process its pickings. When word spread that the Culver brothers were lugging one of Colorado's first stamp mills across the plains by oxcart destined for Black Hawk, Gold Hillers intercepted them and redirected the mill to their community. It arrived in time for the town's Fourth of July festivities, celebrated with a parade, speeches, and pies made with fruit supposedly crushed in the new stamp mill.

Gold Hill's famed Miners Hotel opened in 1872, immortalized by Eugene Field's poem "Casey's Table d'Hote":

> The bar was long 'nd rangy, with a mirror on the shelf,
> 'Nd a pistol so that Casey when required, could help himself;
> Down underneath there wuz a row of bottled beer 'nd wine,
> 'Nd a kag of Burbun whiskey of the run of '59;
> Upon the walls wuz pictures of hosses 'nd of girls,—
> Not much on dress, perhaps, but strong on curls!

Gold Hill sprang up as Boulder County's first major treasure trove. DENVER PUBLIC LIBRARY, WESTERN HISTORY DEPARTMENT

Gold Hill never had a railroad, and pack animals were essential to move goods in and ores out along the steep, rocky, narrow trails. That necessity spawned a bunch of burros. Several herds of twenty-five to fifty each ran wild in the town. George Cowell, a Gold Hill old-timer, told local historian Lynne Walter: "People would put their eggshells and coffee grounds and potato peelings out in the street. About 6 o'clock at night the burros would come down out of the timber and eat up all this garbage, even the paper off the cans. Then they'd go down to the well in front of the saloon and drink from the watering trough. If you wanted a burro, you never bought one. You picked out one that you liked and put your brand on him."

Prospectors exploring the Arkansas River headwaters with Abe Lee, an experienced California miner, also had good luck. When panning in the spring of 1860 on a tributary of the Arkansas River, Lee suddenly let out a whoop and yelled, "Lookee here, boys, I got all of Californy in this here pan!" The "boys" promptly christened California Gulch and launched a rush of some 5,000 gold seekers to the upper Arkansas. Oro City, named after the Spanish word for gold, became one of Colorado's first large boomtowns. For miles up and down the gulch, people were living in brush huts, in or under wagons, and—only occasionally—in log cabins. Log cabins, after all, took a

Horace and Augusta Tabor: The Gold Era

The fabled Tabor "rags to riches to rags" tale began in Oro City. Horace Austin Warner Tabor and his wife Augusta, together with their baby boy Maxcy, had joined the '59ers on a six-week trek across the prairie and were among the first families to reach the early town of Denver. After a brief and relatively unsuccessful effort as a shopkeeper, Horace was struck by the gold bug, and they headed into the mountains. The miners were so delighted by the arrival of Oro City's first respectable woman, Augusta Tabor, in 1861 that they built a cabin for her and her husband.

While Horace dabbled in prospecting, the gold camp selected the conscientious Augusta as their postmistress and patronized the Tabor store and boardinghouse. Women-starved miners came into the store just to see a woman and, even more fascinating, her baby. Augusta also had the only scales in the gulch, and miners trusted her to measure the gold dust they used in payment.

The Tabor store became the center of Oro City as log cabins, saloons, and other businesses sprang up. Augusta also served as a town banker, and folklore has it that her brassiere was the gulch's first cash depository. In her diary, Augusta reported that "ordinary workmen were paid $6 a day in gold. They received their pay every night and the majority had spent it all by morning. The miners would spree all night and return to the mines in the morning." Before Augusta, the only women seen in the gulch were itinerant prostitutes who worked out of wagons and tents as miners lined up outside, hungry for female companionship.

As the gold-mining boom ebbed and the silver boom began, Oro City was quickly transcended by nearby Leadville. There, the Tabor story would continue.

few days to build that would distract from mining. One entrepreneur set up a circus tent, sold beds for a dollar a night, and made a good living.

As with other gold camps, the California Gulch miners set up a mining district and drew up laws, then elected a justice of the peace, a sheriff, a stake driver, and a recorder, Abe Lee. Recorder Lee was instructed to keep California Mining District records in a notebook and not "loose sheets of paper." California Gulch was not as severe in its laws as some other districts which sought to avoid trouble by banning lawyers. Many mining districts allowed women to own claims and even vote—radical achievements in those days. Miner's courts handed out quick justice ranging from expulsion to lynching. "Judge Lynch" acted quickly, and there was no appealing his decisions. When locals were killed by lead poisoning (bullets), the judge was known to prescribe rope burn (hanging).

California Gulch had produced $5 million in gold by 1865. Oro City became one of the most populated places in Colorado Territory and the first county seat of Lake County, one of the original seventeen Colorado counties. In the two-mile-high town, winters were fierce and long. Many went to lower elevations when the blizzards arrived, but kept returning in late spring until the mid-1860s. By then, miners were finding less and less gold. By the late 1860s, hordes were abandoning California Gulch as fast as they had come in the early 1860s. Oro City became Colorado's first great ghost town, a prototype of boom and bust towns to come.

Oro City shriveled into a skeleton. Miners blamed the town's problems on a heavy black sand that clogged gold operations. Not until 1875 would that black sand be assayed and found to be lead carbonate, an ore rich in silver. That silver gave birth to neighboring Leadville, richest of all the Rocky Mountain silver cities.

BRECKENRIDGE: DREDGING THE RIVER BOTTOMS

On Colorado's Western Slope, prospectors washed gold out of the Blue River, a tributary of the Colorado. The gold camp there was named for then–US vice president John C. Breckinridge, but the first *i* in his name was changed to *e* after he joined the Confederacy. Prospectors first prowled the area in 1859. Fearing the Utes and the weather, they built a stockade called Fort Mary B, for Mary Bigelow, the only woman in the party.

After obtaining a post office in 1860 and capturing the Summit County seat in 1862, the town of Breckenridge began a series of bonanzas and busts. Gold in the 1860s, silver in the 1880s, and gold dredging in the early 1900s bankrolled flush times. Breckenridge yielded Colorado's largest gold nugget, a whopping twelve-and-a-half-pound beauty called "Tom's Baby" because its owner carried it around in a blanket to show it off. During hard times, some who had built homes and institutions on the outskirts of town moved them closer to the center. As many structures had no foundations and most were made of wood, Breckenridge could accommodate its shrinking and stretching with this game of musical buildings.

By the end of the nineteenth century, placer mining of the riverside gravel had played out and deep rock shaft mining had exhausted the hillside veins in and around Breckenridge. Still, over the eons, heavy gold sediment had settled at the bottom of the gulches, creeks, and rivers covered by deep layers of boulders, gravel, dirt, and sand. At watery depths of thirty to ninety feet, this placer gold was inaccessible by ordinary mining techniques. To recover this gold, Breckenridge became Colorado's center for dredge boat mining beginning in 1898.

At its height, nine dredge boats gouged the Swan and Blue Rivers in what became known as the "Breckenridge Navy." These huge floating mills, some hundreds of yards long and floating on their own constantly moving man-made lakes, chewed up waterways with giant continually rotating steel bucket shovels supported by large forward boom-like gantries that could reach depths as great as seventy feet. Dirt, sand, gravel, and boulders were scooped onto conveyor-fed ore-processing machines on deck which separated promising ores from waste rock, which the boat discharged behind. These left streams and rivers literally turned upside down, expelling massive piles of rocky tailing in their wake. The valley floors were long scarred by these scoured riverbeds, and wide boulder tailings are still very evident today. Still, such environmental destruction made fortunes for men such as Ben Stanley Revett, hailed as "The Father of Gold Dredging in the United States."

Revett, a graduate of the Royal School of Mines in London, started gold dredging on the Swan River, a tributary of the Blue. Next to his operations, he built an expansive frame house befitting his flamboyant lifestyle and immense girth. "Swan's Nest," as he called it, had extra-wide doors, as one local noted at the time, "so the dignity of its owner need not suffer by passing through a door sideways." Beyond a grand entry hall lay four family bedrooms for his wife and child, quarters for his Japanese gardener and Filipino house servants, two indoor bathrooms, and a billiard room. Finding stones for the massive fireplace was no problem: the view from the veranda across the now-defunct croquet and tennis courts ends in massive rock piles left in the wake of Revett's dredge boat operations. Swan's Nest survives as a resort, and the nearby preserved Swan River Dredge No. 4 is another historical reminiscence.

Gold dredging boomed in the Breckenridge District up until the 1940s. Trying to save a flagging economy during the Depression, Breckenridge officials sanctioned the plowing by one of these two-story pontoon monsters, called the Tiger No. 1, from the northern town limits to the south end of

Main Street, destroying most of the original downtown west of the Blue River. By 1950, Breckenridge had shrunk to a population of just 254 and seemed destined for ghost town status. Today, the historic town has been restored, and surrounding land is rapidly becoming subdivisions and resorts. The old gold camp has become a major winter sports haven and summer resort thanks to the Breckenridge Ski Area, opened in 1961.

CRIPPLE CREEK: "THE WORLD'S GREATEST GOLD CAMP"

Ironically, prospectors took thirty years to discover the bowl of gold hidden near the mountain that gave the 1859 Pikes Peak gold rush its name. Not until 1890 did "Crazy Bob" Womack, a poor and occasionally sober cowboy, find an outcropping of color in what would become the richest-ever Colorado gold district. It lay at a breathtaking 9,500 feet, ten miles west of Pikes Peak.

Womack had come to Colorado from Kentucky at the age of seventeen, hoping to make his fortune in the Clear Creek mines around Idaho Springs. When his mining dreams didn't bear fruit, a busted Womack took a job

Although "Crazy Bob" Womack first discovered Cripple Creek gold, others made fortunes there while he lived in this Poverty Gulch shack. DENVER PUBLIC LIBRARY, WESTERN HISTORY DEPARTMENT

tending cattle on a ranch along Cripple Creek, a tiny, stony stream notorious for tripping animals and men. While herding cows, Womack also hunted gold. He would take promising ore samples to an assay office in Colorado Springs and spend the proceeds at the nearest saloon. Few believed his furry-tongued tales of Cripple Creek pay dirt.

After Womack located the El Paso mother lode in Poverty Gulch in 1890, with ores eventually assaying at $250 a ton, gold fever struck in 1891 as word of his previously dubious but now verified strike spread. His shack and the cattle ranch were soon overrun by gold seekers. Unfortunately, Womack lived up to his "crazy" reputation and quickly sold his claim for a pittance over drinks. The renamed Gold King mine eventually produced over $5 million in gold.

Poverty Gulch and environs were platted as the city of Cripple Creek in 1891. During the next decade, thousands of people and three railroads rushed in and located two dozen million-dollar mines. Cripple Creek blossomed as an instant city complete with streetcars, suburbs, and a stock exchange. Even two devastating fires, both in 1896, did not stop growth of this golden city. Miners' homes climbed the hills in every direction. Fancy hotels and splendiferous saloons lined Bennett Avenue, the main street, while an opera house, elegant brothels, and gilded gambling halls crowded Myers Avenue.

A dozen gold camps sprang up in the surrounding Cripple Creek District, a twenty-five-square-mile region whose population peaked at around 23,000 in 1900. Gross gold production also peaked in 1900 at $18 million, making Cripple Creek "The World's Greatest Gold Camp." To earn that title at its 1900 peak, the Cripple Creek District outproduced Witwatersrand, South Africa; Porcupine and Kirkland Lake in Ontario, Canada; the Homestake Mine in Lead, South Dakota; and every Russian mining district.

Victor, founded in 1894, became the second-largest city in the Cripple Creek District and prided itself on being "the City of Mines and Miners." Miners were initially independent get-rich prospectors but, once the mother lode was discovered, extraction and milling required capital and equipment, transforming miners into a working class of largely immigrant and poorly paid laborers who reaped little of the wealth of the mine owners' boom times. In the mid-1890s, they began to unionize, especially after silver mining crashed in 1893, creating a surfeit of miners and the consolidation of mine ownership in a depression-era economy. Victor, like Cripple Creek, was at the center of the 1894 and 1903–4 labor wars, fighting over wages, hours, and working conditions.

Winfield Scott Stratton

Of the thirty-three men made millionaires by Cripple Creek, the most notable was Winfield Scott Stratton. Once a poor carpenter, Stratton had prospected the Colorado Rockies for years and even studied metallurgy and geology. He was part of the rush that flooded into Cripple Creek in the aftermath of Bob Womack's discovery and filed a claim for the Independence Mine on July 4, 1891. Its output made Stratton Cripple Creek's first millionaire. The miner-turned-mogul had reaped a fortune during its production, and he ultimately sold his Independence Mine to British interests for $11 million in 1899, the highest price ever paid up to that time for a Colorado mine.

Stratton, an eccentric bachelor, fancied women, whiskey, and philanthropy. He supposedly bought a bicycle for every laundry girl in Colorado Springs, gave $5,000 to poor "Crazy Bob" Womack, and, upon his death in 1902, left $6 million to establish the Myron Stratton Home for aged indigents in Colorado Springs. In the Cripple Creek District, the towns of Stratton (1900) and Independence (1895) were named for him and for his legendary gold mine.

Labor conflicts, the rapid extraction of easily recovered gold, and the frequent flooding of the mines slowly brought Cripple Creek's golden days to an end by the 1920s. Despite occasional revivals and the introduction of new processes such as cyanide leaching to reprocess old mine dumps, the district's population and production declined steadily.

The district hoped for a comeback when President Richard Nixon removed federal restrictions on the private ownership of gold and allowed the price to float in 1975. It shot up to $875 an ounce. Some gold mines reopened, but many closed again when the price fell to between $300 and $400 an ounce in the 1980s. Gold soared again in the 1990s, reaching almost $2,000 per ounce in 2015 and falling to around $1,100 before bouncing back to $1,940 in 2020 in an ever-fluctuating market. Between 1858 and 1958, Colorado produced gold valued at $914,717,009, about 3 percent of the world's total supply. Over half of Colorado's gold came from the Cripple Creek District.

Gold finally made a comeback with the 1994 reopening of the Cresson Mine between Cripple Creek and Victor. As one of the world's largest heap cyanide leaching pads and open-pit mines, the fabulously rich Cresson,

The Cresson Mine in Cripple Creek still produces over a million dollars a day in its massive open pit mine while devouring many of the former nearby mines and mining camps. TOM NOEL COLLECTION

originally opened in the 1890s bonanza days, has returned boom times to "The World's Greatest Gold Camp." Whereas gold extraction a century ago recovered only about half the gold in Cripple Creek ores, modern cyanide techniques recover over 90 percent. Today, the Cripple Creek & Victor Mining Company (CC&V) operates twenty-four hours a day, seven days a week. With annual production averaging well over 258,000 ounces and gold prices elevated, the CC&V has become the richest gold mine in Colorado history and one of the world's top ten producers. Since 2015, CC&V has been owned by Newmont Mining Corp., headquartered in Greenwood Village, a Denver-area suburb, and is the largest mining company in the world.

As during earlier mining frenzies, there has been environmental damage. Victor residents complain of mine blasts that rattle their homes and worry about cyanide leaks from CC&V's heap leaching pads into groundwater. Ghost town fanciers are appalled that CC&V's enormous pit mine has completely swallowed Altman, Anaconda, Cameron, Elkton, Independence, Midway, and Stratton (aka Winfield). These ghost towns, which once made the Cripple Creek District a prime target for ghost town tourists, have vanished in a hole in the ground that measures ten miles by seven miles. This gold pit is still growing and still swallowing historical sites. Such inconveniences, CC&V maintains, are the price to be paid for the return of prosperity and high-paying mining jobs.

Limited-stakes gambling, introduced in Cripple Creek in 1991, has, like the Cresson Mine, partially revived the City of Gold. Some older structures have been restored outside and converted to casinos inside. Victor, a city without gaming and with mostly abandoned buildings, is a reminder that the Pikes Peak gold rush left many towns busted. Of the ten post office towns once flourishing in the Cripple Creek District, only Cripple Creek and Victor are alive today. Most of Colorado's once glittering gold towns are ghosts. Gold has seen its booms and busts, and its current revival echoes the original rush when fortune seekers first bet on a golden gamble called Colorado.

CHAPTER TWO

Silver Boom

COLORADO'S EARLY GOLD STRIKES PROVED MAGNETIC. GREEN RUSSELL'S discoveries on tributaries of the South Platte River, George Jackson's find at Idaho Springs, and John H. Gregory's bonanza at Central City lured thousands of fortune seekers into the mountains. Prospectors who had initially combed the hills for gold also began finding silver. Though it started out slowly, silver output climbed to $3 million per year by 1874, when it outstripped gold for the first time. As the gold boom began sputtering, the silver boom began.

National currency policy was also being pushed by western silver interests, claiming that silver was just as good as gold. "Bimetalism," as it was then called, was replacing the previous gold standard. In 1878, Congress passed the Bland-Allison Act, requiring that the Treasury start again issuing silver dollars in addition to "greenbacks" (paper money) and also stipulating that the feds purchase substantial amounts of silver each month. From 1879 to 1893, the Centennial State became known as "The Silver State" with $82 million worth of silver mined.

Boom times bounced higher with the Sherman Silver Purchase Act of 1890, again increasing the amounts of silver to be purchased by the federal government. Such federal subsidies further buoyed the silver boom. Colorado prospered as the leading producer of silver in the country. Euphoria reigned briefly. Three years later, it would go bust—badly.

GEORGETOWN: FAMILIES WELCOME
The first major gold rush had begun on the north fork of Clear Creek. The first big silver strike came on the south fork of Clear Creek, where Georgetown, Colorado's most genteel mining town, would sprout. Georgetown started out as a gold camp but emerged as Colorado's first major silver

George Griffith laid out George's Town, seen here in 1867, in one of the few valleys in the Clear Creek Valley broad enough for a level town and a baseball field. The post office changed the name from George's Town to Georgetown in 1866. TOM NOEL COLLECTION

city. George Griffith of Bourbon County, Kentucky, had succumbed to the "Sudden-Riches Disease" and joined the 1859 rush to Colorado. However, Griffith pushed beyond overcrowded, overclaimed Central City and took Clear Creek's south fork up to Idaho Springs. Then, rather than stop there, he continued eighteen miles farther upstream to an evergreen-fringed valley rimmed by 12,000-foot-high mountains There, Griffith discovered the gold lode named for him on the mountainside above the town which also bears his name.

When the aspen trees turned golden and snow began to blanket the mountains, George Griffith left Colorado to return to his family in Kentucky. Come spring, he brought his wife, his parents, and his brothers and their wives and children out to what they originally named George's Town. From the outset, George's Town grew as a sanctuary for families, unlike the rough-and-tumble bachelor-dominated mining camps proliferating elsewhere.

Though Georgetown had its roots in gold, in 1864 prospectors exploring southwest of town along Leavenworth Creek discovered high-grade silver ore deposits. The discoverers named their find on Mount McClellan the Belmont Lode, French for "beautiful mountain." More silver was found on both sides of nearby Argentine Pass in the Argentine District, both of which were named for *argentium*, the Latin word for silver. A few years later, two miles up Clear Creek from Georgetown, a mountainside north of Clear Creek was found to have high-grade silver, giving rise to the boomtown of Silver Plume.

The silver rush was on. Small mining camps soon dotted both sides of Clear Creek around Georgetown, including Alice, Brownsville, Dumont, Elephant, Empire, Lamartine, Lawson, Silver Plume, and Waldorf. Georgetown became the refined home of the rich mine owners and their families, as well as the area's commercial, cultural, and entertainment center. After wrestling the county seat for Clear Creek County from Idaho Springs, Georgetown became known as "The Silver Queen of the Rockies."

Georgetown was queenly. Griffith had encouraged other families to settle there, offering free town lots to "respectable" women, which made it different from most male-dominated mining towns. The ladies fancied clapboarding log cabins, then painting them. They also crusaded for schools, churches, a library, two opera houses, and other refinements. Whereas most mining towns dedicated little, if any, land to parks, Georgetown set aside a full block as a city park, with a bandstand, playground, metal fence, and wrought-iron entry arches. Tree-lined streets and gardens mixing wild and cultivated flowers also made Georgetown exceptional among usually raw, bleak, weedy mining communities. Why, penny-pinchers asked, waste land on parks that you could not tax or mine? Men might not care for green space or notice the wildflower-clad mountain beauty, but the ladies did.

Georgetown's flush times faded with the start of the 1880s Leadville boom, when many residents left the relatively meager mines of Clear Creek County for the diggings on the Arkansas River headwaters. Leadville exploded into one of the richest silver cities ever, while Georgetown's population, which had peaked at some 3,294 in 1880, dropped off precipitously with the Leadville boom and the 1893 silver crash. By 1950, there were a mere 301 residents in Georgetown. Since then, the population has climbed to a little over 1,100.

Twentieth-century Georgetown residents perpetuated the civic-minded beautification of the original settlers. The town welcomed creation of the Georgetown–Silver Plume National Historic District in 1966, and Georgetowners formed one of Colorado's first private preservation groups in 1970, Historic Georgetown, Inc., and enacted one of Colorado's first and toughest

Isabella Bird

One woman especially impressed with Georgetown was a world-traveling writer from Britain named Isabella Bird. Of the pioneer Colorado silver city of Georgetown, she wrote: "It reminded me slightly of a Swiss village. It is the only town I have seen in America to which the epithet picturesque could be applied." While glorifying Colorado's mountain scenery, she found that greed and raw exploitation of its mineral resources made mining an ugly business. "Mining," she wrote, "destroys and devastates, turning the earth inside out, making it hideous and blighting every green thing, as it usually blights men's heart and soul."

Lady Bird, as she was sometimes called, was a prim and proper, unmarried, middle-aged English world traveler who showed up in Colorado in 1873 wearing a huge sunbonnet and Turkish trousers over her bloomers. She reported the good, the bad, and the ugly in her classic, still-in-print book, *A Lady's Life in the Rocky Mountains* (London, 1879).

Isabella began traveling the world for her health at age forty and wrote travel books on Europe, Asia, Australia, and Hawaii. In 1873, she arrived in Colorado, where she frowned on most communities, calling Denver "the great braggart city of the plains" where "I should hate even to spend a week" and Colorado Springs "a queer embryo place." She candidly compared other cities and mining camps with unspoiled Estes Park, with which she fell in love and rhapsodized over its beauty in florid Victorian prose:

> The sky was all one rose-red flush, on which vermillion cloud-streaks rested, the ghastly peaks gleamed like rubies, the earth and heavens were new created. . . . Grandeur and sublimity, not softness, are the features of Estes Park. The glades which begin so softly are soon lost in the dark primeval forests, with their peaks of rosy granite and their stretches of granite blocks piled and poised by nature in some mood of fury.

local preservation ordinances. In the 1980s, the town even bought out a condominium developer on the Guanella Pass Road to keep development from creeping up the surrounding mountainsides.

Since the 1970s, Georgetown has lost only 2 of 211 nineteenth-century structures in the downtown historic district. Despite such misadventures and new development on the north side of the old town, it reigns as Colorado's best-preserved silver city. Located along the busy I-70 corridor, Georgetown has been saved as a now-popular tourist destination.

CARIBOU

Boulder County is home to another major early silver-mining town, Caribou. At 10,000 feet, it became infamous as one of the coldest, snowiest, and windiest of all Colorado mining communities. "The town where winds are born" was snow-blanketed nine months out of the year. Caribou residents joked that summer lasted two days and winter three years. In winter, residents used second-story windows to climb over snowdrifts that buried one-story buildings. Entering the town over a rise by horse-drawn sleds, winter visitors could often only discern the town by the smoking stovepipes and chimneys poking out of the snow.

Sam Conger, a veteran of California and Nevada mining, was hunting elk on the site when he noticed blossom rock like the silver ore of Nevada's fabulous Comstock Lode. Conger and partners George Lytle and William Martin began big-time silver extraction in August 1869. Lytle named the place Cariboo for the rich Cariboo Mining District of British Columbia, where he had mined earlier. In Colorado, the post office changed the spelling to Caribou.

The Conger party extracted a silver payoff before autumn blizzards set in. By the next summer, 1870, Conger had company, as reported by the *Rocky Mountain News* article on Caribou:

> *Its hotels are the Cariboo House, kept by Mrs. Wilson who sets a good table, but lacks accommodations. Mrs. Lyons . . . is keeping a hotel, having some beds and rooms. Mrs. Gilligan and Mr. Berger have boarding houses. Messiers Tony & Fritz have a bakery and brewery, and Press W. Pierce, a fine, well filled butcher-shop, with an ample supply of vegetables, enough to last till next June. Leo Donnelly has a store with cellar attached, and a well selected, though small, stock of groceries, provisions, miner's goods, camping utensils, hardware. Sears, Werley & Co. have the largest building in the place, a fine, two story, well-finished frame house. The lower story is devoted to billiards and a saloon, while the upper story furnishes about a dozen rooms*

suitable for offices and sleeping rooms. . . . There are at present neither doctors, lawyers, preachers nor school, though the presence of a score of youngsters indicates great need of the latter.

Despite the inhospitable climate, Caribou strove for respectability. The Sherman House, a three-story edifice erected in 1875, became the town's social center, offering lyceum lectures and Caribou Silver Coronet Band performances. Townsfolk opened a school and a Methodist church and, in 1881, persuaded the city fathers to close the notorious Shoo Fly Saloon and run its prostitutes out of town. These enterprising ladies set up shop two miles downhill in well-named Cardinal, where red lights and scarlet ladies were welcome.

The baby silver city glittered brightest of all the Boulder County camps in the 1870s, attracting eastern investors such as Abel Breed of Cincinnati. Breed's background as a highly successful patent medicine and casket salesman left him with investment capital for the business of mining. He bought Caribou mines and built his own Breed Smelter. As a publicity stunt, Breed paved the steps of Central City's Teller House with silver bricks from his Caribou Mine. When President Ulysses S. Grant visited Central City in 1873, he stepped from the presidential coach onto Breed's shiny product. With this nationally reported silver carpet, Breed's fame and stock soared. When potential investors called upon Breed, he offered them refreshment from a coffee and tea service made of Caribou silver.

Breed, who had bought the Caribou Mine from Sam Conger in 1870 for $50,000, sold it to a Dutch company three years later for $3 million—the largest amount paid up to that time for a Colorado mining operation. When Cornish miners and mill workers struck against Dutch management, the owners called in Chinese laborers, who became a target in the labor dispute. The Chinese worked for less and worked more efficiently, leading to much working-class resentment against them and their banishment from many mining camps. The Chinese were soon kicked out of Caribou too.

Like the Chinese, Breed disappeared. Caribou struggled without him around to puff the town. After its mid-1870s boom, it shriveled and began to blow away in hundred-mile-an-hour gusts roaring down from the nearby Continental Divide.

The Dutch abandoned Caribou in 1876. Denver entrepreneurs Jerome Chaffee and David Moffat subsequently picked up the $3 million operation

Caribou proved to be a short-lived silver town where buildings had to be braced against ferocious winds. The whole town has blown away except for a few stone structures and foundations. DENVER PUBLIC LIBRARY, WESTERN HISTORY DEPARTMENT

at a sheriff's sale for $70,000. These two Denver high rollers restructured Breed's empire as the Caribou Consolidated Mining Company and unloaded it on New York capitalist Robert G. Dun, who later became half of the famous Wall Street house of Dun & Bradstreet. Dun may have sunk as much as $1 million into his Caribou Mine, according to mining historian Duane A. Smith in *Silver Saga: The Story of Caribou, Colorado* (Boulder: Pruett Publishing, 1974). Dun wrote of his Caribou misadventures in 1877: "That d—d old mine has harassed me almost to death aside from embarrassing me pecuniarily. I only wish I were out of the operation and had back one quarter of what I have in it." Dun retreated to Wall Street, where he found far safer and more lucrative investments than Colorado mining.

Early prosperity could not save Caribou from the silver crash of 1893. Major wind-whipped fires struck in 1879, 1899, and 1905, and a 1903 earthquake also rattled the town. After peaking with an 1880 population of 549, Caribou declined to 44 by 1900 and became a ghost town by the 1920s. Survivors moved nine miles down Coon Track Creek into Nederland. Nowadays, only summer ghost town hunters prowl the dead silver camp, scrutinizing the stone ruins of a boardinghouse, a brewery, and the cemetery where residents slumber, free at last from the chilly winds.

Leadville

Heavy black sand had bedeviled California Gulch gold grubbers from the beginning. This worthless black stuff gummed up gold extraction apparatuses, although some had found it could be melted into musket balls. Some blamed it for the demise of the early gold rush town of Oro City. Not until 1875 did William H. "Uncle Billy" Stevens and Alvinus B. Wood have that blasted black sand assayed. Whoopee! It assayed as heavy lead carbonate containing a rich silver ore.

A mad rush brought thousands back into California Gulch. Silver seemed to be everywhere. Because the Leadville silver ores lay in mostly horizontal rather than in upright veins, almost anyone could dig down almost anywhere on Iron, Carbonate, and Freyer hills and make a strike. One laborer stumbled upon a rich vein while digging a grave and rushed off to file a claim, leaving the corpse for others to bury. Colorado's silver boom times soared with the Leadville discovery.

When the city was created in 1878, there was much to-do about what it should be named: California Gulch? Oro City? Sow Belly Gulch? Slabtown? Bucktown? Boughtown? Stringtown? Poverty Flats? The Poor Man's Camp? Cloud City? The Magic City? Two-Mile-High City? In the end, residents named it Leadville for the prominent and profitable lead ore which was mined along with the silver.

Leadville became Colorado's Magic City and the Mother of Millionaires and Carbonate Kings. This booming overnight metropolis soon had ten suburbs, all with post offices: Adelaide, Alexander, Climax, Howland, Ibex, Iron Hill, Oro City, Soda Springs, Tabor, and Wortman. Another ten nearby mining camps never earned a post office. Today, all are gone except a much-shrunken Leadville. No one described the Leadville phenomenon better than the nationally known writer Helen Hunt Jackson:

> *In six months a tract of dense spruce forest has been converted into a bustling village . . . the upturned roots and freshly hacked stumps are still in the streets . . . the middle of the street was always filled with groups of men talking. Wagons were driven up and down as fast as if the street was clear. It looked all the time as if there had been a fire. . . . Everybody was talking, nearly everyone gesticulating. All faces looked restless, eager and fierce. It was a Monaco gambling room emptied into a Colorado spruce clearing.*

31

Leadville popped up in the middle of a spruce forest almost overnight, built so rapidly that Harrison Avenue, the main street, in 1879 still had spruce tree obstacles. By 1880, it was the second-largest city in Colorado, behind only Denver. DENVER PUBLIC LIBRARY, WESTERN HISTORY DEPARTMENT

The terrain for miles all around is still raw, denuded of the spruce forest that once thrived there. Every tree in sight was cut down to build the city, shore up mines, or serve as charcoal in Leadville's smelters. Seventeen of these hot, smoky plants rimmed the city. What few trees did not feed smelters or help construct mines or buildings were used to heat homes and businesses in one of Colorado's coldest cities. The all-time record high was eighty-six degrees and minus thirty-six the record low. The growing season is only forty-three days, and it can snow any day of the year. Leadvillites say they have three seasons of winter and one of mighty late fall.

In 1880, according to the federal census taker, Leadville's population had skyrocketed to 14,800. It emerged as the largest and richest of all the

32

Colorado mining towns. Yet it was remote and isolated, buried deep in the mountains at an elevation two miles high—the highest incorporated city in the United States. Getting there was not easy. It cost more to ship freight from Denver to Leadville than it did to ship from Denver to San Francisco.

Leadville was soon overrun by eastern tenderfeet, western ruffians, and a wave of European immigrants "fresh off the boat," all eager to test their luck. Oft-maligned Irish immigrants swarmed into the area, chasing their elusive lucky charms. Greenhorns such as the Gallagher brothers, Charles, John, and Patrick, soon struck it rich. The Gallagher boys arrived in 1876 and by winter had staked the Pine, Camp Bird, and Young America mines. They found rich ore assaying as much as 934 ounces per ton for silver, far more than the usual concentration, as well as lead, which also was saleable. During the winter of 1877–78, they sold their property to the St. Louis Smelting and Refining Company for $225,000.

If the Gallaghers could do it, anybody could. They became branded as the prototypically dumb Irish in the *Leadville Daily Chronicle*, which teased them about their upward social climbing by improbably quoting Mrs. Patrick Gallagher: "Och. Pat tisn't Irish at all. He is a Inglishman, but comin' over to Ameriky in a shteamer he got in wid a lot o' Irish, and got their damned brogue; and faith, he can't git over it. Shure, the Irish up the gulch here are not fit for we'uns to assosheat wid. We are going to move down to Leadville and put up a brick house in the latest style, be Jasus."

Leadville became one of the most Irish cities in the country. Whole communities of unemployed Irish miners in the British Isles moved to Leadville, where the east side was predominately Celtic. When the noted Irish playwright and critic Oscar Wilde came to Leadville in 1882, his countrymen flocked to hear his lecture. In his book *Impressions of America* (Sunderland, 1906), Wilde recalled his trip to the Rocky Mountains,

> *on top of which is Leadville, the richest city in the world. It has also got*
> *the reputation of being the roughest, and every man carries a revolver.*
> *I was told that if I went there they would be sure to shoot me or my*
> *traveling manager. I wrote and told them that nothing they could do*
> *to my traveling manager would intimidate me. They are miners—*
> *men working in metals, so I lectured them on the ethics of art. I read*
> *passages from the autobiography of Benevento Cellini and they seemed*
> *much delighted. I was reproved by my listeners for not having brought*

The Tabor Silver Saga

With the demise of Oro City and the rush to Leadville, Horace and Augusta Tabor moved a few miles northwest of Oro City to the new silver city in 1877. They opened a relatively prosperous general store and thrived, thanks to Augusta's hard work.

Augusta Tabor

One day in the spring of 1878, two German indigents, August Rische, a shoemaker, and his sidekick, George Hook, trudged into town with their scruffy dog hoping to learn how to tell silver ore from everyday rock. To simply shoo them away from the store, the Tabors grubstaked the duo with picks, shovels, food, and supplies worth about $58. Grubstaking was a form of gambling whereby those with means risked "grub" (food) and sundry mining supplies to down-and-out but potentially promising prospectors in exchange for a share of whatever they uncovered. In their bargain, the Tabors would receive a third of anything the miners found—a long shot with these two drifters.

According to legend, a jug of whiskey was added to the deal. Once out of sight, the two found a comfortable hill and sat down to indulge. After emptying the jug, they thought why look further? Why not dig there? As luck would have it, they were on the one spot of Fryer Hill where a silver streak came closest to the surface. A few feet to either side of their shallow hole, they would have missed it completely. They dug deeper and found a vein of extremely rich silver carbonate ore. They called it the Little Pittsburg Mine, named for Hook's hometown, but misspelled without the *h*.

Horace Tabor

Tabor quickly bought out his new partners, eventually making him a millionaire. Investing in other Leadville silver mines, the Tabors were deluged with spectacular daily income from the

Baby Doe Tabor ALL
BILL HANSEN COLLECTION

prospering mines and huge returns from buying and selling silver-mining properties. Tabor soon became "Leadville's Silver King" and, by some sources, one of the five richest men in the country.

Horace rode his good fortune into becoming Leadville's first mayor, Lake County treasurer, the lieutenant governor of Colorado (1878 to 1883), and then in 1883 the ultimate reward for a Gilded Age tycoon—a US senator. In January 1883, he divorced his hard-working wife of twenty-five years, Augusta, in favor of a beautiful, divorced mistress half his age—Elizabeth McCourt, nicknamed "Baby Doe" for already being the sweetheart of the local miners.

The divorce was still making headlines when Tabor married his mistress in March 1883 in a lavish wedding in Washington, DC, at the Willard Hotel. Despite the scandal, President Chester Arthur was among the wedding guests, gasping at Tabor's gift to his bride—a $75,000 diamond necklace, allegedly pawned by Queen Isabella of Spain in 1492 to finance the first voyage of Christopher Columbus to America.

Horace and Baby Doe moved to Denver, where they spent lavishly and foolishly, maintaining an extravagant lifestyle, epitomizing Gilded Age wealth. Besides their block-long Denver mansion boasting a hundred peacocks strutting among nude statuary, Tabor built the grandest building Denver had seen to this day, the Tabor Grand Opera House, as well as the city's finest office building, the Tabor Block. Both are gone. Their reckless spending and the fact that all of their wealth was built on silver would later become a prime example of how shortsightedness and lack of wise diversification devastated people in the silver crash of 1893.

Cellini with me. I explained that he had been dead for some little time which elicited the inquiry "Who shot him?" They afterwards took me to a dancing saloon where I saw the only rational method of art criticism I have ever run across. Over the piano was printed a notice:

PLEASE DO NOT SHOOT THE PIANIST
HE IS DOING HIS BEST

I went to the theatre to lecture and I was informed that just before I went there two men had been seized for committing a murder, and in that

*theatre they had been brought on to the stage at eight o'clock in the eve-
ning and then and there tried and executed before a crowded audience.*

Wilde was not the only public speaker to brave Leadville's wild masses.
Even suffragette Susan B. Anthony boldly came to lecture the miners in
Leadville on women's rights.

John L. Routt, the last territorial and first state governor after Colorado became the thirty-eighth state in 1876, exchanged his three-piece suit
for overalls to work the Morning Star Mine, which he bought for $10,000.
Coloradans cheered this politician who actually worked in a mine instead
of just sitting behind a desk. Despite initial losses, Routt declared, "A miner
will never quit until he has put in his last shot." In April of 1879, he exulted,
"We broke into the 'blanket' of ore and my troubles are over." By 1880, when
Routt was president of the Consolidated Morning Star Mining Company,
the mine was paying around $70,000 a day. In 1889, Routt and company sold
out for a reported $1 million. Routt retired to Denver with his share of more
than $600,000.

Governor Routt was among many who gambled on Leadville and won.
David May founded his first May Company department store in Leadville.
Meyer Guggenheim's ascent to one of the wealthiest men in the world began
with Leadville mining and smelting. Leadville also bankrolled many of the
state's other wealthiest clans—the Browns, Campions, and Grants.

Some came to Leadville not to mine but to mine the miners. Charles
Boettcher shunned mining and instead made his first fortune running a
hardware store supplying the miners. He opened in 1879, with the slogan:
"Hardware, Hard Goods, Hard Cash." The hardworking German later remi-
nisced that Leadville was infested with "any number of reckless people here,
lounging around doing nothing; just living on excitement ... men would
sleep on chairs and be glad of one ... people were living right on the streets
or in mere shelters covered with brush ... the place was so crowded that you
could barely wedge your way through." The shortage of beds and the eternal
hullabaloo led one reporter to claim that "good men and women are leaving
this city every day simply because they are sleepy."

Leadville was the wildest of all the Rocky Mountain mining towns.
Besides drawing the elite, the popular, and respectable residents and visitors,
it was also the epitome of a Wild West mining boomtown and the haven for
every sort of rogue, scoundrel, and desperado. Con man Jefferson Randolph

"Soapy" Smith and gambler-gunfighter Doc Holliday were among the many prowling the saloons and gambling parlors looking for a fight or an easy way to get rich without working. Prostitutes openly brawled in the brothels over men eager for their services. Murders, shootings, robberies, and violence often dominated the scene, with some town marshals run out of town, shot dead in the streets, or later killed for their earlier efforts at law enforcement.

Unlike many other mining towns that tried to regulate, if not suppress, wickedness, Leadville bragged openly of its vice. In 1879, the *Leadville Daily Chronicle* announced proudly that the city had 120 saloons, 115 gambling houses, 35 houses of prostitution, and 19 wholesale liquor businesses. Further down the page, the *Chronicle* admitted there were also 51 grocery stores, 12 hardware stores, 12 shoe stores, 4 banks, 3 newspapers, 9 book and stationery shops, and 1 music store.

STRIKE!

Hard rock mining in the 1880s and 1890s entailed long hours of brutal, dirty, and hazardous work in the dark among dangerous gases, poor ventilation,

Hard rock miners worked underground in dark, dusty, and dangerous conditions. DENVER PUBLIC LIBRARY, WESTERN HISTORY DEPARTMENT

and the ever-present fear of explosions, fires, flooding, tunnel collapses, and equipment failures. Candles gave off the only light until electricity was introduced in the late 1880s. Caged canaries were used to forewarn of depleted oxygen or poisonous gases. Dust from pneumatic drills caused incurable silicosis and an ever-present miners' hacking cough.

Miners suffered while mine owners prospered. Most of the actual working class were poor immigrant miners trying desperately to chase the American dream in the cold, dark depths of the mines or the smoky heat of the smelter's blast furnaces. The miners producing the wealth began to realize that others were making most of the money, not those working for ten to twelve hours a day, six days a week, for $3 a day or less.

Leadville miners organized Colorado's first hard rock miners' union, the Miners' Co-operative Union, associated with the national Knights of Labor union. When the Chrysolite Mine banned smoking and forbade "talking or loitering by miners on duty," that was the last straw. On May 26, 1880, the Miners' Co-operative went on strike.

Soon other mines also experienced striking workers. The mine owners' response would become a standard approach for many more strikes to come. They persuaded the governor to declare martial law and send in the National Guard to protect strikebreaking scabs and stop any interference by striking miners. On June 18, 1880, the union called off the strike. Some historians suspect that the Chrysolite, then an overcapitalized, underproducing mine, had deliberately provoked a strike to cover up its failed production. A strike could be used to explain the shortage of dividends to investors.

Strikes and labor conflicts became intensified following the silver crash of 1893. Most of the silver mines were shut down, most miners lost their jobs, and soup lines formed for the surviving few workers. Those desperate mine owners trying to hang on took on even more-desperate miners trying to survive, and both sides became better organized. Once the largest and richest of silver cities, Leadville almost overnight went bust, experiencing a decline almost as dramatic as its rise. The population has shrunk to a little over 2,000. It lost its magic after the silver crash of 1893 and continues to dwindle to this day, a ghost of its former self.

ASPEN
As Leadville's population exploded, miners swarmed over the region looking for new prospects. They traveled down the Arkansas River to Dayton and

Twin Lakes. From there, some headed west over 12,095-foot Independence Pass. At the west foot of the pass, prospectors found promising silver deposits. They laid out the town of Ute City, soon renamed Aspen, in 1880. As exploratory holes began paying off, many other Leadville miners made the sixty-mile trek from Leadville to Aspen.

Along with miners came the usual small army rushing into bonanza towns—saloonkeepers, businessmen, gamblers, and the brides of the multitude (to label prostitutes discreetly). By 1890, Aspen had become a flourishing city of 5,108. During the early 1890s, just before the silver crash of 1893, Aspen actually outproduced Leadville in silver.

Aspen mines became legendary. The Smuggler produced the largest silver nugget in the Rockies, a 2,054-ounce hunk of ore that was 93 percent silver. A single bedroom-sized chamber in the Emma Mine netted its owner half a million dollars. By 1889, Aspen mines were producing $10 million a year. At night, the sides of Aspen Mountain were ribboned with lines of twinkling lights, as miners wound wearily down the mountain for home, using their mine headlamps as flashlights.

A major problem in Aspen, as in some other mining towns, was the flooding of mine shafts. Shafts sunk down as far as a mile would be flooded by groundwater. Pumps and diversionary tunnels were built. When flooding continued at the Smuggler Mine, the mine manager brought in deep-sea divers from the East. Although skeptics scoffed, the team of divers soon had the pumps repaired, and the Smuggler dried out. The East Coast divers were kept around long enough to teach locals deep-sea diving.

As silver gushed out of the earth, Aspen grew into a city of 7,000. A major investor, Jerome B. Wheeler, built the splendiferous Hotel Jerome, which he equipped with newfangled electric lights and an elevator that the passenger operated by pulling on ropes. He also constructed the Wheeler Opera House and his own mansion, which now houses the Aspen Historical Society. The hotel, opera house, and residence have all been restored as popular attractions in this reborn silver city. Wheeler also built the Aspen Mountain ore tram, bankrolled the Colorado Midland Railroad, and opened the first Aspen bank.

During its thirteen bonanza years, Aspen boasted ten churches, six newspapers, three schools, a large hospital, innumerable saloons, and the first electric lights in Colorado. Good times began unwinding in 1893. Aspen would have to wait another half century for a different snowy white gold to launch another era of flush times.

The Colorado Cannibal

Silvery success prompted prospectors to begin a statewide search that even penetrated the remote, rugged, and largely uncharted San Juan Mountains of southwest Colorado. One early party of five fortune hunters hired a guide named Alfred (sometimes misspelled as Alferd) Packer. When they reached the Uncompahgre River Valley encampment of Chief Ouray, leader of the Ute tribe, he warned them to wait until spring. But the Packer party had a bad case of the "Sudden-Riches Disease" and ignored the weather-wise chief. They headed into the maze of 14,000-foot peaks and the treacherous weather of the San Juan Mountains in the fall of 1873.

Come spring of 1874, only one of the party emerged—Packer. Stumbling into Chief Ouray's Los Pinos Ute Agency, Packer claimed that he had become separated from the other five and subsisted on roots, plants, and bark. But Packer's face looked full and greasy, like that of a carnivore. And the first thing he asked for was not food but whiskey. Although broke when last seen in the fall, Packer now had money to spend. He also had weapons that had belonged to the other five men.

Late that spring, when the snow finally melted, a reporter-illustrator for *Harper's Weekly* magazine stumbled upon the hacked-up and gnawed-on remains of Packer's five companions. Their skulls were crushed and strips of flesh were missing from their bodies. Packer changed his story and said that starvation had driven some members of the party to begin butchering each other. He claimed he had killed the last survivor, but in self-defense. He said it was a matter of eat or be eaten.

No one knew exactly what happened, but no one believed Packer. He was hauled into the Lake City Courthouse in Hinsdale County, a small mining county in the silver- and gold-rich San Juan Mountains. Packer was tried for murder, as cannibalism is not, to this day, a crime. The judge sentenced him to be hung with the famous, according to legend, words: "Packer, you man-eating son-of-a-bitch, there were only seven dimicrats in Hinsdale County and you, you, you et five of 'em!" Packer later found a friendlier judge who modified his sentence to life imprisonment. Later released for good behavior, he settled down in Littleton, Colorado, where he died in 1906 and is buried in the Littleton Cemetery.

THE SILVERY SAN JUANS

Spanish explorers named the major mountain range of southwestern Colorado for Saint John and found traces of gold and silver there. Folklore haunts the San Juans with lost Spanish mines and buried treasure. Its remote location and rugged refuge for the indigenous Utes made the San Juans a promising but initially elusive target for extraction of its precious metals.

Humbugs galore began with Charles Baker, who led a party up El Rio de Las Animas en Perdido (the River of Lost Souls) in 1860. Baker was determined to launch a gold rush, with or without gold. Another boomer, William Gilpin, the first governor of Colorado Territory, also puffed the San Juans, claiming in his 1859 guidebook that the mountains were "a veritable arcanum of metalliferous elements." Who could resist such a flowery invitation?

Like Alfred Packer (see sidebar), the Baker party headed into the San Juans in winter. Baker got as far as the level valley floor where Silverton would be founded in 1874 before turning back. Finding no pay dirt, the party returned to their homes that spring sadder, poorer, and wiser. At least they had not resorted to cannibalism. Disillusioned prospectors swore that Baker should be hung for creating "the San Juan humbug."

The well-publicized humbug eroded interest in the San Juans. Yet, the ever-optimistic Governor Gilpin continued to proclaim "the richest treasures lie where the incandescence of country has molded the carbon into the sparkling gem in the Sierra La Plata of the San Juan Country."

As fortune hunters poked into the San Juans in the late 1860s and early 1870s, they met with opposition from the Utes. Not only had the tribe occupied Colorado for centuries, but an 1868 treaty gave them ownership of the San Juans "in perpetuity." As usual, miners trampled any treaty and the Utes were forced to accept a new agreement in 1873. With a promise of $25,000 a year, the Utes reluctantly agreed to surrender the silver- and gold-rich areas around the future mining towns of Lake City, Ouray, Telluride, and Silverton.

Silverton, founded in 1874, flourished with the Sunnyside Mine, the region's richest and longest-lived producer, first staked in 1873. Silverton became the target of the Denver & Rio Grande Railroad, which steamed into town in 1882 and has been running ever since. This narrow-gauge scenic rail route has become a popular tourist attraction that draws some 200,000 passengers a year.

Silverton and other mining towns in the San Juans fared better than Leadville and Aspen when the silver crash came. The San Juaners simply shifted their focus to gold, zinc, lead, and other profitable metals. Silverton's population did not hit a census year peak until 1910 with 2,153 souls. Durango outgrew Silverton by becoming the smelting center and supply town for Silverton and other San Juan mountain mining towns.

Once there were close to a hundred post office mining towns in the San Juans. Today, most of them are ghosts. In San Juan County, for instance, Silverton is the only town left of sixteen once-lively communities. While many silver cities were dying, one newcomer would squeak through the tough times—Creede.

CREEDE

"Holy Moses!" shouted Nicholas C. Creede upon striking a silver lode on Willow Creek two miles above its junction with the Rio Grande. His 1889 discovery started a stampede that brought an estimated 10,000 people into a remote chasm that became Creede, which soon replaced Wason as the Mineral County seat.

Creede, the man, struck pay dirt again with the Amethyst Mine. He sold his Holy Moses Mine (whose ruins may still be seen three miles up East Willow Creek) to David H. Moffat, president of the Denver & Rio Grande Railroad, which built a spur line to Creede in 1891. Moffat claimed that this spur line from Alamosa via Wagon Wheel Gap to Creede paid for itself within the first four months of operation.

Seven camps thrived in the extremely narrow gorge of Willow Creek: Amethyst, Bachelor, Creede, Jimtown, North Creede, Stringtown, and Weaver. As Richard Harding Davis marveled in his book *The West from a Car Window* (New York: Harper Brothers, 1892), Creede had "hundreds of little pine boxes of houses and log-cabins, and the simple quadrangles of four planks which mark a building site. . . . There is not a brick, a painted front, nor an awning in the whole town. It is like a city of fresh card-board."

This "card-board" town squeezed in between towering basaltic cliffs was scorched by fires and drowned by several major floods. But Creede was too tough to die. Nothing stopped the eternal hubbub of mining and ore processing, of gambling and carousing in some thirty saloons strung out along Willow Creek. Creede attracted a rogue's gallery of western characters, including Poker Alice Tubbs, Bob Ford, Calamity Jane, Bat Masterson, and Soapy Smith.

Born in a silver rush and graduating to gold, Creede was a wild child. Saloons, dance halls, and whorehouses opened in tents to capitalize on the rush. Many brides of the mining masses showed up, including Killarney

Creede, last of the major silver cities, was another instant city, squeezed into a narrow chasm on a tributary of the Rio Grande. DENVER PUBLIC LIBRARY, WESTERN HISTORY DEPARTMENT

Kate, Lillis Lovell, Marie Contassot, Slanting Annie, and Timberline Rose Vastine, a six-foot-tall doll who towered over most of her customers. Creede Lil, one of the town's first soiled doves, graduated from a hillside tent to a log cabin, where it was easier to provide horizontal recreation. Lil stayed busy with customers around the clock until her death in 1892. The town's underworld gambling establishment, headed by con man Jefferson Randolph "Soapy" Smith, paid for her burial in Sunnyside Cemetery.

Cyrus "Cy" Warman was a lifelong lover and chronicler of railroading. Moving up from roundhouse laborer to engineer on the D&RG, he eventually left railroading to finally heed the beacon of journalism. In 1892, he set out for Creede to illuminate that town with his *Creede Candle*. There he published his often-quoted poem, "Creede":

> Here's a land where all are equal,
> Of high or lowly birth—
> A land where men make millions,
> Dug from the dreary earth.
>
> Here the meek and mild-eyed burro
> On mineral mountains feed—

It's day all day in the daytime,
And there is no night in Creede.

The cliffs are solid silver,
With wondrous wealth untold—
And the beds of running rivers
Are lined with glittering gold.

While the world is filled with sorrow,
And hearts just break and bleed—
It's day all day in the daytime,
And there is no night in Creede.

Creede was the last big flash among Colorado's silver cities. With the silver crash of 1893, most of them would shrivel and many would die.

Chapter Three

The Panic of 1893

Colorado's mining boom lasted until the silver crash of 1893, known both locally and nationwide as the Panic of 1893. By then, silver had replaced gold as the state's most lucrative resource, and its mines provided almost 60 percent of the nation's silver. Yet, its price had fallen after 1873, when the federal government demonetized silver, taking the United States to the gold standard. Washington politicos did this under pressure from eastern capitalists trying to control inflation. Inflation hurt bankers and other capitalist lenders who were being repaid in inflated currency worth less at repayment time than it had been when they loaned it. This pitted wealthy easterners against westerners, notably farmers, ranchers, and miners looking to borrow.

The federal government lowered its demand for silver at the same time that Colorado's production began soaring. Colorado and other western silver-mining states, notably Nevada and Utah, began pressuring Washington for subsidies. So did agrarian interests in the Midwest and the South, which also wanted cheap money. The result was passage of the Bland-Allison Act in 1878. This required the US Secretary of the Treasury to make monthly silver purchases of at least $2 million at the market price then hovering at around $1 an ounce. "Bimetalism," as the combined silver and gold standard was referred to, encouraged production of both precious metals as a currency standard.

Silverites rejoiced in 1890 with passage of the Sherman Silver Purchase Act, named for its champion, Senator John Sherman. This federal law hiked the US Treasury's required monthly purchase to four million ounces of silver at the prevailing market price. In trying to address a growing worldwide depression and what was considered an unsound money policy, newly elected president Grover Cleveland and Congress repealed the Sherman Silver

By the late 1880s, railroad cars stacked with Leadville silver bullion were shipped out of Buena Vista, a town downstream on the Arkansas River, showcasing Colorado's reliance on the silver boom. TOM NOEL COLLECTION

Purchase Act in 1893. With the return of the gold standard and removal of silver subsidies, the price of silver plummeted almost overnight, falling from roughly a dollar to around 50 cents an ounce.

Colorado crashed with the silver crash—worse than any other state in the country. Panic ensued. By July of 1893, roughly half the banks in the state had closed as depositors stampeded to pull out their savings. Those too late lost everything. Businesses also failed, as many of them depended one way or another on silver mining. Overbuilt and undercapitalized railroads serving the mining towns went into receivership.

Denver was hit especially hard. The real estate boom collapsed. Ambitious commercial construction downtown and residential development in expanding streetcar suburbs ceased overnight, leaving partly completed brick skeletons and vacant foundations dotting building sites. Prairie dogs moved back into projected subdivisions. Foreclosures were rampant, and real estate became available to anyone who would pay the back taxes. Architects fled the city. Realtors and construction workers joined the ranks of the unemployed. Only 124 Denver building permits were issued in 1894, compared to 2,338 in 1890.

Governor Davis H. Waite, a Populist from the silver city of Aspen, proposed a novel solution. He suggested that the state use its sovereign power to buy all of Colorado's silver and send it to Mexico to be minted into silver dollars. This got around the law against minting money in the United States. These dollars would then be used as a local circulating medium in Colorado. Opponents called the idea of "fandango dollars" crazy and illegal and shot it down in the legislature.

Meanwhile, unemployed miners from all parts of the state drifted into Denver. They clogged the streets, and some turned to crime or suicide. A frightened city established a refugee camp along the South Plate River bottoms at Riverfront Park. The city set up tents for some 400 men and fed as many as 1,000 a day.

Worried Denver officials sought to get the swelling ranks of destitute men out of town. Denver already had enough indigents among its own population. The city issued one-way railroad passes to anywhere but the Queen City of the Plains.

As more and more unemployed poured into Denver, the city also came up with another scheme, giving the indigents lumber to make flat-bottom boats to take their troubles downstream. This ragtag armada finally pushed off but did not get far before hitting sandbars, fallen cottonwood trees, and other obstacles. A few boaters died, but some actually reached destinations far to the east. There they joined Coxey's Army, a national protest march on Washington to demand relief from President Grover Cleveland and the federal government. Some of these protestors camped on the White House lawn, only to be arrested for trespassing.

These homeless, unemployed men gathered in Denver's South Platte River bottoms on June 2, 1894, to protest and beg for assistance. DENVER PUBLIC LIBRARY, WESTERN HISTORY DEPARTMENT

Mines and smelters, Colorado's biggest employers, ceased production. The Colorado Bureau of Labor Statistics Report for 1894 was gloomy: Aspen had 2,000 unemployed with 50 mines closed and "the situation is bad and couldn't be very much worse. If we get no favorable legislation, Aspen and vicinity is a goner." Leadville had 2,500 unemployed with 90 mines closed and "business is completely stagnated. The people are leaving as rapidly as their friends in other places can send them money to get away." Georgetown had 600 unemployed and 45 mines closed. Statewide, the bureau reported 377 business failures, 45,000 people out of work, and almost half of all mines closed.

Of Colorado's busts, this rivaled the Great Depression of the 1930s for the misery it caused. It would take over a decade for Colorado to recover. Only the Cripple Creek gold bonanza of the 1890s largely sustained the state's economy until it could become more diversified and less reliant on the mining of precious metals.

LEADVILLE'S ICE PALACE

Leadville came up with a novel, chilly solution to boost itself out of its gloomy 1890s silver depression. If Montreal, Quebec City, St. Paul, and St. Petersburg could create ice palaces, why not the two-mile-high city? After all, 10,152-foot Leadville was the highest city in the United States and usually one of the coldest. Usually.

With $1 subscriptions from ordinary folk and generous contributions from the well-heeled, Leadville put its unemployed miners to work to build its ice palace in the winter of 1895–96. This great, frosty Norman castle crowned a three-acre realm. A pair of ninety-foot-high towers guarded the entrance, and smaller towers crowned each corner between crenellated parapets. Ice blocks three to five feet thick formed the walls. Electrical lights embedded in the ice provided a shimmering glow inside and out. A toboggan ran downhill from the Ice Palace into town. Inside the icy exterior lay a frame building with a ceiling of ice crystals. Therein visitors found an ice rink, dining rooms, and a dance hall.

No sooner did the Ice Palace open than Leadville began experiencing freakishly warm weather. Temperatures that winter reached a daytime high of sixty-five degrees. The ice palace sank into mud puddles. On March 28, 1896, the Ice Palace closed, never to reappear. Rarely had a boom busted so quickly.

TROUBLE IN THE MINES

Even a still-frozen ice palace (see section above) could not relieve the trouble in the mines and smelters. With sinking profits and so many unemployed miners, the owners claimed an excuse to cut wages to $2.50 per day and require ten-hour days while organized miners fought to keep wages at $3 for an eight-hour workday, as well as improved working conditions.

To address their grievances, in 1893, the Western Federation of Miners (WFM) was formed and would grow into the most powerful union ever seen in the Rockies. In 1894, the WFM claimed an early success in a five-month strike in the Cripple Creek gold district, where pro-union Populist governor Davis Waite called out the National Guard to support the miners.

A different outcome came in 1896–97, when the WFM was soundly defeated by silver mine owners in Leadville. A familiar pattern emerged over that nine-month strike. The mine owners unified and retaliated with lockouts, blacklists, spies, and detective agencies and brought in private armed guards to protect "scabs" hired to replace the strikers. A pro-management governor

The Tabor Saga Concludes

Of the many silver crash tragedies, the fate of Horace, Augusta, and Baby Doe Tabor is best known. Horace and Augusta had attained moderate prosperity during the Oro City gold boom. They were at the forefront of the Leadville silver boom and had attained undreamed-of wealth. Horace traded in his austere wife, Augusta, for a trophy bride, Baby Doe, and squandered millions on luxurious Gilded Age silver trappings.

Tabor had blindly invested everything in silver mining, and then heavily mortgaged his holdings to support his lavish lifestyle. Mired in foreclosures and lawsuits, he lost his mines, his Denver opera house, his office buildings, and his mansion. Baby Doe's jewelry, furs, and silk finery were pawned. Despite their dire circumstances, Baby Doe stuck with him, surprising those who thought she would leave when the money dried up. As it turned out, she was no "gold digger" or, more appropriately, no "silver digger." She stuck with him to the bitter end. Shortly after friends promoted him to Denver's postmaster, Tabor died in 1899 in the city's Windsor Hotel, which he once owned.

Baby Doe lived for another thirty-six years in poverty in a twelve-by-sixteen-foot shack at the Matchless Mine on the east side of Leadville. Her elder daughter, Lillie, soon abandoned her and moved to the Midwest. The Tabors' younger daughter, appropriately called "Silver Dollar," desperately tried to make it on her own as a poet, songwriter, and novelist but drifted into alcohol, drugs, and burlesque before dying mysteriously in a flophouse in Chicago in 1925.

Baby Doe's story is romanticized in "The Ballad of Baby Doe," but her real life played out even more sensationally than any opera. Once the toast of the president of the United States and the talk of all Colorado, she descended into dire poverty. In her isolated Leadville shack next to the played-out Matchless Mine, she somehow survived blizzards and scared off bogeymen with her shotgun. She newspapered the shack's windows to stop peepers chasing rumors that her $10,000 wedding dress and $75,000 diamond wedding necklace lay inside.

Her hellish life in that shack is explored by Judy Nolte Temple in her book *Baby Doe Tabor: The Madwoman in the Cabin* (Norman: University of Oklahoma Press, 2007). Nolte used the Tabor Collection at History Colorado to unravel the often-bizarre scribblings of a deranged woman clinging to her lost daughters, her Catholicism, and her fabulous, if sinful, past. Nolte suggests that Baby Doe was doing penance at the Matchless Mine until the day her body was found there, March 7, 1935, frozen to death, arms spread out in the shape of a cross.

She was last photographed dressed in rags, living reluctantly off whatever charitable offerings people would leave at her door. Today she lies with her beloved Horace in a connubial grave at Mount Olivet Cemetery in Wheat Ridge, a west Denver suburb. Her Matchless Mine shack is now a popular tourist attraction.

Ironically, Augusta Tabor flourished financially following her 1883 divorce and weathered the crash. She initially rented out her twenty-room mansion to fourteen boarders and parlayed her business acumen and frugality into a wide range of diverse investments from her divorce settlement. At the time of the silver crash, she had become one of the richest businesspeople in Denver. She resided comfortably in the Brown Palace Hotel, which their son Maxcy was then managing. Augusta donated heavily to charity, helped build a new Unitarian church, supported the suffragette crusade, and died a wealthy woman at the age of sixty-two in 1895 in Pasadena, California. Diversifying wisely had paid off, and she left Maxcy an estate estimated at between $500,000 and $1.5 million.

Elizabeth McCourt "Baby Doe" Tabor tumbled from beauty queen millionaire to living in a Leadville mine shack. TOM NOEL COLLECTION

Governor Frederick W. Pitkin, sympathetic to the mine owners in Leadville, called out the National Guard to quell the 1896–97 strike by the Western Federation of Miners, handing it a major defeat. Such union-busting tactics became standard practice in Colorado. TOM NOEL COLLECTION

sent in the National Guard to side with the mine owners and declared martial law. Killings, injuries, damaged property, and arrests ended in arbitration and a major defeat for the WFM.

The Western Federation of Miners' star organizer was William Dudley Haywood, but everyone, friend or foe, called him "Big Bill." Like many poor youths, Bill Haywood started working in the mines at the age of nine. He graduated to underground mining at sixteen and then chased mining booms and busts throughout the West. He was one of many who soured on the dream of rushing west and striking it rich. Mining had evolved into a depression-cursed, corporate world of huge underground ore-extraction factories and hot, smoky smelters.

In 1894, Haywood joined the Western Federation of Miners. He became a zealous convert and preached the union gospel everywhere—down in the mines, in the saloons, and in union halls. Long before the "closed shop" became legal, Big Bill made it the law in Colorado mines by routinely telling miners to join the WFM or hit the trail.

Haywood and other unionists rejoiced when Colorado passed an eight-hour maximum workday for mine and smelter workers in 1899. In 1902, however, the Colorado Supreme Court declared the law unconstitutional. That court held that everyone should have the right to work as many hours a day as they wished. This left miners working ten- and twelve-hour days, which allowed owners to hire two, rather than three, shifts a day.

Haywood decided the time had come to strike. On July 4, 1903, he and the WFM declared a statewide strike that spread from Denver to Cripple Creek, Idaho Springs, Telluride, Durango, and elsewhere. Haywood declared openly socialist views and welcomed class warfare. He argued: "Barbarous gold barons did not find the gold, they did not mine the gold, they did not mill the gold, but, by some weird alchemy, all the gold belonged to them."

As the WFM had organized smelter workers as well as miners, Haywood launched the 1903–4 strike in Globeville. That area, just north of downtown Denver, was originally an independent town and had become the

The Globe Smelting and Refining Works gave its name to what is still the working-class Denver neighborhood of Globeville. TOM NOEL COLLECTION

53

state's smelter hub thanks to the Globe Smelter but also housed a half-dozen others. Haywood fired up the strikers, telling them: "There are no rest days, no Sundays, no holidays, for smelter workers [because] the fires that melted the ores, like the fires of hell, must never cool."

Strikers also walked out of the huge Grant Smelter, allowing the fires to cool and causing the molten metal and the slag to congeal and freeze the furnaces. After this sabotage, the American Smelting and Refining Company never fully reopened the Grant Smelter.

"Now that we had to fight for the eight-hour day," Haywood wrote later in his autobiography, "it would involve one strike after another, some of which would become very bitter." That was exactly what happened. Colorado's most widespread labor war raged for a year between July 1903 and July 1904. As before, mine owners hired private guards and persuaded Colorado governor James H. Peabody to send in the National Guard. Both armed forces roughed up strikers and protected the so-called scab miners who replaced strikers. The governor, a conservative banker from Cañon City, blasted "the socialistic, anarchistic objects and methods of the Federation ... under the evil influences of a criminal leadership." He meant, among others, Haywood, who responded satirically in the WFM's *Miners' Magazine* with a bogus letter to "His excellency the Governor of Colorado from Czar Nicholas II of Russia," confiding, "I have the same insubordination to deal with in the convict mines of Siberia."

Violence and murder flared. Peabody blamed it on the WFM, which he called the "Western Federation of Murderers." Much of the public sided with Peabody. He used the National Guard to shut down pro-union newspapers, raid union halls, and deport strikers. By July 1904, nearly all mines and smelters were working with non-union labor. Haywood reluctantly called off the strike. He left Colorado for Chicago, where he was jailed for his socialist views and radical union organizing, before fleeing to Russia to join the Communist Party that successfully staged the kind of workers' revolution that he had tried to inspire in the United States.

Chapter Four

Booming Populism, Suffrage, and Women's Achievements

The Panic of 1893 busted Colorado's economy and social structure. During the recovery, there was a transformation of society's views with growing populism and social consciousness. Consequently, women's suffrage and efforts at political and social reform became boons of such a societal boom.

Colorado's economic busts rebounded into social gains. Labor unrest and economic distress inspired radical political solutions and reform crusades. The Populist Party attracted many disillusioned Democrats and Republicans, who found fault with the "gold bugs" who controlled both political parties. Founded on a national level in 1891, the Populist Party garnered strong support among farmers and factory and smelter workers, as well as miners. They all had been hurt by the 1893 depression. The Populists were particularly successful in Colorado, where they elected a Populist candidate as governor, the aforementioned Davis Waite. An Aspen newspaper editor, former schoolteacher, and union organizer, he championed the Populist program with concrete, if then radical, ideas:

1. Have the federal government buy up all the silver that could be produced at $1.28 an ounce.
2. Nationalize the railroads and lower their rates.
3. Establish a maximum workday of eight hours.
4. Establish a minimum wage of $3 a day.
5. Start taxing people's income rather than their land.
6. Have richer folks pay a larger share of their income for taxes.
7. Allow voters to petition to change laws or make new ones to get around obstructionist members of both parties opposing reform measures.

8. Use the secret ballot in elections.
9. Establish direct election of US senators by all voters and not by state legislatures.
10. Give women the vote.

This last "radical idea" was the first to become reality. In 1893, the year of the crash, Colorado men voted to enfranchise women. Women argued that they could not do any worse than the men. Suffragettes adopted a broom as their symbol, indicating that they intended to clean up government at a time when political corruption prevailed.

Wyoming had given women the vote in 1890, but that vote had been to approve a large constitutional package with women suffrage merely among

DON'T FORGET THE WOMEN WHEN YOU VOTE ON TUESDAY.

Equal Rights! Equal Responsibilities! Equal Suffrage!

Colorado men voted to give Colorado women the vote in 1893, long before national women's suffrage was enacted, enabling them to campaign for other reforms. TOM NOEL COLLECTION

Freewheeling Women

A new contraption, the bicycle, became another symbol of the women's movement. The bicycle was all the rage in the 1890s and early twentieth century. Bicycles allowed women independence and freedom of movement, no longer reliant upon their menfolk or distant and sometimes unreliable mass transit systems or the relatively rare access to a horse and buggy. They could now travel freely wherever and whenever they wanted, to the market, to work, to clubs, or to social or political events.

The bicycle also transformed women's fashion from heavy, uncomfortable corseted dresses with bustles to more accommodating bloomers and loose-fitting pants, blouses, and jackets. Bicycle frames were even redesigned to accommodate the change in women's style and dress.

Susan B. Anthony proclaimed, "I think [bicycling] has done more to emancipate women than anything else in the world. It gives women a feeling of freedom and self-reliance." Seeing a female on a bicycle presented "the picture of free and untrammeled womanhood."

one of hundreds of provisions. In Colorado, on the other hand, men voted solely on enfranchisement. So, Coloradans boast that they were the first state to deliberately give ladies the vote. Susan B. Anthony agreed, as she wrote one Colorado suffragette: "Oh how glad I am, that at least we have knocked down our first state by popular vote." This came twenty-seven years ahead of the Women's Right to Vote amendment to the U.S. Constitution in 1920.

Women's suffrage was probably the most important and significant Populist reform because it had so many other ramifications. Women tended to focus on moral issues, political reform, education, and family concerns. The ladies battled everything from promiscuous expectoration to child labor to prostitution. Social reforms included the rise of kindergartens, welfare benefits for single mothers, a Colorado Civil Rights Act in 1895, early juvenile justice laws in 1899, a juvenile court system in 1903, and finally, child labor laws in 1911. Women helped some labor causes succeed after long and bitter labor wars, ultimately legitimizing unions, the eight-hour workday, and $3 a day minimum wage.

Prohibition of alcohol became a major women's issue. Many supported Prohibition because they saw it reducing poverty, crime, domestic abuse, and

Time-Saving Innovations

Women had more time for political activity, pursuing employment opportunities, and joining social clubs because of the many new goods and appliances that reduced the time needed to run a household. Electric refrigerators, gas stoves, sewing machines, vacuum cleaners, and many other inventions freed women from housework.

Even the many women living on Colorado farms and ranches could mail-order labor-saving devices through Sears Roebuck catalogs. In that seductive booklet, women could buy clothing rather than make it themselves. Anything a person might want, even an entire house, could be ordered from Sears. Women were thereby liberated from the drudgery of a lonely and overworked home life to primarily serve the needs of their breadwinning husbands and freed to pursue their own goals and ambitions.

other social problems. Women, supported by many churches, finally achieved their goal by passing the Prohibition Amendment outlawing the sale of alcohol, which Coloradans adopted January 1, 1916, three years ahead of national Prohibition.

Once Colorado women got the vote, many of them became politically active, and some ran for office. Three captured seats in the Colorado House of Representatives in 1894, making them the first women in the world to be elected to a state or territorial legislature. By 1900, ten women served in the General Assembly. Helen Ring Robinson became the first state senator in 1912 and championed women's and children's causes. Colorado has long prided itself on politically active women. Although the state has yet to elect a female governor or US senator, about half of the state legislators are now women.

WOMEN JOIN THE WORKFORCE

The ratio of men to women had drastically changed since the gold rush days where men outnumbered women 20 to 1 according to the 1860 census. By 1890, that ratio had grown to 4 to 3. Hundreds of women had originally come to Colorado during the gold rush as schoolteachers. In female-scarce Colorado, teachers were often snatched up as wives. Toward the end of the nineteenth century, more favorable employment opportunities abounded.

Many women worked as maids, laundresses, dressmakers, domestic servants, waitresses, factory workers, or shopgirls. While miners were fighting for $3 per day in wages, shopgirls were often eking out a living at $3 per week. The 1900 Colorado Bureau of Labor Statistics reported one conversation overheard among two shopgirls sitting down for a 15-cent meal:

"Oh Mary, you can't afford such a high-priced meal as that."

"It's too bad if I can't eat a decent meal once a week."

Poverty drove some women to prostitution. Other women, who had secured an education, could pursue a career and not simply hold a job. Many became teachers, nurses, midwives, office workers, or stenographers, positions more respectable and suitable for the "fairer sex." Wage disparity between men and women remained common, as men were viewed as the primary and necessary breadwinners. The lack of "equal pay for equal work" was apparent among teachers. By 1899, urban male teachers in Colorado averaged $82.30 per month while female teachers earned only $58.21 per month.

Emily Griffith, Colorado's best-known schoolteacher, helped many poor children through hard times. She taught English as a second language to immigrant kids as well as job training and placement. In 1916, she founded Denver's Opportunity School "For All Who Wish to Learn." After discovering that many parents also needed help, she opened her free school on nights and weekends for adults needing language and job training. When she found both children and adults were underfed, she opened a soup kitchen at the school's front door, knowing it is easier to learn on a full stomach.

Some women broke into the male bastions as professionals. By 1900, 17 percent of Colorado's physicians were women. They not only specialized in obstetrics, gynecology, and pediatrics but also often branched out to pulmonary diseases such as consumption, which had lured many physicians to Colorado.

One general practitioner, Dr. Justina Ford, completed medical school back east in 1899, then came to Colorado. When she applied for a medical license, the examiner told her, "I feel dishonest taking a fee from you. You have two strikes against you to begin with. First of all, you're a lady and second, you are colored." Denied hospital privileges, Dr. Ford worked out of her home or made house calls. She delivered more than 7,000 babies, catering not only to African Americans but also to others of color, notably Asians and Hispanics. Her home office in Denver's Five Points neighborhood now serves as the Black American West Museum.

Margaret "Unsinkable Molly" Brown

Margaret "Molly" Brown not only survived the 1893 silver crash but prospered in its aftermath, thanks to her husband's gold mining. The poor, uneducated Irish Catholic became a model of women's independence and philanthropy, even though snubbed by Denver's high society. Born in Hannibal, Missouri, in 1867, Margaret Tobin started out as "Maggie" in a poor family but posthumously came to be called "Molly." At nineteen, the red-haired, blue-eyed, buxom young woman headed west to Leadville, finding work sewing drapes. There she fell in love with a handsome mining manager, James "JJ" Brown, whom she married in 1886.

After the silver crash of 1893, Brown's resourceful mining efforts paid off. He found gold in the Little Jonny and other mines, making them wealthy. Molly shared that wealth by supporting the soup kitchens serving unemployed miners. The Browns moved to Denver's swanky Capitol Hill neighborhood and purchased a stylish Queen Anne–style

Margaret "Molly" Brown epitomized the rise of poor immigrant women into prosperous respectability. TOM NOEL COLLECTION

house at 1340 Pennsylvania Street. Molly became a charter member of the Denver Women's Club and joined other society ladies in fundraising for St. Joseph's Hospital and Immaculate Conception Cathedral, where pew number 6 was reserved for the Brown family.

The mythical Margaret "Molly" Brown, a creation of writers Gene Fowler and Caroline Bancroft, and Broadway's and Hollywood's *The Unsinkable Molly Brown*, was an airhead social climber. This was hardly the case, as Kristen Iversen points out in her award-winning book, *Molly Brown: Unraveling the Myth* (Boulder, CO: Johnson Books, 1999). Molly campaigned for women's rights, came to the aid of troubled miners, supported labor unions, and raised funds for French troops in World War I.

Marital bliss eluded her, as JJ was in the public spotlight for several extramarital affairs. In court, there were allegations of JJ's "moroseness" and at least two attempts to shoot Molly. "I got the gun both times and prevented my being killed, while he wept and afterward cried, begging me to go away where he could not kill me." They permanently separated in 1909.

Molly began a life of world travel that led to her 1912 heroics aboard the *Titanic*. As the ship sank after hitting an iceberg, Molly courageously calmed the passengers in her lifeboat and urged the coxswain to return to pick up survivors. After the disaster, she helped care for and raise money for some of the poor passengers from steerage, earning her widespread praise. She gained fame as the "Unsinkable Molly Brown." Her Capitol Hill residence has become Colorado's most popular house museum. Tour guides there celebrate Molly as a model of how a poor, uneducated woman from an ostracized ethnic group could rise to the top in a male's world.

Diminutive Mary Lathrop graduated summa cum laude from the University of Denver Law School and was licensed as an attorney in 1896, passing the bar exam with the highest score not to be beaten until 1941. She became the first female member of both the Colorado and American Bar Associations. She once said: "I'm either a lawyer or I'm not. Don't drag being a woman into it." When not successfully keeping a client, gambling czar "Big Ed" Chase, out of jail, she focused on probate law, protecting women and children.

Lathrop's first case in the Colorado Supreme Court established the law of charitable trusts, upholding the Clayton Trust for orphans. The Clayton Trust's red sandstone dormitories still exist on the west side of Colorado Boulevard in Denver across from the former Park Hill Golf Course, previously owned by the Clayton Trust and now heavily contested for development or preservation as open space.

WOMEN'S CHARITIES AND CLUBS

An 1894 *Rocky Mountain News* article condescendingly noted: "Denver is a city of women's clubs. There are clubs for every subject of which the feminine mind has ever had to grapple." Instead, women's clubs emerged as a major instrument of social change as the "fairer sex" not only grappled with but confronted and overcame many of society's ills.

Many women's organizations devoted themselves to charity. Elizabeth Byers had organized the first charity, the Ladies Union Aid Society, in the 1860s to assist Union soldiers. After the Civil War, the society focused on the hungry, sick, homeless, and destitute. In 1874, it changed its name to the Ladies Relief Society. While her husband, *Rocky Mountain News* editor William Byers, used his paper to promote Colorado as a gold mine for immigrants, Elizabeth worried about the many indigents, widows, and orphans who did not strike it rich. In 1883, she set up the Working Boys' Home and School to provide troubled youths "as pure and homelike an influence as can be obtained in any institutional atmosphere." She joined Margaret Gray Evans, wife of second territorial governor John Evans, to establish in 1872 the Denver Children's Home, which still pursues its founding mission.

The depression of the 1890s gave new purpose to the Denver Women's Club, a veritable "Who's Who" of Denver society. The club sponsored community vegetable gardens to feed the poor, a traveling art gallery to educate children, and a summer baby clinic in City Park to promote health. It also helped form the State Home for Dependent Children in 1895 and a Civil Service Reform Bill in 1899.

Perhaps the most forgotten of all the women working in early-day Colorado were the Catholic nuns who established hospitals, orphanages, and schools. A hospital for the poor and overworked miners in Leadville was one of their earliest successes. Even before St. Vincent's had windows or doors, sick and dying miners were dumped off there. To care for them, the Sisters moved into the unfinished hospital and awoke under a blanket of snow. After that, they slept on mattresses in the kitchen around the stove. Their first patient died from frostbite, saying he was "thankful to die with the sisters" rather than on the cold, dirty streets of Leadville. The Sisters hung up canvas and paper to create rooms and found themselves invaded by twenty-seven measles patients, all of whom they nursed back to good health.

Sister Marceline McGrath recalled the hospital in the early days:

There were sick people in every corner—in the halls because there was not room enough, and on the floors because there were not beds enough. . . . Poor dying men would beg, when there were no more beds,

"O Sister, for God's sake take me in; let me lie on the floor; let me die with the Sisters."

The 1893 crash left many poor, unemployed sick miners in the Sisters' care. The nuns worked not only on the body but also on the soul, converting dying miners to Christianity and sending their souls off to heaven. Besides St. Vincent's in Leadville, nuns opened a dozen other Colorado hospitals, of which St. Joseph and St. Anthony in Denver, St. Francis in Colorado Springs, St. Mary's in Grand Junction, and Mercy in Durango are prominent survivors.

Like hospitals, public libraries typically originated as a cause of women's clubs. Women believed in libraries as a crucial avenue to self-education, advancement in society, and job training. Free public libraries gave even the poorest victims of bust times a way to educate and advance themselves.

In Monte Vista, women raised money from the fewer than 1,000 residents to build this fine stone library in 1894. TOM NOEL COLLECTION

Small-town libraries often shared space in town halls and courthouses, were combined with schools or museums, or found homes in train stations (Lyons). Other innovative locations have included a redesigned grocery store (Castle Rock), a former Catholic church (Kiowa), a former residence (La Veta), a former bank (Collbran), and an old school (Crested Butte). The Fort Morgan library shared space with a museum. In Fairplay, the library is located in the former county courthouse and jail.

A typical tale is that of the Women's Literary Club in the small town of Monte Vista in the San Luis Valley, which started a circulating library in 1885. Mrs. Lillian Fassett kept that collection in her house for the first ten years and served as the town's first librarian. In 1894, the town constructed a free-standing stone library as one of its first major improvements. In 1919, the librarian and collection moved into Monte Vista's present Carnegie Library, built with a generous grant from the Carnegie Foundation.

After envisioning a library, women typically raised money, formed a literary or reading group, started collecting books, selected a site, and then sought support from the Andrew Carnegie Foundation. The foundation made community donation of a prominent site and community financial support a condition for its funding. Andrew Carnegie, whose Carnegie Steel Company became one of America's largest and most profitable corporations, made support of libraries the centerpiece of his various philanthropic endeavors. Carnegie insisted on architect-designed fine buildings, usually in a Neoclassical style.

The Carnegie Foundation supported the construction of 1,689 public library buildings in the United States. Thirty-six of these were built in Colorado between 1901 and 1929, as Colorado emerged from one depression only to fall into another. Four of the Colorado Carnegies have been razed, two are vacant, and ten have been used for other purposes such as an events center (Denver), a museum (Rocky Ford), a bed-and-breakfast (Sterling), and a restaurant (Littleton).

With women's suffrage and their active, socially conscious club activities, other Populist reforms also succeeded. Tax reform was a particular priority—replacing property taxes with progressive income taxes became a reality in 1913. Dramatic Gilded Age inequality of wealth favored rich city folks on often-small tracts of urban land while farmers, ranchers, and other rural endeavors were often land-rich but cash-poor. Election reform also came with direct election of US senators in 1913. Wealthy Colorado tycoons such as Simon Guggenheim, Nathaniel Hill, and Horace Tabor had commonly bought their seats from the state legislature. Progressive reform at the local level eventually led to national reforms. From the state most badly damaged by the 1893 silver crash, panic, and bust, Colorado recovered and boomed as one of the most progressive states in the country.

CHAPTER FIVE

Economic Diversity: Ranching, Agriculture, and Manufacturing

THE SILVER CRASH AND THE PANIC OF 1893 TAUGHT COLORADANS THAT mining alone could not carry the state. Economic diversity was essential. As mining declined in the early 1900s, agriculture replaced it as the state's top economic enterprise. Ranching and farming blossomed, as did industry. A diversifying economy also led to a more diversified population, as growing agricultural and industrial enterprises not only attracted but demanded immigrant and ethnic labor. Foreign immigration also reached its peak in the latter part of the nineteenth century, with many flocking to Colorado to feed the needs of the state's labor-starved but booming diversified economy.

RANCHING

From the territory's beginning, Colorado offered opportunities other than mining. The largest economic alternative by the 1870s was the ranching industry, which could feed the miners and the growing population supporting the mining industry.

Like many who initially tried gold prospecting, John Wesley Iliff found his fortune in other ways. He had been bitten by the gold bug at age eighteen. His father had offered him a $7,500 interest in the family farm back in Ohio, but young Johnny replied, "No, just give me $500 and let me go West."

Shortly after his arrival in Colorado, Iliff sensed that mining was a long shot and opened a general store in Denver. There, he provided groceries, clothing, money, and supplies to emigrants, often in exchange for their livestock. Cattle, he found, could be left out, like buffalo, to graze on dried prairie grasses during Colorado's usually mild winters. He rested and fattened the animals on the open range and then sold their beef.

Iliff captured large contracts to provide beef to Indian reservations and to railroad construction crews. In 1868, he began supplying meat to Union Pacific teams constructing the transcontinental railroad through Wyoming. To fulfill this very large order, Iliff bought many of the longhorn cattle that Charles Goodnight brought up from Texas along the Goodnight-Loving Trail on the eastern base of the Front Range, where I-25 is roughly situated today. By the 1870s, Iliff annually bought 10,000 to 15,000 Texas longhorns, paying $10 to $15 a head for cattle weighing 600 to 800 pounds. He fattened them on western prairie grass for a year or two until they reached 1,000 to 1,200 pounds and then sold them for $30 to $50 a head.

With the profits, Iliff kept buying up large chunks of northeastern Colorado. Much of it was either along waterways or adjacent to vast tracts of still unclaimed open range on the public domain. He also hired ranch hands and had them file homestead claims, which he then bought from them. Cowboys paid a measly $30 a month could use the cash from selling their homesteads. They could also find jobs with Iliff, who by 1878 owned a ranching empire of 35,000 cattle and 15,558 acres along the northwest side of the South Platte River between Greeley and Julesburg.

Iliff's control of the river and its tributaries gave him a virtual monopoly on the drylands beyond as well. Before homesteaders intervened with farming and the open range was fenced off by newly patented barbed wire in the late 1870s, no other rancher or farmer could survive on waterless land. There, Iliff's cattle grazed on an estimated 650,000 acres of public domain. He became Colorado's first rancher millionaire. Yet the cattle business compromised his health. He died of an obstructed gall bladder from all of the alkaline water he had consumed on Colorado's dry open range.

After Iliff died in 1878, his widow, Elizabeth Sarah Fraser Iliff, took over his vast spread. Elizabeth had come to Colorado from Chicago as the Singer Sewing Machine Company's manager for the western region. She had a storefront in Denver, but also sold sewing machines out of a buckboard wagon. When her buckboard broke down out on the plains one day, she was rescued by the tall, handsome, brown-haired, blue-eyed Iliff. They fell in love, and she left the sewing machine business to learn ranching after they married. Following his death, Elizabeth soon had their cattle empire humming as smoothly as one of her sewing machines. One of an estimated 500 women running Colorado ranches by 1900, Elizabeth Iliff's success in cattle raising also allowed her to become a philanthropist. She gave $100,000 to endow the

Iliff School of Theology at the University of Denver, whose southern campus boundary is Iliff Avenue.

John Wesley Prowers became Colorado's second-most-successful cattleman as ranching became a terrific boom business. Born in 1838, he came from Missouri to Colorado as a teenager, hauling goods on the Santa Fe Trail to Bent's Fort on the Arkansas River. In 1861, Prowers married Amache, the daughter of a prominent Cheyenne peace chief, Ochinee (Lone Bear). That same year, he bought a hundred Missouri cattle and began acquiring prime land along the Purgatoire and Arkansas Rivers.

Prowers, like Iliff, acquired riverside and creekside lands that gave him control of adjacent waterless uplands. By 1881, he owned 80,000 acres along forty miles of Arkansas River frontage and controlled 400,000 acres of rangeland and 10,000 head of cattle. Prowers did much to improve cattle breeding in Colorado, where he introduced some of the first Herefords in 1871 to replace scrawny longhorns. At his death in 1884, Prowers had become

The National Western Stock Show

The cattle industry changed not only Colorado but also all of America. Inexpensive western beef transformed the US diet. Before the 1880s, few Americans could afford beef. But cowpokes, feedlots, stockyards, meat processing, and refrigeration changed all that. Fresh beef in refrigerated railroad cars flooded eastern grocery stores and meat markets. Americans became beef eaters as steak and hamburgers became the all-American meals.

Cowboys, who fed the miners, railroad crews, and town builders, left a legacy celebrated with Colorado's largest and longest public celebration: the National Western Stock Show. Beginning in 1906, this annual event still attracts more than 700,000 visitors to Denver for sixteen days every January. Starting out as a show to display, buy, and sell all forms of livestock, and to learn new and improved breeding and veterinary skills, the event has grown into a trade show selling everything imaginable, from pickup trucks to kitchenware. A rodeo was added in 1931, and a Mexican Rodeo Extravaganza added in 1987 beefed up attendance and brought in new audiences of Hispanics, eager to celebrate their culture as Colorado's first ranchers of sheep, cattle, horses, and other livestock.

Colorado's second millionaire rancher. Prowers County in southeastern Colorado, where his cattle once roamed, bears his name.

While the cattle barons grew rich, the cowboys and ranch hands led a life far different from that portrayed in Hollywood westerns. Paid a mere dollar a day, tending cattle and riding the range was hard, monotonous, and dangerous work on a diet of coffee, biscuits, and beans. Although surrounded by cattle, cowpokes could not even enjoy steaks, as that would cut into the owner's profits.

Prowers's and Iliff's success, later supported by British capital, rode the railroad boom. Railroaders once focused on mining towns began to build to ranching communities, where millions of cattle and sheep needed transportation to markets. After railroads arrived in the 1870s, Colorado beeves could be shipped to markets back east, including Kansas City and Chicago. By 1880, Colorado produced more beef than any state but Texas, and more sheep and wool than any state but New Mexico.

This cattle boom led to overstocking the American West with more than seven million head by 1885. After cattle exhausted the prairie grasses, it was replaced by sagebrush, salt brush, Russian thistle, and other less nutritious plants, if not by dusty wastes of naked soil. Overgrazing and the absence of fresh grasses left cattle weakened and malnourished when the great blizzard struck.

Beginning with a snowstorm in November, the extreme winter of 1885–86 gripped the high plains for five months. Howling winds, deep snow, and bitter cold temperatures, as low as minus forty-six degrees Fahrenheit, kept ranchers and cowboys confined to their houses and bunkhouses while blizzards wiped out their herds. A million or more cattle starved or froze to death. Texas longhorns, with their thin hides, lack of body fat, and light fur that reflected rather than absorbed sunshine, proved especially vulnerable. At the same time, much of the open range on the public domain was being fenced off by homesteaders intent on dry farming and later irrigated farming.

The days of the large-scale cattle barons were coming to an end, and smaller fenced-off ranches abounded. These setbacks for ranchers enabled sheepherders who were moving north from Colorado's San Luis Valley and New Mexico to establish themselves in areas formerly dominated by cattlemen.

Demand for wool to make Civil War uniforms had sparked a sheep-raising boom in the early 1860s. Sheep required less water than cattle and fed on plants that cattle shunned. Cattlemen fought the sheep invasion, as they were convinced that sheep ruined grazing land for cattle. Range wars led to violence as thousands of sheep were massacred or driven over cliffs. Sheepherders' camps and wagons were attacked. Colorado's cattle-sheep wars were as murderous as the more famous Johnson County, Wyoming, and Lincoln County, New Mexico, conflicts. As ranchers tended to be Anglo and sheepherders Hispanic, racial differences led to underreported violence against Hispanics. Cowboys were seldom prosecuted or punished.

Despite cowboys slaughtering whole flocks and terrorizing or murdering sheep men, the sheep industry grew. By 1900, Colorado boasted two million sheep, with the count rising to three million by 1914. Sheep, in fact, were more numerous than cattle in Colorado between 1900 and 1950. Cattle have since regained the lead, and beef products are now Colorado's leading international export.

Farming and Agriculture

In his official 1820 exploration report, Major Stephen Long labeled Colorado's eastern plains as the "Great American Desert." He claimed that the lack of water and wood would render the area unsuitable for agriculture.

William Byers, a land agent for the Denver Pacific Railroad, preached a rosier view. Pointing out that the 1862 Homestead Act allowed anyone, including women and immigrants, to apply for 160 acres of land, Byers repackaged the area as a veritable Garden of Eden. He helped convince easterners, including the utopian-minded Nathan Meeker and *New York Tribune* editor Horace Greeley, that an agricultural colony north of Denver would flourish. This led to the 1870 establishment of the Union Colony, later renamed Greeley, along the Denver Pacific line. It would eventually dig twenty-seven miles of water canals capable of irrigating 250,000 acres.

Not to be outdone, the Kansas Pacific Railroad set up agricultural experiment stations in eastern Colorado to coax settlers to settle on the high plains in towns such as Cheyenne Wells, Kit Carson, and Strasburg. Between 1880 and 1890 the number of farmers in Colorado grew by 300 percent, and dozens of new farm and ranch towns sprouted on the eastern plains.

Initially, dry farming pushed westward out of Kansas and Nebraska. Wheat was the primary grain crop. Irrigated farming, supported by numerous irrigation and ditch companies, made Colorado acreage second only to California and greatly expanded agricultural production. By 1900, there were 10,000 miles of irrigation ditches in Colorado irrigating 150,000 acres of land. Key inventions like windmills to bring up aquifer water and barbed wire to keep out unwanted cattle helped make an agricultural boom possible. Later inventions such as high-volume pumps and center-pivot irrigation, invented by Strasburg farmer Frank Zyback in 1952, have transformed much of the high plains and the San Luis Valley into giant irrigated crop circles in square quarter-section plots.

Still, there have been ups and downs. In 1910, Oliver Toussaint Jackson, a successful Boulder businessman, filed a homestead claim and advertised for African American colonists to promote Dearfield in Weld County, named for the precious value of the land. Dearfield initially prospered in the 1920s, but its dreams turned to dust in the 1930s as its precious soil blew away during the drought years of the Dust Bowl. Like many other small farming communities on the eastern plains, Dearfield is today a mere ghost town. Colorado floriculturists, specializing in carnations and roses, thrived after World War II, but have wilted in recent decades due to foreign competition. Mink raising also flourished before floundering.

The Arkansas Valley in southeast Colorado has become famous for its Rocky Ford cantaloupes, first developed in the 1870s by George W. Swank. Firms such as D. V. Burnell Seed Company, founded in Rocky Ford in the 1860s, have made the Arkansas Valley a major source of flower and fruit seeds. Today, Colorado's agricultural bounty is celebrated in numerous state-wide festivals such as Rocky Ford's Watermelon Days, Palisade's Peach Festival, Paonia's Cherry Days, Glenwood Springs' Strawberry Days, Olathe's Sweet Corn Festival, Greeley's Potato Days, and Pueblo's Chile and Frijoles Festival.

Charles Boettcher—Diversification Personified

No one exemplified successful economic diversification in many fields of business better than Charles Boettcher. Once a poor German immigrant, Boettcher emerged as Colorado's premier businessman and industrialist. His diversification and smart approach to business opportunities proved to be bust-proof.

Boettcher was born in 1852 in Prussia, where his father, Frederick, ran a hardware store. Charles came to the United States in 1869, joining the thousands of poor German immigrants fleeing the warfare and unrest in their native Fatherland. With the help of his brother Herman, he entered the hardware business. After working for his brother, Charles opened his own

Charles Boettcher shined as Colorado's best example of a well-
diversified industrialist, a diversification that allowed him to ride out
busts. TOM NOEL COLLECTION

hardware store in Boulder, Colorado. That two-story brick store at the main intersection of Pearl Street and Broadway still stands, with a carved stone inscription over the corner entrance, "C. Boettcher A.D. 1878." R. G. Dun, the credit rating entrepreneur who later became half of Dun & Bradstreet, first appraised Boettcher in 1875 as "a tinner by trade . . . industrious and economical and we think his prospects fair."

In 1879, Charles set out for Colorado's fabulous new boomtown—Leadville. In the two-mile-high "Cloud City," he avoided the silver-mining fever, which had reached epidemic proportions, and built another hardware store. When asked why he never ventured into mining, Boettcher replied, "Axes and hammers, picks and shovels don't go out of style."

Boettcher also put his money into ranching, banking, and the Leadville Electric Light Company. Hanging on to investments paid big dividends: when the Public Service Company of Colorado, the state's largest energy provider, acquired the Leadville Electric Light Company in 1923, he became a major stockholder and a director of Public Service (now Excel Energy). In Leadville, he became one of a dozen millionaires created by that city's boom, including the Tabors and the Guggenheims. Boettcher, however, made his bundle not by mining but by supplying the miners and everyone else with what they needed.

To supply his growing hardware store empire in 1884, Boettcher bought a large wholesale company in Denver and began dealing in mining, milling, construction, and agricultural supplies. In 1890, he moved to Denver and listed his occupation in the *Denver City Directory* as "loans and investments," rather than listing his multiple businesses. These included Boettcher & Company Investments, one of Colorado's largest stock brokerages, and the Denver U.S. Bank (now part of Wells Fargo Bank). Tired of buying dynamite from the DuPonts and others for his mining supply business, he formed the National Fuse and Powder Company in Denver in 1901.

Charles's wife, Fannie, finally persuaded her workaholic husband to take a vacation to Germany in 1900. To Fannie's dismay, the trip turned into a tour of German sugar beet industry sites. Charles studied the fields and the factories where the big ugly beets were grown to be reduced to pure white sugar. According to legend, he had Fannie empty out one of her suitcases in order to take home beet seed. In 1900, Charles, his son Claude, and a few other partners set up the Great Western Sugar Beet Company (GW).

From the 1910s to the 1950s, sugar beets emerged as Colorado's primary agricultural crop. The McKinley (1890) and Dingley (1897) tariffs

Ethnic Diversity

Booming economic diversity brought ethnic diversity and was virtually driven by a booming number of immigrants, not only by business leaders such as Boettcher and Mullen, but also by large pools of skilled and unskilled laborers who rushed to the United States in the latter half of the nineteenth century and early twentieth century. Not just easterners sweeping west to avoid the depression and strife back east, but people from all over the globe headed to gold rush Colorado in 1859 and the boom times that followed.

Many of Colorado's early miners came from mining communities in their native lands, such as Ireland, Scotland, Cornwall, Wales, Silesia, Austria-Hungary, Poland, Russia, the Slavic countries, Italy, Greece, the Balkans, Scandinavia, and even Canada. As agriculture took over, former farmers from such places as the dry Russian steppes and eastern and western Europe quickly moved in, as well as Japanese and Mexicans, with their vast farming and ranching experience.

Former freed slaves escaped the perils and Jim Crow laws of the post–Civil War South to take up farming, ranching, mining, and working for the railroads, hotels, and restaurants, as well as serving as menial common laborers. Sheepherding attracted Mexicans,

Hispanic migrant workers, shown here in 1908, have long done much of Colorado's heavy work. COURTESY LIBRARY OF CONGRESS

Greeks, and Basques. Chinese were enlisted to work on Colorado's railroads and then moved on to mining and independent laundry businesses throughout the state. Germans dominated the beer industry.

Perhaps most importantly, much of the capital for Colorado's expanding economy, including mining, railroading, cattle ranching, real estate development, and industry, came from British, German, and other western European countries because the expected yields could far exceed those available in their homelands' stagnant economies. With such foreign capital came immigrant managers, overseers, and even some of the original investors.

Colorado became the proverbial booming melting pot of multitudinous peoples, bringing their own skills and many often still speaking their native languages, maintaining their own cultures and religions, and congregating in their own communities. Most were readily accepted and embraced and soon seamlessly integrated into Colorado's growth. Others remained stigmatized, marginalized, and oppressed, with vestiges of such discrimination remaining to this day.

on imported sugar boosted the domestic sugar beet business. Three giant firms—Great Western, Holly, and National—transformed the South Platte and Arkansas River drainages into beet kingdoms. These massive farms were usually tended by migrant labor actively enlisted from Mexico, where civil war and poverty drove many hardworking Mexicans north to toil in the sugar beet fields. Their labor in Colorado's sugar beet fields enabled Boettcher's Great Western Sugar Beet Company to become Colorado's second-largest employer after Colorado Fuel & Iron in the 1920s. By 1926, sugar beets replaced wheat as Colorado's number one cash crop and led the nation until the industry turned sour in the 1960s.

To process his ranch's cattle and those of other Coloradans, Charles Boettcher and some partners set up the Western Packing Company in 1901, which he sold to Swift & Company in 1912. Instead of buying insurance from someone else for his many enterprises, Boettcher formed the Capitol Life Insurance Company in 1905. It became Denver's biggest hometown insurance company. Boettcher also became a major stockholder in the Denver Tramway Company, which monopolized the city's streetcar service.

The Colorado Fuel and Iron Company in Pueblo reigned as the state's biggest industry from the 1890s to the 1950s. That Pueblo plant produced much of the railroad track and the barbed wire that shaped Colorado and the Rocky Mountain West. TOM NOEL COLLECTION

Yet stories of Boettcher's frugality delighted Coloradans. In 1922, he bought Denver's finest hotel, the Brown Palace, where he lived for the rest of his life. Daily, he walked from the Brown Palace six blocks down 17th Street to his Ideal Building office. His son Claude also worked at the Boettcher Investment Company, but did not walk to work like his father; he arrived in an enormous, chauffeured Packard and dressed in fashionable conservative suits. Asked why he didn't ride and dress like his son, ninety-year-old Charles replied: "Unlike myself, Claude has a rich father."

Boettcher died in his sleep on July 2, 1948, at the age of ninety-six. He left an estate of $16 million to the Boettcher Foundation with the provision that all its proceeds be given exclusively to Colorado causes.

John Kernan Mullen—Grain Tycoon
Another contributor to Colorado's agricultural economy was John Kernan Mullen. Mullen, a poor Irish immigrant, put together a vast Colorado-based milling empire stretching from Texas to Oregon, from Missouri to California.

Mullen had arrived in Denver in 1871 seeking a mill in need of a miller. He then opened his own mill in 1875. Employing the tough business practices of other tycoons of his era, Mullen crushed and then bought out competitors to create a near monopoly on grain, flour mills, and grain elevators by 1885. His empire is now a part of the global giant ConAgra.

Branching out into the land and cattle industry and later the financial sector, Mullen quickly became a millionaire. Yet his name is still remembered in Colorado because of his philanthropies, including the Mullen Home for the Aged and the Mullen School for Boys, now Mullen High School.

Shaking hands with J. K. Mullen was unforgettable. After working in flour mills since the age of fourteen, his hands were imbedded with millstone shards. That evidence reminded everyone of his rough upbringing. Mullen never forgot his heritage and did much to employ and uplift Colorado's Irish community. His philanthropy, much of it anonymous, helped build Immaculate Conception Cathedral, Mount Olivet Cemetery, St. Joseph Hospital, St. Cajetan's Church, and many other Denver institutions. His five daughters and their descendants also embraced the family's charity work, leaving Mullen better remembered today for his giving than his taking. His rise from poor Irish immigrant to millionaire grain tycoon reflected on both ethnic and economic booms.

MANUFACTURING

Manufacturing, along with ranching and farming, grew into big business. Again, Charles Boettcher rose to prominence. Waste and inefficiency had always annoyed Charles Boettcher—especially when he was paying for it. During construction of GW's first sugar beet plant in Loveland, he questioned why the cement was imported from Germany at extremely high cost. He was told that Germans made much more reliable cement than anyone in the United States. So, Charles began investigating. He discovered that all the ingredients—limestone, sand, gravel, clay, and silica—could be found in Colorado. In 1901, he started what would become Ideal Basic Cement to mass-produce high-quality cement.

SURVIVING THE INFAMOUS COAL WAR OF 1913–1914

By 1903, Boettcher's cement company was worth $1 million, and he began building a headquarters building on downtown Denver's "Wall Street of the West," 17th Street. Denverites watched the eight-story Ideal Building rise as Colorado's first concrete-reinforced structure with a steel skeleton. When the cement had dried, Charles had the wooden forms set afire. Everyone in town, including the local press, rushed down to see the new building destroyed. After the wooden forms burned, all were amazed to see the concrete building still standing, undamaged. Boettcher had dramatically made his point about steel and concrete construction being fire resistant. From that day forward, most large downtown buildings would be cement and steel instead of wood framing and masonry.

The largest firm of all, the Colorado Fuel and Iron Company (CF&I) in Pueblo, employed one out of every ten Coloradans in its statewide, vertically integrated network of mines, mills, smelters, steel plants, and company towns. CF&I began with William Jackson Palmer, of Denver & Rio Grande Railroad fame, who consolidated three smaller firms in 1880 to form Colorado Coal and Iron to manufacture rails for his booming network of tracks. His company mined and marketed Colorado's vast fields of much-sought-after bituminous coal, produced iron and steel, and manufactured coke. Coke, a form of high-grade coal made by roasting out impurities, burns at an extra-high temperature needed for use in steelworks and smelters.

Palmer, who was better at organizing businesses than at keeping them, was eased out of the company by 1884. John C. Osgood came on board in 1892 and combined his Colorado Fuel Company, the largest coal producer in the Rocky Mountain West, with Colorado Coal and Iron to form CF&I.

CF&I ultimately owned 69,000 acres of coal lands and produced twelve tons of coal a day, half of the state's output. Besides innumerable coal mines, CF&I ran two iron mines, four coking plants, and one of the most advanced steel plants in the West. CF&I absorbed smaller coal mines to raise its share of Colorado coal production to 75 percent. It modernized the Bessemer Works at Pueblo at a cost of $20 million between 1899 and 1903 and tripled the output.

From Wyoming to New Mexico, CF&I employed an army of 15,000 workers, from clerks to coal weighers—a majority of whom lived in the proverbial company towns and owed their souls to the company store. Following the 1893 crash of silver, suddenly unemployed and desperate immigrant miners flocked to the coal industry and were initially eager and willing to enjoy the benefits of these company towns. CF&I's early company towns included Primero, Segundo, Tercio, and Cuarto—four efficiently if unimaginatively named and numbered CF&I coal towns west of Trinidad. The homes there were frame boxes with three or four rooms for the often-large families of workers. Houses at Morley, another company town, were better built from concrete blocks molded to imitate stone and sported porches and hip roofs.

The most progressive of some sixty CF&I towns, Redstone, lay along the picturesque Crystal River in central Colorado. There, CF&I president John C. Osgood built a model company town of Queen Anne–style cottages with electric lights, indoor toilets, and running water. In the same complex he erected an elegant Tudor-style boardinghouse for single male workers. A mile farther upstream he built his personal forty-two-room mansion, Cleveholm Manor. All of these buildings survive, restored for residential and tourist uses.

Surviving the Infamous Coal War of 1913–1914

Soon after Osgood created his idyllic town, he lost control of it. To raise funds to modernize CF&I, he had begun borrowing from John D. Rockefeller Jr., then one of the richest men in the United States. This arrangement ultimately gave Rockefeller the opportunity to snatch up CF&I. In 1903, Colorado's largest business became a part of the nation's largest business empire—Standard Oil. Southern Colorado coal miners, paid an average of $15 a week, further subsidized Rockefeller's millions.

Rockefeller owned CF&I when it became involved in the deadliest labor war in US history—the Coal War of 1913–1914, culminating in the Ludlow Massacre. From 1884 to 1914, over 1,700 men had died in Colorado's coal mines—the highest death rate in the United States. Colliers were paid by the ton, often set at 2,200 pounds, and not paid for "dead time" for basic safety measures such as shoring up unstable mine roofs. For "live time," they were paid solely in scrip redeemable at the company-owned stores, which set their own prices and readily extended credit to ensure indebtedness that might never be paid off.

Curfews were set in the company towns, rules governed everyday life, loyalty was demanded with dissent and efforts at labor organization squelched, incoming and outgoing mail was tampered with, and armed guards patrolled the perimeters to prevent ingress and egress. Segregation of the workforce by race or country of origin was also demanded. In one company town, thirty-two nationalities speaking twenty-six separate languages compromised both safety and labor organization. Most were from southern or eastern Europe, but Hispanics, Black people, and even Japanese people joined the mix.

While the supposedly altruistic corporate paternalism of the company towns provided housing, stores, recreational facilities, schooling, and health care, it also maintained total control over the exploited labor force in an isolated locale, prompting some historians to call such towns a "feudal domain."

After the Ludlow Massacre, the Red Cross showed up to help survivors, including many immigrant families. TOM NOEL COLLECTION

The United Mine Workers of America (UMWA) and 8,000 largely immigrant coal miners struck CF&I's vast southern Colorado coal fields in September 1913. Poor pay, long hours, the loss of liberty and human dignity under the feudal system, and dangerous working conditions led miners to join the UMWA, a national union. Founded in 1890, this still-active organization has long been a champion for coal miners. The union provided tent homes for striking miners and their families after CF&I evicted them from their company towns.

As with most other Colorado miners' strikes, the pro-management state governor sent in the National Guard to protect scabs (nonunion strike breakers) and control strikers. An improvised armored car, the "Death Special," assembled at CF&I and mounted with a machine gun, patrolled the company's property and the perimeter of the union's encampment.

On April 20, 1914, after weeks of violent clashes, the National Guard began firing machine guns into the tent camp of Ludlow. Miners' families who lived there dug out cellars beneath the tents to avoid the bullets. Next, the Guard set fire to Ludlow. Two women and eleven children suffocated to death hiding under one of the tent homes. Infuriated strikers fought back with guerrilla warfare for a week. The Greek strike leader, Louis Tikas, was openly murdered. An estimated one hundred strikers, family members, and National Guardsmen lost their lives before federal troops were called in by President Woodrow Wilson to disarm both sides.

By December 1914, the strike was finally called off. John D. Rockefeller Jr. was excoriated in the press. Headlines nationwide brought this atrocity to public attention, earning the strikers popular support previously lacking. Yet the UMWA and other unions did not get the recognition and power they sought until the New Deal and the National Labor Relations Act of 1935.

CF&I survived both the Panic of 1893 and the Coal War of 1913–14, and continued to reign as the state's largest employer. It made its hometown of Pueblo the state's second-largest city, the "Pittsburgh of the West." Like other steel mills nationwide, CF&I began a slow decline after World War II. The coal fields and company towns followed the pattern of most of the earlier gold and silver camps and became ghosts.

In 1982, suffering from foreign competition and an aging plant, as well as natural gas replacing coal, the steelmaker idled its four large blast furnaces. In 1984, it shut them down permanently and by 1993 was bankrupt. Most of the once-vast works have been demolished, although a few smaller firms continue to operate on a reduced scale. The stylish Southwestern-style administration building was recycled in 2007 as the Steelworks Center of the West. A major legacy of CF&I's glory days is Pueblo's richly diversified population.

Chapter Six

The Gilded Age Rush to Respectability and the 1918 Flu Pandemic

GILDED AGE COLORADO

The Gilded Age between the Civil War and the early 1900s was a time of opulent materialistic excess, conspicuous consumption, and business dominance. This was also a time when Colorado struggled to elevate itself from a Wild West frontier state in a rush to respectability. Denver also joined the rush, eager to emerge from its reputation as a backward cow town and smoky, smelly smelter and mining supply hub to become the wealthy, cultured, and sophisticated business center of the Rocky Mountain West.

Social status and recognition were everything. Rigid class stratification created a time of clawing social mobility, with the slowly emerging middle classes attempting to emulate and climb the social ladder to the wealthy upper crust. The wealthiest 1 percent of society owned over 25 percent of the wealth, the upper 10 percent owned three-quarters of the wealth, while the bottom 50 percent owned less than 4 percent. Although some of the middle class were rising, most Coloradans lived in poverty.

While the mansions had indoor plumbing, toilets, and running hot and cold water and were isolated in tree-lined affluent enclaves, the masses relied on wells and outhouses. They survived in often densely packed, seedy, rat-infested, and crime-ridden neighborhoods where packs of stray dogs and gangs of wild youths ran amok amid effluence, filth, and pollution. The Gilded Age was therefore a time of both boom and bust, depending on one's status in society.

After Colorado became a state in 1876, Coloradans pursued respectability with the same zeal they sought gold. Those who struck it rich rushed to flaunt their success with architect-designed mansions, elegant schools, grand churches, lavish private clubs, and opulent opera houses. Luxurious grand hotels also served as status symbols, luring wealthy residents, business travelers, and tourists, as well as the most modern technological advances and creature comforts such as elevators, telephones, hot water radiators, and flush toilets. Examples included Denver's Oxford and Brown Palace, the Jerome in Aspen, the Boulderado in Boulder, the Broadmoor in Colorado Springs, the Strater in Durango, the Hotel Colorado in Glenwood Springs, and the Beaumont in Ouray.

Horace A. W. Tabor opened his Tabor Opera House and Vendome Hotel in booming Leadville before moving to Denver and opening Tabor's Grand Opera House in 1879. At the time, it was Denver's finest building and a statement that Denver had arrived. Other cities and towns, big and small, erected opera houses as status symbols celebrating both their boom times and their newfound respectability. Central City boasted one of the state's most impressive opera houses, opened in 1878, and it remains an important venue for opera enthusiasts to this day. Aspen had its Wheeler Opera House, and even Longmont offered its Dickens Opera House, first opened in 1882.

Following the opening of the Tabor Grand Opera House, theaters sprang up along Denver's Curtis Street, offering live theater, burlesque, and vaudeville. Legend has it that Thomas Alva Edison himself, on a 1915 visit to Denver, called Curtis Street "the best lighted street in the world." In 1908, the Princess opened as a movie house showing Denver's first six- reel film, *Queen Elizabeth*, starring the French tragedienne Sarah Bernhardt. Other silent-picture houses followed, making Curtis Street the vibrant hub of Denver's nightlife.

The first fine residential district for Colorado's movers and shakers sprouted on 14th Street in what is now part of Denver's Central Business District. By the end of the nineteenth century, Denver's elite moved east of Broadway and uphill to residential enclaves in Capitol Hill. At her opulent 1906 mansion at East 10th Avenue and Sherman Street, Louise Sneed Hill reigned over Denver society with her "Sacred Thirty-Six," an elite social club that excluded Jews and Catholics and attempted to emulate Mrs. John Jacob Astor's "Four Hundred" set of New York City.

The Gilded Age obsession with all things high class found expression in upscale social clubs. The upper crust measured their riches not only by the size of their mansions but by their inclusion in many elegant and exclusive clubs, complete with ornate dining halls, thirst parlors, ballrooms, and luxurious libraries, squash courts, and billiard, smoking, and card rooms. Some graduated to country clubs, such as the Denver Country Club, founded in 1887, which claims to be the oldest country club west of the Mississippi River. Originally a club dedicated to horse racing and polo, it eventually moved to a 120-acre former wheat farm that offered Denver's finest golf course, as well as a swimming pool and tennis courts. Soon, the eponymous Denver Country Club and Polo Club neighborhoods sprouted nearby as new enclaves for Denver's elite. Social climbers sought to elevate their self-importance by flaunting their biographies and club memberships in social registers and Louise Hill's *Who's Who in Denver Society*.

However, beneath the shiny veneer of such impressive monuments of wealth, as well as the massive town halls, courthouses, and other public buildings, cities like Denver lacked basic infrastructures to provide health care, sanitation, water and sewer systems, or improved roadways, sidewalks, and public parks for the masses. The patina of booming success and respectability masked the reality for most Coloradans.

Mayor Speer's Beautification Dreams

While other political machines often perpetuated the problems, Denver's mayor Robert W. Speer attempted to change all of that toward the end of Colorado's Gilded Age. Denver's rush to respectability inspired a machine Democrat to transform Denver into a beautiful, progressive city that would appeal to tourists, while bolstering the city's infrastructure with improvements for the masses.

Robert Walter Speer came to Colorado in 1878 to recover from tuberculosis. The Colorado cure worked for Speer, who regained his health and gained weight, a beaming smile, and a firm handshake. Jumping into Democratic Party politics, he rose rapidly through the ranks as city clerk, postmaster, a member of the Fire and Police Board, and then head of the Board of Public Works, which controlled nearly half the city's budget. Speer used his authority to hire and fire employees, sign contracts, issue saloon licenses, and work with the underworld to build up the most powerful political machine Colorado has ever seen.

As mayor of Denver from 1904 to 1912 and from 1916 until his 1918 death in office, Speer transformed a drab, ordinary city into what he liked to call "Paris on the Platte." At a time when the silver crash was still slowing private-sector growth, Speer launched massive public spending projects as

Mayor Robert Walter Speer between 1904 and 1918 transformed a dusty, drab Denver into an urban oasis, a so-called "City Beautiful" of parks, parkways, and stately public buildings. He drew inspiration from the 1893 Chicago World's Fair, which transformed a swampy lakefront into a dreamy landscape of Neoclassical buildings. As Denver's most powerful boss, with a well-oiled political machine, he made things happen over—or under—the table. DENVER PUBLIC LIBRARY, WESTERN HISTORY DEPARTMENT

part of his "City Beautiful" movement. He doubled the city's park space, gave away 110,000 shade trees, and even created mountain parks outside the city limits. Speer loved lights. In front of Union Station, the city built a Welcome Arch, eighty-six feet wide and sixty-five feet high, illuminated with 1,294 lightbulbs. Even more spectacular was the electric light fountain in City Park Lake (since renamed Ferril Lake for Colorado's premier poet, Thomas Hornsby Ferril).

Speer cleared the slummy heart of the city for Civic Center Park, which would stretch from the State Capitol on the east to what would become the City and County Building on the west. Around the grassy landscaped park, other government buildings were eventually clustered: the Colorado History Museum, the U.S. Mint, the Public Library, and, in future years, a new Denver Public Library, the Denver Art Museum, and state and city office buildings.

One of Speer's proudest achievements, the 12,000-seat municipal auditorium, opened in 1908 to host the first national political convention west of the Mississippi River. There, Democrats nominated William Jennings Bryan for his third and last unsuccessful run at the presidency. Under the national spotlight, Denver strove mightily to shine. Apache Indians regaled the delegates with war whoops and dances. The city brought down mountain snow to dump in front of the auditorium so that delegates could settle differences with snowballs that July. Denver would not host another national political convention for a hundred years. That 2008 convention nominated a more successful candidate, Barack Obama. The original Denver Municipal Auditorium now anchors the Denver Performing Arts Complex as the transformed Ellie Caulkins Opera House.

Between 1904 and 1918, Speer developed and greatly beautified the city's major parks—City Park, Washington Park, Sloans Lake, and Sunken Gardens. Instead of mere showpieces, fences were avoided, "Keep Off the Grass" signs were removed, and playgrounds were added so as to make them available and appealing to the masses. Speer also planned a system of parkways and boulevards connecting many of the parks with flower, shrub, and tree medians under wooded canopies and generous setbacks for broad sidewalks and tree lawns.

Still, the nicer neighborhoods and suburbs in east Denver received the lion's share of these efforts. A prototype was Speer Boulevard, which bordered Cherry Creek and conveniently passed through the wealthy Denver Country Club neighborhood where Speer lived. The creek had become so trashy that some suggested converting it to a trunk sewer since that had become its main use. Speer had a better idea. He cleaned up the creek, confined it to a channel to prevent flooding, and planted ornamental streetlights, grass, vines, and trees along the boulevard.

Speer also recognized the need for mundane improvements. He spent more than $10 million on streets, sidewalks, and sewers. The renowned Denver Zoological Gardens that Denver boasts today began when Mayor Speer freed animals at City Park Zoo from cages and put them in large, natural enclosures. The City Beautiful was for animals as well as people. The Gilded Age was finally transitioning from a mere superficial boom for the wealthy to an era of rising upward mobility and benefits for the previously neglected masses. Denver was transforming from a dusty western cow town and mining supply center to the preeminent business and cultural center of the Rocky Mountains. By building during a bust period, Speer prepared Denver for booms to come. Unfortunately, he would succumb to one of Colorado's biggest busts.

THE 1918 "SPANISH FLU" PANDEMIC

Since entering the Great War in Europe in April 1917, Colorado's sugar beet industry was booming; beef, vegetable, and grain products were in high demand; and steel mills were turning out much needed war materials fed by previously strife-ridden coal mines. While Coloradans were growing Victory Gardens to free agricultural produce for the war effort, they were also joining the army in droves and pushing war bond drives to flag-waving crowds. Little did they know that they would soon be fighting an invisible enemy more dangerous than the Central Powers: the Influenza Pandemic of 1918.

Many believe that the so-called "Spanish Flu" pandemic, responsible for perhaps 50 to 100 million deaths worldwide including 675,000 Americans, originated at Camp Funston, a regional army mobilization center outside of Fort Riley, Kansas, less than 500 miles from Denver. Most Colorado recruits enlisted at Fort Logan in southwest Denver before being transferred to Camp Funston for basic training. In early March 1918, the camp cook fell ill and, before noon, another hundred reported to the infirmary. Deaths soon followed. The military censored any reports of the outbreak to maintain morale and retain focus on the war effort.

The sick American troops were soon shipped off to Europe, where they mingled with other troops from all over the world. In Europe, the influenza outbreak mutated and became more deadly and contagious and was soon killing more troops than the battlefield carnage. The warring countries suppressed any news of the pandemic. Spain was neutral, and its unmuzzled press freely reported the rising death toll. It was rewarded for its candor by most assuming that the epidemic originated in Spain. Kansas was off the hook.

Colorado had several vulnerabilities that doomed it during the 1918 pandemic. As the "World's Sanitarium," much of its health-seeking population was already afflicted with tuberculosis and other lung disorders. Of the approximately 1,733 physicians in Colorado serving a population of 906,000, one-sixth were off serving in the military and many of the rest were deemed medically unfit for active service, often due to pulmonary disease. Miners performing dangerous high-altitude, thin-air labor in confining underground caverns, daily breathing in dust from hammers, drills, and explosives, already suffered all kinds of lung ailments. These ranged from TB and emphysema to black lung disease and silicosis.

The State Board of Health was grossly underfunded, spending more on the health of livestock than the health of its citizenry. It had no emergency fund. After receiving a measly $3,300 from the $1 million set aside by Congress for state relief, the state had to commandeer funds appropriated for fighting venereal disease. The governor and state public health officials failed to act decisively at the outset and ceded control to local governments, with politicians wary of business pressures and public protests, especially during a midterm election year. Disaster loomed for a flu pandemic.

Within ten months, and mostly from October to December 1918, almost 50,000 Coloradans became ill and approximately 7,783 would perish, ranking Colorado's death rate among the top states in the country. Denver, with a population of 213,381, lost about 1,500 citizens and fared better statistically than the rest of the state, but was still one of the worst-hit cities in the United States. The mining town of Silverton has often been deemed one of the deadliest flu communities in the nation, losing almost 10 percent of its population, while Gunnison emerged as an "escape community" and a model for pandemic avoidance.

Some historians believe that Denver's Mayor Speer was one of the earliest victims of the first wave of the influenza pandemic, though this is impossible to prove. Midway through his third term as mayor, Speer developed a spring "cold" on May 2, 1918, which progressed to pneumonia, causing his death on May 14 at the age of sixty-two. Ten thousand mourners turned out

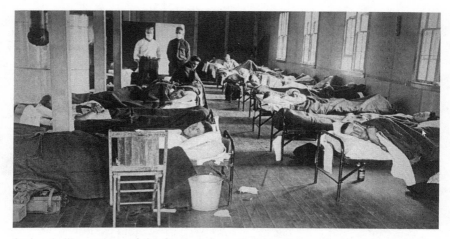

Seriously ill members of the Student Army Training Corps convalesce on cots in the quarantined barracks in Fort Collins as heavily masked orderlies stand help-lessly nearby. Without screens in a cramped and littered general ward, isolation was attempted by alternating head-to-feet positions from bed to bed. NATIONAL ARCHIVES

for his funeral in the Denver Municipal Auditorium that he had helped build a decade earlier. At the time, Coloradans were unaware of the outbreak just 500 miles away.

The second wave struck the American shores in early September 1918 as both sick and wounded troops were rotated home. The naval yard in Boston was the first hit and, by the end of the month, there were 14,000 flu cases and 757 deaths in the Boston area. Other naval facilities along the East Coast and Great Lakes saw the same outbreaks. The pestilence rapidly spread across the country.

Less than a month after the outbreak in Boston, the second wave hit Colorado's college towns. Members of the Student Army Training Corps arrived from Montana for specialized training at the University of Colorado in Boulder, Colorado College in Colorado Springs, and the Colorado Agricultural College (CSU) in Fort Collins. Of the approximately 250 cadets arriving in Boulder around September 19, 1918, over a dozen were already seriously ill. Within five days, seventy-five student soldiers were isolated in Mackey Auditorium and makeshift hospitals in two fraternity houses. Within a week, the number had climbed to ninety-one. Health-care providers could offer no treatment for this unknown contagion, but patriotic women distributed jars of jelly to the quarantined sick.

The first death was reported on October 1, and by October 3, there were three dead. Bodies were stashed in the steam tunnels between Woodbury Hall and Mackey Auditorium. Boulder shut the city down on October 7 with a full quarantine, closing the university and all schools, churches, and movie theaters. Eventually, about 650 Boulderites became infected, with 119 dead.

A similar scenario played out in Fort Collins. Over half of the first 150 trainees were ill upon arrival and were hospitalized at a specially constructed barracks on campus. Fifteen would die. In Colorado Springs, 200 Montanans brought two dozen sick to Colorado College. Three died before the city shut down on October 4 and two more succumbed by October 5.

The *Palisade Tribune* helped spread the alarm:

> *It crept into the armies first, and then into the town.*
> *It surely is a thing accursed—and now they've shut things down.*
> *It causes grief and trouble, too, so you'd best take care I shout,*
> *For the Spanish "flu" will get U if U don't watch out.*

Blanche Kennedy, a twenty-year-old college student at the University of Denver, arrived home from a visit to Chicago with the flu and quickly died on September 27, 1918. Her brother William, an assistant city attorney, succumbed on October 5 as another brother, Charles, fought for his life. Along with the black crepe of death hung over the door, their Park Hill home was placarded and quarantined. The scourge had arrived in Denver.

On October 5, 1918, the State Board of Health warned that this was one of "the most communicable diseases ever," and later that "this disease is the most contagious and virulent ever experienced in the country." After stating it was a "crowd disease," the state "urged" local officials to "prohibit social gatherings of every nature whatsoever." Governor Julius C. Gunter made it an official proclamation on October 7.

Dr. William H. Sharpley, a former mayor of Denver, was Denver's Manager of Health under Mayor William Fitz Randolph Mills. Both tried to initially downplay the onslaught to avoid panic—cases were being misdiagnosed, there was no epidemic, it remained confined to Spain, and it was nothing more than the everyday common flu. They were enabled by the press, as the *Rocky Mountain News* falsely headlined on October 3 "Denver Free of the Flu." By October 5, there had been ten flu-related deaths, including the Kennedy siblings.

Public health announcements were soon tacked on public buildings and posted in Colorado's newspapers. Quips often accompanied such warnings, such as "Nobody says 'God bless you' these days when you sneeze—Bless me!" and "Cover up each cough and sneeze—if you don't, you spread disease!" BILL HANSEN COLLECTION

On October 6, Denver reluctantly joined Boulder, Colorado Springs, and Pueblo but only partially shut the city down. All schools, churches, and indoor places of entertainment were shuttered, including movie houses, theaters, pool halls, dance halls, lodges, and even club rooms and reading rooms. Indoor public funerals were also banned. Shops, businesses, restaurants, and hotels could remain open, and streetcar service remained uninterrupted.

Believing that Colorado's fresh open air was healthy, outdoor gatherings were still permitted and even encouraged by Sharpley. The omission allowed citizens to rush outdoors in packed crowds: 40,000 gathered at Cheesman Park to view a new war plane; 10,000 paraded in a Liberty Loan Drive; and large outdoor funerals and religious services abounded. Despite the state warning, on October 8 Sharpley assured the citizens "the plague is over" and would be gone within a week.

This is not to say that Denver ignored all public health advisories—just some. Federal, state, and local officials urged numerous preventive measures—many tried and true and centuries old: keep away from those with "colds"; isolate the sick; cover your nose with a handkerchief when you sneeze and your mouth when you cough, and regularly clean and disinfect your handkerchief; keep your hands clean and out of your mouth; live and work in well-ventilated areas; don't share drinking cups; and don't spit in public.

Denver's public health warnings did nothing to stem the soaring trajectory of cases, hospitalizations, and deaths. By October 15, there were 257 new cases in just twenty-four hours. The State Board of Health became openly concerned over a lack of sufficient preprinted death certificates. With Denver dithering on banning public assemblies to control this "crowd disease," the governor finally intervened:

> *BE IT RESOLVED: that all public gatherings, both indoor and outdoor, of whatever character or nature, are hereby forbidden and the people are advised and warned against visiting among their friends and acquaintances.*

Sharpley relented and quickly did an about-face, claiming the rise in cases was due to the open-air assemblies and "the criminal neglect of those who participated." Compliance meant that all shops and businesses were ordered closed, except restaurants, food shops, drugstores, and hotels. Streetcars faced limited capacities and restricted schedules. Business hours were curtailed. Gatherings at home were prohibited, as were all public funerals. Gauze masks were recommended but not required when going out in public. Denver was shut down.

On October 17, the *Rocky Mountain News* reported that "every physician in the city is overworked and exhausted." Recently unemployed teachers were pressed into service as nurses. Hospitals were running out of beds, and medical staff were getting sick and dying. Under the executive order, newspapers emphasized that all those with medical training had a patriotic duty to respond.

Placing Denver in complete quarantine seemed to work. Cases, hospitalizations, and deaths peaked and then declined. The populace grew restless after weeks of lockdown, and politicians were pressured by businesses to reopen. From November 8th to the 10th, Denver's city officials proclaimed the disease was "under control" and discussed a cautious and gradual reopening. Sadly, and ironically, it was planned for November 11, when events overtook any attempted measured steps.

Well before dawn on November 11, 1918, Denverites were rousted from their beds by clamoring horns, whistles, and bells, with newspaper boys screeching what everyone had been long waiting for—"Peace!" People poured

March of Democracy on Sixteenth Street After the Armistice Had Been Signed

News of the Armistice in France on November 11, 1918, brought Denverites out of their isolation and swarming into the streets for two days of raucous flag-waving revelry, as Denver officials were forced to lift all public health restrictions. DENVER PUBLIC LIBRARY, WESTERN HISTORY DEPARTMENT

into the downtown streets from their homes, rooming houses, and hotels, on foot and parading in any conveyance available, waving flags, singing, dancing, shouting, cheering, and weeping, building bonfires, setting off sulfurous pyrotechnics amid clouds of confetti, and hanging Kaiser Wilhelm in effigy. All of Denver spontaneously opened up and city officials lifted all restrictions. Speeches and songs enthralled 8,000 cheering citizens crammed into the Denver Municipal Auditorium. The results were inevitable.

Armistice Day cheers were soon muted as November became Denver's deadliest month. Within ten days, over a hundred died. There were 605 new cases and 22 deaths in a single day. Sharpley again tried to discount the toll and reassured the fearful public that death rates would soon normalize. The County Hospital created a special isolation ward as over half of the nurses fell ill.

On Friday, November 22, Mills and Sharpley reinstated the city's closing orders. But seventy-five masked entertainment business owners had formed an "Amusement Council" and marched on City Hall the next day, protesting that they were losing vast sums of money weekly and demanding that masking orders should be sufficient. The city relented and the new closing orders were rescinded within twenty-four hours of their adoption.

In their place, a universal masking order was adopted. Thick, six-ply gauze masks were mandated. Sharpley opposed the masking order because gauze is a loose, open weave and "gauze masks are porous and minute germs pass through the mesh." Masks were soon dubbed "little gauze germ catchers" by some, while others ridiculed the gauze face coverings as so thin and porous that it was "like trying to keep out dust with chicken wire." A shortage of masks immediately followed as the American Red Cross worked feverishly that weekend to fill the expected demand.

Most Denver residents simply ignored the order. Mayor Mills sadly noted that "it would take half the population to make the other half wear masks. You can't arrest all the people, can you?" Tramway operators threatened to strike if compelled to enforce the order. Chaos, confusion, shortages, and inability to enforce the masking order resulted in the order being rescinded on November 30. In its place, more rigorous isolation and quarantine enforcement measures were adopted.

With little trust in public health authorities and the medical profession having little to offer, desperate citizens throughout the state sought anything that might help. Malodorous camphor balls around the neck or flannel pads saturated with camphor oil worn about the chest were common sights, due to

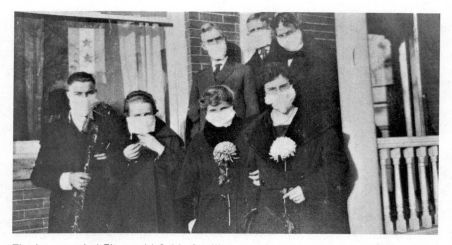

The intermarried Fitzgerald-Cohig families pose for a masked photo on their Denver front porch. The flowers in the coat belts and the two stars in the flag hanging in the window proudly declare that they had two men serving in the military overseas. TOM NOEL COLLECTION

their apparent decongestant properties. Vicks VapoRub was in high demand, with camphor as the primary ingredient. Quinine, a well-known antimalarial drug, was offered as a sure cure for flu, with a money-back guarantee. Garlic and onions were touted for their natural preventive health properties.

Some professed cures were especially dangerous. Katherine Anne Porter, the author of *Pale Horse, Pale Rider* (New York: New American Library of World Literature, 1936), a highly acclaimed fictional account of the flu pandemic in Denver, was administered poisonous strychnine during her own long febrile illness. The October 17, 1918, *Walsenburg World* not only recommended camphor bags but urged the populace to throat gargle with a good disinfectant—e.g., two to three drops of highly toxic formaldehyde in a glass of water. Aspirin, a new "miracle drug," was recommended in such excessively high doses that some health historians now believe contributed to the death toll due to the toxic effects of its blood-thinning properties.

Alcohol was then a well-known disinfectant, as well as a ready palliative for the stricken. Many miners and smelter workers followed their usual habit when sick by retiring to bed and getting drunk on whiskey. Prohibition dried up the availability of liquor, but bootleg whiskey could usually be found almost anywhere.

As Denver was the railroad hub for the rest of the state, the plague moved north, south, east, and west along Colorado's network of rails. All across the state, town halls, schools, hotels, churches, and rooming houses were rapidly turned into makeshift hospitals. Many communities had no physicians, and women were recruited without training to serve as nurses.

Salida, a railroad town, was once again seeing flush times with the surging wartime demand for iron, tungsten, lead, and zinc from the nearby mines. By mid-October, however, hundreds were prostrate and dozens were dying. The hospital was quickly overwhelmed, and the Hotel Denton was transformed into an emergency ward where seventy-three were taken in the first day.

The Red Cross sent out an urgent plea for volunteer nurses. Local madam Linda Evans readily offered her patriotic "working girls" to go above and beyond their usual bedroom endeavors to tend to the bedridden sick. Most "fallen angels" eagerly became "angels of mercy." One even provided what was considered Heaven-sent help to the local minister's family, who afterward gratefully offered her a permanent maid's position. She declined and returned to being a "Hell's belle," even though, with eighty dead, the customer base was significantly reduced.

The mountain mining communities were hit the hardest. Many miners were immigrants who could seldom read or understand English, and relished their frontier, bachelor, and ethnic independence. They still worked hard all day and played hard all night and, after years of labor strife, were resistant to authority. Miners were not going to readily accept alcohol prohibition and certainly not stop sneezing, coughing, and spitting, where and when they wanted to, or stoop to wearing masks. The *Creede Candle* offered this encouragement, likely with tongue firmly implanted in covered cheek:

New Uses of "Flu" Masks
A face bandage that hides your kisser and a handy thing to catch the germs, not only your own special brand, but whatever mavericks may be wandering at large. It is also a handy thing to spit your tobacco juice into, even if it does make your chin and nose a little bit mussy. It may also be used as a chewing gum holder by those addicted to the habit, tho we consider this latter practice to be extremely reprehensible.

By late October, influenza hit the Southern Ute Indian Reservation in southwest Colorado and at least forty Native Americans succumbed to the disease. The nearby *Durango Evening News* naturally chastised the Native population: "They have paid the toll of negligence and disobedience to the advice of their superintendent and nurses and physicians."

Durango had acted quickly after Loisa Bass died on her eighth birthday on October 8. The city went into quarantine as urged by state officials. Incoming train cars were fumigated, passengers were isolated, traveling salesmen were banned, and masking was required. Mail from the East was steamed and sterilized before being distributed, and outside newspapers were burned rather than circulated. Despite such precautions, many became ill and many died. Still, long before Durango's newspapers were hypocritically damning the Native Americans for their death toll, the city was sympathetically trying to help in the disaster taking place fifty miles to the north.

Silverton, a mining town of perhaps 2,500, was isolated high in the San Juans, connected to the outside world only by railroad and telephone service from Durango. It retained its wild and woolly boom-time vices of drinking, whoring, and gambling. Because of its remoteness, the two newspapers somewhat cavalierly downplayed the plague going on in surrounding towns and mining camps. Citing no known flu cases by mid-October, Silverton nonetheless followed the statewide public health order to shut down.

In a bizarre twist of fate, premature rumors reached Silverton on October 16 that the war in Europe had ended. Like Denver almost a month later, a spontaneous celebration swept through town. A piano was rolled into the street, bonfires were set, bells, whistles, and horns blared, and cheering crowds of flag-waving miners and town folk openly shared bottles and kegs of bootleg whiskey while singing, laughing, hugging, and crying in relief. The next day, the *Silverton Standard* headlined "Silverton Celebrates!" The following day, the same newspaper sadly printed a retraction—there was no peace.

Three days after the hoopla, hundreds of Silverton citizens fell ill and many quickly died. Beds were rushed over to the town hall to serve as a makeshift hospital. Twenty-five sick people arrived one day and, the next day, only one had survived. Unfortunately, the undertaker soon perished, and most of the doctors and nursing staff fell ill, with some dying. A physician from Ridgway took over the "City Hall Emergency Hospital." It was quickly also transformed into a morgue. Martial law was declared. All six telephone operators lay prostrate, and teachers filled in to make emergency calls for aid to Durango for nurses, medical supplies, and another undertaker. Durango sent what it could and even supplied pots of steaming broth on the daily trains.

By October 26, the *Silverton Standard*'s headline read "The Worst Week Ever Known in History" and contained pages of obituaries, chronicling over 125 dead. Many miners were unidentified other than by what mine they worked at and their country of origin. Virtually every household in town was affected. Many homes sprouted black crepe draped over the thresholds, with shuttered windows, empty chairs at the kitchen table, and bedchambers filled with pale, sick loved ones. Widows and orphans abounded. A "death wagon" plied the streets each day to collect the dead. Like Salida, the "girls of the line" from the red-light district on Blair Street readily pitched in, and several died. The uphill mines were shut down, but the town soon banned any panicky incoming miners seeking aid. Some miners desperately fled over Red Mountain Pass but were turned back by a "shotgun quarantine" of armed guards protecting Ouray.

As bodies stacked up outside the city hall hospital, an acute shortage of coffins created a demand for rough wood boxes and then simply blankets. As the thermometer dropped, the corpses froze stiff and stacked up because the ground became too hard to dig graves. One burly six-foot-six, 300-pound Swede named Quinton dug graves all night but rapidly fell sick and expired the following day, only to be buried in one of the graves he had just dug. Individual graves could not be dug fast enough, and teams of scrapers eventually had to plow two long, shallow trenches for mass burials of ninety victims in Hillside Cemetery. By the time of the real Armistice on November 11, there was nothing to celebrate. The boys off fighting in the war had been safer and fared far better than those family and friends they had left behind.

Within six weeks, almost 250 had perished—about 10 percent of the population. Another half had fallen ill. Silverton has often been identified as having one of the highest death rates in the country.

As the pale horse of death trampled over Silverton, Gunnison was a horse of an entirely different color. Gunnison County was a low-density, homogenous county of 5,590 self-sufficient ranchers and farmers, with few mines. The town of Gunnison, with a population of 1,209, was a railroad hub, supply center, and college town, with the recently opened Colorado State Normal School (today's Western Colorado University). The entire area was used to independent living at high altitude with its own food supplies and goods such that it was tolerant to home solitude and essentially hibernating during the long, cold winters.

The *Gunnison News-Champion* took a proactive role in alerting the citizens. After reporting the outbreaks and death toll in Sargents, just thirty-two miles to the east, the October 10 edition warned, "The Flu is after us. It is circulating in most every village and community around us." Further, "This disease is no joke, to be made light of, but a terrible calamity." On October 7, Gunnison had implemented the governor's urgings to close up the community. County health officials, however, went further and adopted far stricter measures and basically declared de facto martial law. They ordered "a strict quarantine to be placed in Gunnison County against the world."

Unlike elsewhere, the citizenry readily supported the measures and voluntarily self-isolated. Barricades and fences were placed on all the roads and highways leading into the county, with posted warnings, guarded by armed lawmen during the day and lit by lanterns at night. Two railroads served the town, and conductors forewarned passengers that if they stepped foot on the station platform, they faced mandatory quarantine. This was often emphasized by masked and armed lawmen at the train station.

Enforcement was strict. "We have no flu and do not intend to have any" warned the health officials. A state senator inadvertently stepped off a train and was isolated in the detention ward set up on the college campus. Two Nebraskans tried to sneak in past the barricades and were literally "cut off at the pass" by the county sheriff, who arrested them, disabled their vehicle, and hauled them off to jail. An Alamosa man was arrested and heavily fined $43, a whopping $800-plus in today's dollars.

The results after four months of the quarantine were amazingly effective. There were no cases or deaths in the town and only two cases and one death in the entire county. The quarantine was not lifted until February 1919 and, even then, out-of-town college students had to spend two days in isolation and be inspected each day by a physician before returning to school. Still, a third wave swept through Colorado later in 1919 and the *Gunnison News-Champion* lamented, "The flu has us at last." One hundred cases followed, with nine dead.

In 2006, researchers at the University of Michigan Center for the History of Medicine issued an extensive study funded by the Pentagon to determine how best to protect the military in the event of a future pandemic. After carefully reviewing the nation's efforts during the 1918 pandemic, the report identified Gunnison among a handful of "escape communities" in the country, emphasizing that Gunnison's strict measures were "exceptional" and a model for future efforts.

By January 1919, the second wave of the pandemic finally began burning out. Schools reopened with an extended school year for heavily masked students across the state. The third wave of the flu struck later in 1919 and accounted for 10 percent of the final death toll in Colorado.

Katherine Anne Porter's *Pale Horse, Pale Rider* ended on a sobering but optimistic note:

No more war, no more plague—only the dazed silence that follows the ceasing of the heavy guns, the noiseless houses with the shades drawn, empty streets, the dead cold light of tomorrow. Now, there would be time for everything.

Besides the toll in human lives and suffering, Colorado's booming wartime economy briefly went bust. Surviving businesses began to recover in fits and starts. Despite the loss of many breadwinners and young men in their prime earning years, returning servicemen faced high unemployment, accentuated by low wages and high inflation. The service and entertainment industries saw double-digit losses of revenue. Colorado, as well as the rest of the country, fell into a deep, but brief, recession. Still, a resurgence in demand for consumer goods and rising exports of agricultural products to a war-ravaged Europe swept Colorado and the nation into the "Roaring Twenties," only to face the Great Depression a decade later.

CHAPTER SEVEN

Boom and Bust Gambling

NOTHING MORE TYPIFIED COLORADO'S BOOM AND BUST CYCLE THAN THE mining era and its gambling on natural resources. In that wild-eyed "get rich quick" time of "easy come, easy go," the miners worked hard and played hard with unbridled enthusiasm and optimism. Vice peddlers proved more than happy to accommodate them. Gambling was probably more prevalent in nineteenth-century western mining camps than at any other time or place in American history. Colorado's gambling history followed a time line of wild boom and reforming bust to a more recent resurgent boom, as society became more accepting and tolerant.

Even before white settlers arrived with the gold rush, Native Americans were ardent gamblers. In addition to horse racing, they played dice, lacrosse, shinny, and hoop and pole games. The Utes were among the very first Indian nations to acquire horses from the Spanish as they pushed north into New Mexico and Colorado. They became a horse culture, and horse racing and betting became a cherished pastime.

From the outset, the territorial and state constitutions made gambling illegal. The laws were basically ignored. Gambling was tolerated as a necessary evil and locally licensed, taxed, and fined. When public outrage might briefly arise, or the town's coffers needed replenishment, a short crackdown with fines was the usual solution. Gamblers simply viewed such inconveniences as a cost of doing business. Communities found that gambling fines could support their civic needs. Even respectable folks, like government officials, tolerated gambling joints as a revenue source lightening the tax burden on the citizenry. The town of Silverton, for example, used fines on gambling for over half its expenses.

Colorado's first saloon and gambling hall was reputedly Brown's Saloon, at a fur-trading post at Brown's Hole along the Green River near today's

Colorado, Wyoming, and Utah border. From 1822 to 1840, American, French, Mexican, and Native American trappers, hunters, and traders gathered there to profit from their furry "banknotes"—beaver pelts, animal hides, and bison robes—while celebrating with concoctions such as "Taos Lightning," so-called "fire water" that ignited when poured on flaming embers to prove its high alcohol content. Some called this whiskey "tangle foot," "shake knee," "rotgut," or "bust head."

At the annual mountain rendezvous, the big fur companies paid trappers for their beaver pelts and buffalo robes. Smelling the annual payday profits, gamblers and alcohol vendors gathered for what quickly degenerated into drunken brawls with boisterous betting on horse races, wrestling, fighting, shooting contests, running competitions, and games of chance with cards and dice. Stakes were high and included ponies, weapons, clothes, or even the services of women.

Almost as wild as the rendezvous were some of Denver's first gambling saloons. With the '59ers came an assortment of bummers, loafers, desperadoes, and other riffraff, as well as the saloon keepers and gamblers. Gambling, reported Chicagoan Richard D. Young, was "the most extensive business carried on here and participated in by all classes of citizens." Another visitor to Denver, William Hepworth Dixon, complained that in 1866 Denver, "every tenth house appears to be either a brothel or a gaming house, often both in one."

Colorado's first notorious drinking and gambling establishment was the Denver House. This log-walled, canvas-roofed, one-story edifice provided water from a dirty rain barrel but the back bar also sold murky-looking stuff in reused bottles with ambitious labels. Well-lubricated patrons were lured to the gaming tables, where they seldom won. Boston journalist Albert D. Richardson observed that "at a half dozen tables, the gamblers were always busy day and night." One sleight-of-hand artist made over a hundred dollars in gold dust each day, daring the greenhorns: "I take no money from paupers, cripples, or orphan children. . . . It is my regular trade, gentlemen, to move my hands quicker than the eye. Who will give me $20?" Richardson sat in on one session where the county judge lost thirty Denver town lots in less than ten minutes of card-playing and the county sheriff pawned his revolver for $20 to bet on faro.

New York journalist Horace Greeley spent the night at the Denver House in 1859 on the dirt floor and reported that customers were "allowed as good a bed as his blankets will make." Greeley complained that "gambling

The Denver House became Colorado's first notorious gambling hall where knights of the green cloth fleeced the unwary while a small band struggled to play loudly enough to drown out disturbances. TOM NOEL COLLECTION

and dissipation were universal." Still, he expressed reluctant admiration of the gambling fraternity, where gamblers not only provided charity among themselves and other denizens of the vice industry, but often offered their winnings to helpless women or orphans.

The gambling hall owners usually rented the tables to gamblers for a daily or weekly fee or a share in the profits. If a customer claimed he was cheated, the house could disclaim all responsibility because it simply rented out the tables. Still, some houses provided shotgun-wielding overseers to ensure the house was not cheated and that unruly sore losers were quickly subdued.

Most gambling saloons were rowdy affairs. Whooping, hollering, laughing, cussing, and arguing often competed with a makeshift off-tune orchestra of various banjos, fiddles, tambourines, horns, and the prized piano. Early saloons had no stools at the bars to rest, and the weary miners were drawn to the gambling tables simply to find a place to sit. Amid the dealing of greasy cards, rolling of dice, spinning of the wheel, and counting of chips wandered the dance hall girls and barmaids plying customers with drink and offering other favors. Cigar smoke hung in the air already pungent with the smell of sweating miners, vomit, and spit on the floors where the spittoons were

The Early Broadmoor Casino

Colorado's most elegant gambling casino was created by a Prussian count, James Pourtales, just south of Colorado Springs, which was then dry. Shocked at the dishonest gambling, loose women, ruffians, and shootings that plagued Leadville, Cripple Creek, and other wild towns, Pourtales opened a respectable, model place, the Broadmoor Casino, on July 1, 1891.

Located atop the dammed Cheyenne Lake, the grand casino offered a refined pleasure palace reminiscent of the European casinos at Baden-Baden and Monte Carlo. Admission was charged to keep out the riffraff. Gentlemen could relax in the gaming rooms for genteel amusement amid the finest French cuisine, wine, liquors, and cigars while listening to a fourteen-piece uniformed Hungarian band. The blue-nosed teetotalers and fire and brimstone preachers of Colorado Springs dubbed it a "sunny place for shady people."

The Broadmoor Casino never made a profit and virtually bankrupted Pourtales before the all-wood structure met a fiery end on July 17, 1897. It took over twenty years for the current Broadmoor Resort to rise from its ashes.

The Broadmoor Casino was perhaps Colorado's most opulent gambling parlor. The Broadmoor Resort and Hotel would later rise from its ashes and would once again lure the well-heeled to Colorado Springs. TOM NOEL COLLECTION

often missed targets. Hunting trophies adorned the walls along with specially commissioned paintings of one of the local Jezebels reclining erotically on a divan. In the finer establishments, sumptuous back rooms or second stories were reserved for the high rollers in plush surroundings offering the finest liquors and cigars.

After each new mountain strike, a predictable cast of vice merchants appeared, eager to mine the miners for every ounce of gold extracted. On July 15, 1860, one correspondent from the South Park gold fields wrote home to complain: "Gamblers and thieves are ranged round at their tables playing every game from roulette up to the faro bank. And here, night after night, crowds of the silly ones fill the coffers of these money leeches in the delusive hope of winning a little money easier than they could ever work for it." When a strike went bust, the purveyors of whiskey, wagering, and loose women followed the disillusioned prospectors to the next promising diggings.

Telluride's town marshal leans nonchalantly against the polished mahogany bar, aloof from the crowd of gamblers at the Cosmopolitan Saloon around 1905. Gamblers briefly look up from the gaming and roulette tables under an alluring erotic painting offering further distractions. A potbellied stove provided the only heat, and smoky oil lamps hung from the tin tile ceiling provided feeble lighting. DENVER PUBLIC LIBRARY, WESTERN HISTORY DEPARTMENT

As prosperous mining camps became towns, the gambling saloons graduated from tents to log cabins to false-fronted clapboard structures to imposing brick two-story buildings—often the most prominent structures in the settlement.

In the 1880s, the silver city of Leadville supported 14,000 residents with 120 saloons, 118 gaming houses, and 35 brothels. Entertainer Eddie Foy recalled the early boomtown: "They were gambling in tents and even in the open alongside the sidewalk. You could get any sort of bet, from five cent chuck-a-luck up to a five-thousand-dollar poker pot." Later, the mining moguls traveled to and from the "Magic City" in elaborately furnished Palace Pullman cars, drinking, smoking, and gambling thousands of dollars before continuing their wagering in style at Leadville's finer establishments.

In thriving Telluride, oft referred to as "To Hell You Ride," gaming and lawlessness reigned. The citizens were tolerant, as they paid no taxes. The town marshal would simply raid one of the vice establishments to collect "fines" whenever the town's coffers needed replenishing. The marshal also often served as debt collector for local merchants by rousting those behind on their bills, who could often be found in the gaming parlors.

GAMBLING'S COLORFUL CHARACTERS

Jefferson Randolph "Soapy" Smith II has sometimes been dubbed the "King of the Frontier Con Men." He once declared, "I am no ordinary gambler. When I stake money, it is a sure thing that I win."

He began in Leadville swindling miners with his prestidigitation at the shell game. Moving to Denver, Smith and his band of bunco artists started working other cons, most notably "The Prize Soap Racket." To draw a crowd, Smith flashed his cash by openly rolling $5 to $100 bills around bars of soap before rewrapping them and tossing them into a basket and then singing out of pitch, extolling the virtues of his soap. Smith sold the bars at $1 each. Shills in the audience excitedly and loudly won the first big bills before the suckers started buying. There were no other winners. When the police arrested him, he refused to give his full name so he was booked as "Soapy."

In the late 1880s, Smith bought the Tivoli Club, a Denver gambling house, and posted an entry sign warning "Caveat Emptor." He was confident that few locals knew their Latin for "Let the buyer beware." Barbers near Union Station were enlisted to assess the wealth of newly arriving tenderfeet.

Likely prospects would have a V shaved on the back of their heads before being befriended and guided to the Tivoli to be relieved of their fortune.

Smith soon became the boss of Denver's underworld and immersed himself in most of the city's underworld activities. Graft and payoffs to the police chief, the mayor, judges, and patrolmen on the beat, combined with Smith's large gang of menacing followers, firmly ensconced him in Denver politics. He actively participated in the voter fraud election of Wolfe Londoner as mayor in 1889.

Attempts at reform chased Soapy out of Denver and to the booming silver city of Creede before he returned to Denver in 1892. To protect his empire, he joined the corrupt and heavily armed discharged officeholders holed up in the Denver City Hall and resisting removal which reform Governor Davis Waite had ordered. Ultimately, the governor called out the National Guard in the so-called City Hall War. That battle pitted state government officials against the corrupt city of Denver, where reformers were trying to oust crooks from city hall.

Finally charged with attempted murder for severely beating a saloon manager in 1895, Smith fled to Skagway, Alaska, during the Klondike gold rush. There, he established another criminal empire before being gunned down in 1898 at the age of thirty-seven in a shoot-out with a member of the local Vigilance Committee.

New Yorker Edward Chase had arrived in Denver in June 1860 at the age of twenty-two and over the next fifty years built and ran one of the largest gaming and entertainment empires in the state. He began with the Progressive, a gambling hall with the first floor solely devoted to gaming and the second floor reserved for high-rolling members of the sporting fraternity, with plush private rooms and no limits. In 1868, an R. G. Dun and Company credit report described Chase as a "rich and clever man sometimes good for $50,000, sometimes not so much . . . a notorious gambler, a hard man [who] keeps a lewd and dangerous place . . . a blackleg."

Next to the Progressive, Chase set up the Palace, a celebrated two-story brick gambling hall and variety theater that seated 750 burlesque and vaudeville fans, with an adjacent gambling salon accommodating 200 more with food, beer, and the waitresses alternating as dancers. In its review of the Palace "theater," the *Rocky Mountain News* reported that the performances were "mostly leg art." So many murders occurred at the Palace that the December 6, 1888, *Georgetown Courier* commented, "With the amount of blood spilled in that den, the floors must be a gorgeous gory red color."

Gambling czar "Big Ed" Chase practiced what he preached: "All of the chances are with the man who owns the house. I thought they might as well lose to me as to someone else, and I did the best I could to accommodate them." TOM NOEL COLLECTION

Arrested many times, the impeccably dressed Chase was seldom convicted. He amassed such a fortune that he was able to purchase a Capitol Hill mansion for cash. Chase organized a sizable bloc of voters from the gamblers, saloon owners, soiled doves, transients, derelicts, and drunks of the tenderloin wards. For a dollar and/or a drink, these folks would vote in politicians sympathetic to the vice district. Chase ingratiated himself with officials and respectable folks by providing funds for the needy and other pet social welfare projects. Even as Denver moved into a period of Progressive Era reform after the turn of the century, a blind eye was turned so long as he continued business in low profile and did not abuse his customers. In 1921, Chase died at the age of eighty-three and left a fortune worth $600,000 to his third wife, Florence.

After initially cleaning up several Kansas cow towns with his friend, Wyatt Earp, William Barclay "Bat" Masterson was appointed city marshal of Trinidad, Colorado. He supplemented his $75 monthly salary by moonlighting as a faro dealer. Later, Masterson hooked up with crime boss Soapy Smith in Denver and helped orchestrate various Denver election frauds. At the same time, he ironically served as deputy sheriff of Arapahoe County, of which Denver was then the county seat. By 1886, he was dealing faro for "Big Ed" Chase at the Arcade. The 1893 *National Police Gazette* proclaimed Masterson "the king of western sporting men [who] backs pugilists, can play any game on the green with a full deck, and handles a Bowie knife or revolver with the determination of a Napoleon."

John "Doc" Holliday, a dentist by trade and gambler by choice, fled Tombstone, Arizona, in 1881 following the bloody aftermath of the shoot-out at the OK Corral. He retired to Colorado, seeking a cure for his worsening tuberculosis and to escape a likely necktie party. While dealing faro in Leadville, the emaciated, red-eyed, temperamental, and often drunk Holliday killed his last man in 1884, gambler and former policeman Billy Allen, over a $5 debt. Upon Holliday's death in Glenwood Springs in 1887 at the age of thirty-seven, fellow gamblers chipped in for his funeral and served as pallbearers. His obituary in the *Denver Republican* noted, "Few men have been better known to a certain class of sporting people, and few men of his character, had more friends or stronger champions."

GAMBLING FINALLY DRIVEN UNDERGROUND

Early in the twentieth century, mining was waning, Colorado's economy had diversified, and moralizing and progressive influences began diluting the

Wild West image. A gentler West was championed by Colorado women who had been given the vote in 1893 and demanded political and social reform. Temperance elements strove to dry up the state and curb the vices that went with alcohol. By 1916, Coloradans adopted Prohibition and drove Denver's wide-open vice district underground. Both above- and belowground, gaming and drinking remained frequent companions. Like the speakeasies, gaming could still readily be found.

With the repeal of Prohibition in 1933, organized crime turned from bootlegging to gambling, bookmaking, and loan-sharking. Public taste for drinking and gambling was rekindled. With Prohibition repealed, gambling slowly reemerged and even became socially acceptable.

Hoping to resuscitate the sinking city with tourism, the Central City Opera Association resurrected the derelict 1878 Opera House and staged an annual summer opera festival beginning in 1932. To further draw visitors, the opera persuaded the city officials to allow gambling at the Teller House. Other Central City businesses also started offering gaming in a tacit hands-off agreement with the town's government.

Local tolerance attracted Colorado's most infamous crime family, Denver's Smaldone clan. Besides supplying most of the gaming devices for the local businesses for a percentage of the take, the charismatic Clyde Smaldone opened a small casino that he grandly named the Monte Carlo. During the summers from 1947 to 1949, he offered craps, roulette, and slot machines to eager gambling visitors.

The town welcomed the Smaldones, as Clyde not only arranged gaming that increased the revenues of small mom-and-pop businesses, but also helped local officials finance a desperately needed water system, restore crumbling structures, and finance school lunch programs. State officials were not so happy and staged various raids, but locals were easily tipped off by a network of spies whenever a raid by "outsiders" from downhill was coming. Finally, state and federal pressure forced the closure of Central City's illegal gambling operations in 1950, much to the town's dismay.

Clyde later told his biographer Dick Kreck, "I was glad we went in. We could help all them hungry kids and help other people that needed stuff and fix homes and everything. At least we didn't lose money. I can't complain."

In 1951, a Denver grand jury claimed that Clyde and his partners reaped $25,000 to $50,000 from his Central City operations. Mountain town gambling was again driven underground, but the former "Richest Square Mile on

During Central City's popular summer opera festival from 1947 to 1949, Colorado's underworld crime boss, Clyde Smaldone, raked in a small fortune operating his Monte Carlo Casino and supplying gaming devices for other local gambling operations such as the nearby Keno Club. GILPIN HISTORICAL SOCIETY

Earth," still struggling, had briefly tasted the potential prosperity of jingling cash registers thanks to gaming.

GAMBLING LEGALIZED

In 1947, Colorado voters sanctioned pari-mutuel betting at dog and horse racing tracks. Seventy years later, it has largely proved a bust. The Mile-High Kennel Club opened in 1948 in Commerce City, an industrial suburb of Denver, offering sixty nights a year of dog racing. Muzzled greyhounds chased a scented mechanical hare around an oval sand and loam track while gamblers studied racing sheets before betting. The track's mascot, Rusty, a cleat-footed hare, could not save dog racing from animal welfare officials. Colorado banned greyhound racing in 2009, and the large site is now being developed for mixed use.

Trumpets blared "First Call" at horse racing tracks such as Centennial Racetrack in Littleton, which opened in 1950 and billed itself as "The Santa Anita of the Rockies." It never lived up to expectations, and horses ran their last lap in 1983, before becoming a subdivision along South Santa Fe Drive. Pikes Peak Meadows horse track in Colorado Springs suffered a similar fate and morphed into a race car speedway. Desperate attempts to add sports gambling to racetracks were repeatedly rebuffed. Only Arapahoe Park in Aurora still limps along, struggling to the finish line.

In 1951, voters approved bingo and raffles for charitable, nonprofit, and religious organizations, with the state receiving a 2.5 percent tax. It proved a godsend for Pastor Charles H. Hagus of the Annunciation Catholic Church in poverty-stricken northeast Denver. Bingo nights not only supported the deteriorating church, but also enabled it to buy a nearby abandoned Greek Orthodox church to serve as a much-needed Catholic parochial school. From these beginnings, bingo grew from gray-haired parishioners in church basements to over sixty bingo halls in Colorado in a multimillion-dollar industry. The largest, Slammer's Bingo Hall in Lakewood, provides 14,000 square feet for hundreds of players supporting different charities and community organizations each night.

When charity proved lucrative, gambling and police corruption once again intermingled. Bingo was rocked by scandal in the 1980s as members of Denver's police department were found to have illegally skimmed over $270,000 into a slush fund by paying "volunteers" at games supporting the Denver Police Junior Band. A few years later, another police scandal unveiled incomplete records that could not account for hundreds of thousands of dollars in gross sales, net profits, and missing equipment. Sixteen felony and misdemeanor convictions resulted, and top officers were suspended or fired.

Colorado voters approved a state-run lottery in 1980, with the first scratch ticket drawing on April 26, 1983. Other games have been added over the years, including Powerball in 2001, MegaMillions in 2010, Lucky for Life in 2016, and Lotto+ in 2019. As the pots grow with no winners, long lines form as people throw more money against almost impossible odds.

Some critics argue that lotteries are "robbery by bureaucracy" and are the only consumer product heavily promoted and sold by the state that actually targets the poor and those least able to afford it. They point out that it is the same game, albeit on a far larger scale, that organized crime used to run, known as the "numbers racket," but, ironically, offers worse odds than the street bookies do. The state spends millions on marketing and the payouts are always promoted for the larger annuity value and not the actual cash value, with both being heavily taxed. Still, smaller winnings are regularly paid out.

In September 2017, some lucky Coloradan won $130 million on a Powerball ticket, and several multimillion-dollar winnings have also been claimed.

The real winners of the state lotteries are Colorado's outdoors and recreation, which almost all Coloradans support and enjoy. Fifty percent of the amounts wagered go to the state and, as of 2019, that translated to $3.4 billion. Colorado's unique distribution system provides 50 percent of the tax revenues to Greater Outdoors Colorado, which has funded the restoration of 900 miles of trails, protected 1,000 miles of rivers, added 47,000 acres to state parks, and conserved another 1.2 million acres of public lands. Endangered species are also protected, and 1,600 community parks and outdoor recreation areas have been created or improved statewide. Another 40 percent of the lottery funds goes to the Conservation Trust for open space land acquisition, equipment purchases, facility development, and park maintenance and restoration. The last 10 percent is awarded to Colorado Parks and Wildlife to support and maintain Colorado's more than forty state parks, which continue to grow in number but receive no other tax revenue and are wholly funded by gate admissions and lottery proceeds.

The federal Indian Gaming Regulatory Act of 1988 opened the door for Colorado's two Indian reservations to establish their own Las Vegas–style casinos, free from state controls or taxes. The Mountain Utes opened the Ute Mountain Casino in Towaoc, while the Southern Utes opened the Sky Ute Casino Resort in Ignacio.

Gaming for Historic Preservation

In 1991, Colorado voters were asked to approve a constitutional amendment allowing limited-stakes gaming in Black Hawk, Central City, and Cripple Creek. Inspiration came from Deadwood, South Dakota, where gambling was sanctioned to revive the struggling small mining town and fund historic preservation of its many vintage landmarks. In 1989, Deadwood became one of the first communities to reestablish gaming and soon boomed. Boosters argued that they were merely bringing back the good old days of the frontier mining towns, when gambling was pervasive and accepted. Deadwood's successful model became contagious.

Central City began pushing limited-stakes gambling as a source of historic preservation and reviving the local economy of a long-declining gold city. Nearby Black Hawk soon joined in the chorus, as did Cripple Creek. When gaming efforts failed in the General Assembly, a ballot initiative, supported by massive promotion from outside interests, proposed to amend the state constitution to allow gaming in the three former gold towns. The term "gaming" was substituted for "gambling," and any reference to "casinos" was scrupulously avoided by the proponents during the debates. Cripple Creek councilman Terry Wahrer argued, "We want to bring limited gambling in as an attraction, as part of our history, not as an industry." Proponents sweetened the deal for voters by including a provision to tax casinos at 40 percent and use those funds for historic preservation statewide.

Preservation was stressed in selling gaming to the voters. But, somewhere during the debates, the provision that gaming must take place "in existing historic structures" was changed to "in structures of historic type." Besides preservation, the proponents assured voters that the limits on stakes, devices, and hours would deter big-time Las Vegas–style casinos.

Despite warnings by opponents as to what gaming could do to the former mining towns, the amendment passed 57 percent to 43 percent in 1990, effective in 1991. A reluctant Governor Roy Romer signed the legislation but warned, "We are going to be very diligent to preserve the historic value of these towns." Eighteen years later, with the historic value of the towns already compromised by large casino operations that built non-historic-style structures, the limited stakes were raised from $5 to $100, twenty-four-hour gaming was allowed, and craps and roulette were added.

Still, the complicated distribution of the 40 percent taxes on adjusted gross proceeds stressed preservation: 50 percent went to the state's general fund; 28 percent was distributed to the State Historical Fund, of which 20 percent went for preservation and restoration in the three cities in proportion to their revenues; 12 percent went to Teller and Gilpin Counties in proportion to their revenues; and 10 percent was returned to the three cities in proportion to their revenue to be used however they choose.

Even before the law became effective, boom times returned to the three old gold-mining towns as outside land speculators swooped in and started buying every property they could find. Property values and taxes soared, landlords terminated leases, and "For Sale" and "Going Out of Business" signs appeared everywhere. Elderly pensioners residing in a trailer park along Main Street in south Black Hawk were evicted to clear the land for development. Locals moved out as the new jobs were filled by commuters from metro Denver. Basic needs such as grocery markets and service stations were driven out.

As the law took effect, local utilities were quickly overwhelmed with inadequate water supplies and overflowing sewage systems. Ultimately a large sewerage plant was built downstream from Black Hawk. All of Gilpin County had only a four-person jail but, with gambling revenues, was able to build a new justice center capable of holding over sixty inmates, which soon filled with gambling-related offenders.

Even with major infrastructure improvements, Gilpin County Manager Donna Martin concluded after the first year: "Gambling has not done us any good. We have lost our sense of community. . . . The culture shock for these people was unreal." Local control was key in the new law, and pro-preservation and pro-development factions clashed.

Those betting on beginner's luck by locally owned store owners prospering in resurrected historic structures were quickly disillusioned. The September 23, 1992, *Wall Street Journal* observed that Las Vegas "veterans raced in, along with real estate developers," wiping out "the mom and pop stores." The September 13, 1992, *Colorado Springs Gazette Telegraph* quoted one small Cripple Creek business owner driven to bankruptcy in the first year: "We didn't foresee the openings of these large casinos. Good grief. They have 400, 500, 600 slots, food service and Las Vegas style entertainment. These are things a small place can't compete with."

Most of Central City's largely intact business district was preserved but many storefronts remained empty, the businesses unable to compete with the large casinos farther down the gulch in Black Hawk and closer to the highway traffic from Denver. In response, Central City built the four-lane Central City Parkway from I-70 to the town in 2004. Although it was designed to circumvent Black Hawk, many used it to get there and bypassed Central. While Black Hawk built giant parking lots, Central City did not. Traffic control and large tour buses in the narrow, winding streets deterred others. In the end, only a half-dozen casinos survived and Central City's gaming revenue accounts for less than 10 percent of the state's overall proceeds.

When Colorado's casinos opened their doors in October 1991, one Black Hawk establishment had a dirt floor and served beer from an ice-filled trough that horses had used for drinking water. Black Hawk, unlike Central City, had few intact historic structures and large expanses of open space. Ruins and stone foundations remained of "The City of Mills," populated with only about 200 permanent residents. Black Hawk opted for a pro-development approach, and city officials had their personal residences restored with gaming funds.

The thirty-three-story Las Vegas–style Ameristar Casino Resort and Spa towers over Black Hawk's business district. BILL HANSEN COLLECTION

Playing somewhat fast and loose with the new law, Black Hawk justified massive new casinos with modern towering structures as akin to the former large mills that dominated the skyline, particularly in the southern area along Clear Creek and Main Street. Contributing historic structures were moved, "accidentally" burned down, expanded with only the facades remaining, or openly demolished to make way for Las Vegas–style hotel-casinos and necessary parking facilities. "Preservation" often consisted of relocating historic structures such as the iconic 1863 "Lace House" to what some describe as a "building zoo" in the newly created hillside Mountain City up the gulch, totally destroying each structure's historical context.

Some have suggested that more mountainside blasting has taken place in Black Hawk for casino development than ever occurred during Gilpin County's gold-mining and milling heyday. The September 23, 2019, *Denver Post* quoted local resident Judy Laratta as saying, "Black Hawk still had dirt roads. There was no parking, and there was a creek that ran along the side of the road. But it's a booming place now. It's like a little Las Vegas."

Black Hawk's overflowing profits make up over three-quarters of Colorado's overall gaming revenue, and the slot machines in its thirteen casinos earn twice as much as those in either Central City or Cripple Creek.

When legalized gambling came to Cripple Creek in the 1990s, the town's more distant, slow, two-lane mountain road connection to Denver and Colorado Springs population centers led to slower rebirth and preservation. Burros, long-gone fixtures in other mining towns, still wander the streets as unofficial garbage collectors. Bennett Avenue's main street business district remained relatively intact. The Imperial Hotel with its Gold Bar Theater survives, as does the historic Butte Theater. The Teller County Hospital became the Hospitality House, and the old high school was reborn as the upscale Carr Manor. Such overnight accommodations enabled Cripple Creek, as of 2020, to support twelve casinos, with additional hotel space being constructed by the larger casinos. Cripple Creek still garners just under 20 percent of Colorado's gambling market.

As of 2019, gambling's annual revenues had continued to climb and totaled $840 million, not including the tribal casinos. Almost $17 billion in revenue had been generated along with $2.5 billion in taxes since gambling was legalized. Thanks to gambling, Colorado has the largest state grant program for historic preservation in the country. The State Historical Fund (SHF), an arm of History Colorado, as the State Historical Society has been renamed, has spent more than $300 million on about 1,500 different projects in all sixty-four counties. Although Black Hawk turned into a preservationists' nightmare, Central City and Cripple Creek remain fairly intact. The rest of Colorado came out a big winner thanks to the preservation funding generated in the three towns.

To be eligible for SHF grants, properties must be listed on the national, state, or local register of historic places. Colorado has more than 1,500 sites and historic districts on the National Register of Historic Places. Many cities, towns, and counties also have their own locally designated landmarks and districts. Denver, for example, boasts more than sixty historic districts and 350 individually designated landmarks. Even the smallest and poorest communities are eligible for funding to professionally restore their treasured landmarks.

Colorado lingered behind a growing wave of legalizing sports betting nationally. Competitive team sports are a booming business and high entertainment in sports-crazy Colorado, at both the collegiate and professional level. Denver is one of only twelve cities in the country to host all four major professional sports—the Denver Broncos, the Denver Nuggets, the Colorado Rockies, and the Colorado Avalanche. Millions were lost each year to black-market bookies, offshore website accounts, or Nevada gaming tourism by eager Colorado sports junkies. In 2018, the United States Supreme Court struck down the Professional Amateur Sports Protection Act, leaving it to each state as to whether and how to regulate sports gambling.

Colorado voters in 2019 narrowly approved legalized sports betting beginning in May 2020. Residents over twenty-one can place sports bets through online or sports betting platforms operated by Colorado's mountain casinos in Black Hawk, Central City, and Cripple Creek, which will also offer in-person sports betting. Some studies project hundreds of millions of dollars to Colorado's economy, with millions collected annually in tax revenue. The first $130,000 of the 10 percent tax will go to treatment of gambling addiction, while most of the remainder will fund various needed water projects. The timing couldn't have been better. Despite professional and college sports nearly going bust in 2020, the online sports betting exceeded all expectations and boomed during the pandemic.

Overall, Colorado's love of gambling has been a boom, and betting on its continued growth is a safe bet. Casino gaming, the lottery, and other gambling have supported charities and helped preserve Colorado's great outdoors, water resources, unique cultural heritage, and historic places and is a win-win for almost everybody. With 2020 pandemic-related changes in the law to save floundering gambling communities, Colorado's mining camp casinos now hope to compete with Las Vegas! That might perhaps be a long-shot bet.

CHAPTER EIGHT

Transportation: From Stagecoaches to the Space Age

COLORADO'S GREATEST CHALLENGE HAS LONG BEEN TRANSPORTATION. Some 700 to 800 miles of "the Great American Desert" separated Boulder, Colorado Springs, Denver, Pueblo, and other Front Range cities from "civilization" and the navigable Missouri River towns of Kansas City, Leavenworth, Atchison, and Omaha.

This remoteness and rugged interior stunted development and growth. The vast plains and impenetrable Rockies forced the various transportation systems to initially go around Colorado, which was originally left off rail, auto, and then aviation routes. Pioneer trails, trains, highways, and planes originally bypassed Colorado to traverse the much lower passes of Wyoming. To bring a boom, Coloradans put their money on transportation as the key to shining times. No industry could prosper and no town could long survive without adequate, fast, and cheap transportation links to the outside. Because of lack of adequate transportation, Colorado has more dead towns than live ones.

WAGONS AND PACK ANIMALS

Gold rushers swarmed across the prairie in Conestoga and large freight wagons or just their old farm wagons tugged by teams of oxen or mules. Some traveled on foot pushing handcarts. Penetrating Colorado's high, rugged Rocky Mountain wilderness to tap its mineral resources initially was on foot or hoof, clambering over animal or Native American paths up precipitous canyon walls. Gold rushers built steep, rough, winding, and narrow roads to accommodate wagons and stagecoaches drawn by sturdy teams of mules.

119

Coloradans depended on wagon trains for vital supplies. In 1860, 10,000 tons of freight in three-ton wagons pulled by ten to twelve oxen lumbered across the plains. One single wet goods shipment to Denver of 160 barrels of liquor and 270 cases of champagne required eighty wagons. This animal-powered transportation was slow, hazardous, and expensive. High freight rates and passenger fares in the 1860s made it difficult to supply miners, to attract settlers, or to export gold ore.

STAGECOACHES

Before railroads, a stagecoach network kept some towns plugged in. Colorado's first stage company, the Leavenworth and Pike's Peak Express, spent $250,000 on fifty-two Concord stages, 1,000 mules, a 687-mile network of stations, and salaries for "sober, discreet and experienced" drivers. On May 7, 1859, the first two coaches, traveling in pairs for protection, reached Denver, bringing passengers, mail, and express freight. On the return to Leavenworth, Kansas, the stages carried out passengers, mail, and gold—sometimes as much as $40,000 in bullion—and a guard riding shotgun.

Stagecoach lines soon crisscrossed Colorado, connecting major population centers. The stage's arrival became the high point of daily life. At the sound of the rumbling coaches drawn by four to six horses or mules, a ruckus that could be heard a mile away, townspeople rushed to the depot. Only high rollers, politicians, journalists, gamblers, fancy ladies, and financiers could afford stage rides, but everyone could enjoy the spectacle as passengers tumbled out and dusted themselves off. Mail was quickly taken to the post office, where homesick folk waited in long lines. The stage company charged 25 cents per letter in addition to federal postage, inspiring some to read their mail, then return it as someone else's and demand a refund.

Frequent accidents, Indian raids, robberies, and heavy expenses bankrupted the Leavenworth and Pike's Peak Express stage company in less than a year. Its successor, the Central Overland California and Pike's Peak Express (COC&PP), shortened the Leavenworth to Denver trip to six days, reduced the round-trip fare from $200 to $75, and extended service up Clear Creek Canyon.

The overextended COC&PP also ran out of money, prompting employees to dub it the "Clean Out of Cash and Poor Pay." It was sold at auction in 1863 to the western stagecoach king, Ben Holladay. His Holladay Overland Mail and Express Company further shortened the South Platte route,

The Wells Fargo stage stop in Denver helped make it Colorado Territory's transportation hub even before railroads arrived. Its first floor still survives at 15th and Market Streets in Lower Downtown. TOM NOEL COLLECTION

expanded service to mountain towns, and spruced up the depot at 15th and McGaa Streets in Denver. Happy with Holladay, Denverites honored him by renaming McGaa Street as Holladay Street. Two decades later, after that street became a notorious red-light district, the name was changed again at the Holladay family's request. It became Market Street in 1887 and remained a place where intimacy was marketed. As Market Street wore the red-light stigma, folks changed its name west of Cherry Creek and east of 23rd to Walnut Street.

The Wells Fargo stage line bought out Holladay in 1867. It served parts of Colorado lacking rail service well into the twentieth century. Wells Fargo remains prominent in Colorado to this day and reigns as Denver's largest bank.

Stagecoach travel was not comfortable. The Concord stages in common use were simply cradled, swinging wooden boxes. As many as nine passengers

121

were crammed into each coach, which thus provided human padding and kept people from bouncing around too much when the going got rough.

RAILROADS

Increasingly, stage lines faced competition. Ever since 1848, when "Pathfinder" John Charles Fremont first attempted to chart a rail route through Colorado, surveyors tried to squeeze a route through the Rockies. William Byers in his *Rocky Mountain News* assured the Union Pacific Railroad (UP) that the "hilly" land west of Denver could be crossed by rail easily. Grenville M. Dodge, the UP chief engineer, reached a different conclusion after his surveying party encountered a September 1866 blizzard on Berthoud Pass. Heeding Dodge's advice, the UP ran its transcontinental tracks across southern Wyoming, where the "hills" were much lower and gentler.

The UP laid out Cheyenne in 1867 as the road's Rocky Mountain headquarters. Hundreds of Denverites moved to the instant Wyoming city. It boomed as Denver dwindled, prompting the *Cheyenne Daily Leader* to crow that "Denver is too near Cheyenne to ever amount to much."

To save Denver, worried businessmen, including former Colorado territorial governor John Evans, editor William Byers, and other civic leaders, organized a Board of Trade on November 13, 1867. The board, a predecessor of the Chamber of Commerce, resolved that if the railroads would not build to Denver, then Denver must build to the railroads. Six days later, Evans, Byers, Walter Cheesman, David Moffat, and others created the Denver Pacific Railway (DP). Byers warned in his *Rocky Mountain News* that unless the road were built, "everybody would move away. We could not afford to pay our enormous freights. . . . We should break ground tomorrow." Within three days, the DP sold $300,000 in stock, some shares being exchanged for promises to work on the roadbed or supply ties.

Denver declared a holiday for the ground-breaking on May 18, 1868. Almost a quarter of the town's population gathered as kegs of beer were tapped and a band struck up "The Railroad Gallop." Two ladies guided the plow that first broke the virgin prairie, then men and mules went to work grading a roadbed. Denverites worked feverishly, knowing that Golden, fifteen miles west, had already incorporated a railroad, the Colorado Central (CC). Like the DP, it aimed to connect with the UP's main line at Cheyenne. Denverites bet on the DP to win the rail race, while Goldenites wagered on their CC.

Golden's chief booster, William Austin Hamilton Loveland, hoped to make his town Colorado's rail hub. Loveland capitalized on the animosity toward Denver shared by many smaller towns. "There is little of the Denver egotism about the Golden City folks," declared the *Central City Colorado Times*. "We can hope for advantages from Golden City that Denver in her exclusiveness would never grant."

Evans and the Denver crowd out-jockeyed Golden in the iron horse race. Working with UP allies, Evans helped persuade Congress to give the Denver Pacific a land grant consisting of the usual forty-mile strip of alternating square-mile sections along the road's right-of-way between Denver and Cheyenne. This enabled the DP to secure loans and raise capital through land sales. Through deals with the UP, Evans got that company to help lay the tracks and provide rolling stock for the DP, but the price of outside help came high—by 1880, Evans and other local capitalists would lose control to the UP.

Evans presided over the completion of the DP on June 22, 1870. A silver spike, symbolic of railroad prosperity, also became symbolic of the improvisations that brought the line to Denver. Evans had to wrap an ordinary iron spike in white paper and pretend it was silver, because the miners bringing the genuine spike from Georgetown had lingered in a saloon and pawned the precious nail to pay their bar bill.

Two months after the arrival of the DP, the Kansas Pacific (KP) became the second line to reach Denver. To motivate KP track layers, on August 15, 1870, a large barrel of whiskey was placed on the prairie at what is now Strasburg. Five miles to the east a construction crew at Byers began laying track westward; five miles to the west another crew began working eastward from Bennett. The two gangs of track builders set a record that day, completing 10.25 miles of track by 3:00 p.m. The workers got free drinks; Denver got a direct connection with Kansas City and St. Louis.

John Evans and other Denver boosters hoped to make it the transportation and supply hub for the booming mining districts deep in the mountains. Enormous amounts of capital were required to survey, blast, grade, or tunnel over or through the precipitous canyon walls and often impassable passes of the Rockies. The cost of wood ties, steel rails, engines, and rolling stock caused many of the newly incorporated railroads to never develop beyond paper railroads or run out of steam far short of their ambitious destinations.

Narrow-gauge railroads were an answer to cost cutting and terrain-conquering, and Colorado developed the largest network of narrow-gauge

By the early 1870s, Denver emerged as the rail transportation hub of the Rocky Mountain West with two standard-gauge railroads, the Denver Pacific and the Kansas Pacific, linking it to the north and east, and the narrow-gauge Denver & Rio Grande heading south and west to serve the mountain mining districts. Transfer coaches moved passengers and freight from one rail depot to the other until scattered stations for each line were consolidated in 1881 as Union Station. TOM NOEL COLLECTION

railroads in the country. At three feet wide opposed to the standard four feet eight and a half inches, narrow-gauge railroads cost less to build, could be built quicker, and could move around tighter curves and more precipitous mountain rail beds than the standard-gauge railroads.

With each arrival of a railroad, towns and mining camps celebrated assured prosperity with brass bands, parades, and long-winded speeches. Colorado's railroad history is full of boom and bust trains that eventually either went bankrupt or merged and consolidated into the big boys.

Late in 1870, the CC finished the first stretch of its road, a narrow gauge spur connecting Golden with the standard-gauge DP four miles north of Denver. The sulky Golden crowd did not build into Denver, hoping that their town still might become Colorado's rail nucleus. The financially feeble CC slowly inched north through Boulder, Berthoud, Longmont, Loveland, and Fort Collins, not connecting with the UP at Cheyenne until 1877. By then, Denver, with five railroads, had clearly won the soot-and-cinders competition.

Golden did, however, win the race to the mining towns up Clear Creek Canyon. Boston capitalists financing the CC decided to save construction time and money by using the narrow-gauge system and bought small narrow-gauge steam locomotives previously used for filling in Boston's Back Bay, reconditioned them, and shipped them west to tackle the Rockies.

By 1872, the CC had reached Black Hawk and Central City. In 1877, the baby road puffed into Georgetown, Colorado's first silver city, fifty miles west of Denver. Seven years later, the road completed its most fantastic feat, the Georgetown Loop. This engineering marvel used 4.7 miles of track, making three and a half complete loops over towering trestles, to climb the 2 steep miles from Georgetown to Silver Plume.

The CC soon had competition. Evans, Moffat, and Cheesman also wanted to share in the new mountain rail boom. They incorporated the narrow-gauge Denver, South Park & Pacific Railway (DSP&P) in 1872. It laid rails up the South Platte Canyon and through the mountains to Kenosha Pass, which it finally reached in May 1879. From that pass, a spectacular vista awaited travelers then and now—an immense flat valley rimmed by snow-capped mountains. South Park, as this beautiful region is called, had gold as

The Georgetown Loop, seen here around 1890, has been reincarnated by History Colorado to take passengers back to the glory days of yesteryear railroading. TOM NOEL COLLECTION

well as scenery and was the railroad's first namesake destination. Fairplay and other gold camps were among the first major strikes.

After tapping South Park's goldfields, the DSP&P branched out to climb over Boreas Pass to the Summit County gold-rich towns of Breckenridge, Dillon, and Keystone. Meanwhile, the main line ran through Fairplay and down Trout Creek to the Arkansas River, which it followed north to Leadville, arriving in 1880. In its quixotic quest for the Pacific, the DSP&P built the Alpine Tunnel in 1881, the first bore under the Continental Divide. Exhausted by that engineering feat, the railroad ran out of steam in 1883, never getting beyond a mountain valley north of Gunnison. Like so many of Colorado's "Pacific" railroads, the DSP&P never got anywhere near that ocean.

The Denver & Rio Grande (D&RG) became the most important railroad in assuring Colorado's regional dominance. This narrow-gauge line was organized in 1870 by thirty-four-year-old William Jackson Palmer. Having supervised construction of the KP and having watched other roads build east to west, Palmer reckoned that a north-to-south line along the Front Range would be a moneymaker. He hoped to ultimately reach Mexico City, but the D&RG never got farther south than Santa Fe, New Mexico.

The federal government gave the D&RG a 200-foot right-of-way but refused a land grant, so Palmer turned to town-building to help finance construction. If existing towns refused to donate land and other incentives, the D&RG acquired property nearby for a depot and town site. When Colorado City balked, Palmer founded nearby Colorado Springs in 1871. When Animas City spurned him, he bypassed it and founded Durango. All told, the D&RG founded around a hundred towns along its tracks.

Although the D&RG started out going south, silver rushes turned two of its branches to the west. After the Leadville boom began in 1877, the road raced west to Cañon City and followed the Arkansas River through the Royal Gorge up to Leadville in 1881. With the rush to the San Juan Mountains, the D&RG built another extension west over La Veta Pass, crossed the San Luis Valley, dipped into New Mexico, and then steamed through southwestern Colorado to Durango and Silverton.

Palmer's road also became the first to span Colorado, linking Denver with Grand Junction via a route through Pueblo, Salida, and over Tennessee Pass to the Colorado River in 1883. The road followed the river into Grand Junction and on to Utah. It was reorganized as the Denver & Rio Grande Western Railway (D&RGW) in 1920. The D&RGW completed a more direct route to Grand Junction via the Moffat Tunnel under Rollins Pass as of 1934. Unable to compete with the UP's faster route through Wyoming, the D&RGW offered a more leisurely "rail cruise" with glass-domed observation cars through scenic Colorado, including the California Zephyr, later taken over by Amtrak.

The DP, KP, CC, DSP&P, and D&RG were the pioneers among over a hundred different lines to lay track in Colorado. Other later, larger lines—the Atchison, Topeka & Santa Fe; the Chicago, Rock Island & Pacific; the Chicago, Burlington & Quincy; the Missouri Pacific; and the Union Pacific—all chugged into Colorado by the 1880s. With their coming, Colorado expanded its sway over its Rocky Mountain hinterland. Railroads also transformed the Colorado high plains into a booming agricultural region.

Railroads facilitated not only agricultural and mining booms but also a population explosion. Arrival of the railroads in 1870 had an immediate impact. Colorado, which had stagnated during the 1860s, grew by almost 500 percent during the 1870s, reaching a population of 194,327 in 1880. The population more than doubled to 413,249 by 1890, only to be slowed by the 1893 silver crash. Today, Colorado's population hovers over 5.8 million but few travel by train.

Only two major rail lines survive—the Burlington Northern Santa Fe and the Union Pacific. Today, Amtrak and six summer excursion trains provide the shrunken available passenger service.

BICYCLES

The late nineteenth-century cycling craze led many Coloradans, both men and women, to two-wheeling. With the development of the chain-driven "Safety Bicycle" in 1885 and the pneumatic tire in 1893, cycling transformed Colorado's local transportation. It not only spurred women's liberation, but became cheap, reliable transportation for the masses. Early cycling clubs made it a sport for the wealthy, but common folk soon relied on it to go freely to and from work, markets, parks, and any other local destination they desired, without being dependent upon less reliable and highly scheduled streetcar service.

By the turn of the century, Denver claimed the highest concentration of bicycles in the country. Cyclists were an early proponent of the "Good Roads Movement." Today, cycling remains one of Colorado's most popular recreational activities, and state and local governments are encouraging greater use

The bicycling mania infected Colorado in the late 1800s and proved to be one form of local transportation and recreation enjoyed by many women and all segments of the population. TOM NOEL COLLECTION

of bicycles as healthy alternatives to polluting automobiles and a solution to chronic traffic congestion and downtown parking woes.

AUTOMOBILES

Colorado's automotive history began with David W. Brunton, a mining engineer and inventor of the Brunton compass. He tested several contraptions at the Mechanics Institute in Boston in 1899 before selecting a Columbia Runabout electric. Shipped west by rail, the vehicle arrived at Denver's Union Station in a big box. Brunton brought it to his house at 865 Grant Street on Capitol Hill. It took him a day to assemble, and his diary reads "May 10, ran electric carriage in the streets of Denver." During that 1899 spin, a gang of boys, dogs, and newspapermen followed him. What did he feed it? How fast would it go? How could it be stopped? What kind of waste did it leave behind?

Rich and adventuresome people began buying horseless carriages. Lawrence C. Phipps, Sr., imported a $17,500 Mercedes tonneau, which came with a German chauffeur-mechanic to drive and service it. With a sixty-horsepower engine capable of ninety miles per hour, Phipps was king of the road. He soon had a rival in Spencer Penrose of Colorado Springs, who added a new car every year to his stable. To test his new toys, he spent nearly $250,000 to build an automobile road to the top of Pikes Peak in 1915. To promote his road and mountain motoring, Penrose began staging an annual Pikes Peak Hill Climb auto race that continues every summer.

Highway construction was left to private parties, such as Penrose, or local governments until 1914, when the state levied the first property tax for highway improvement. Further state support came with passage of a gasoline tax in 1919.

Colorado also put convicts to work building roads—more so than any other state. Prisoners enjoyed the temporary reprieve in the great outdoors

Early automobiles faced many obstacles on unpaved roads over rough terrain which seemed to be either dusty or muddy and unbridged streams that were often impassable. DENVER PUBLIC LIBRARY, WESTERN HISTORY DEPARTMENT

Back to the Future—
The Fritchle Electric Car

FRITCHLE GARAGE

From 1909 to 1917, over 500 elite Fritchle Electric cars were manufactured and sold out of the plant at Colfax and Clarkson in the Capitol Hill neighborhood. Today it is the home of the popular Fillmore Auditorium. BILL HANSEN COLLECTION

The earliest automobiles were propelled by steam, electric batteries, or gasoline. Initially, electric cars were particularly popular, as they were quiet, odorless, and easy to handle, as compared to the noisy, rattling, hand-cranked, smoke-belching, and complicated internal combustion engines. Oliver P. Fritchle, a Denver electrical engineer, was fascinated by batteries. In 1908, he opened his electric car factory.

The "100 Mile Fritchle Electric" soon became an industry leader and set the tone for high-society ladies, offering wide seats and high roofs to accommodate large dresses and wide-brimmed hats. Ads boasted that the "100 Mile Fritchle Electric holds all records for hill climbing, mileage per charge, durability and economy of upkeep." At a whopping cost of over $3,500, they soon became a status symbol for social climbers such as Molly Brown, one of Fritchle's first customers. As internal combustion engines gained in popularity, Fritchlie even developed a hybrid gas and electric model.

The facility closed in 1917—a victim of the availability of inexpensive Texas and Oklahoma petroleum, the lack of sufficient charging stations, and the cheaper mass-produced Model T Fords introduced in 1908. It would take a hundred years before soaring oil prices and polluting emissions would once again revive interest in electric cars.

and a chance to earn good behavior merits, but private contractors lobbied successfully to be freed of this competition. Inmates still make Colorado license plates at the state penitentiary in Cañon City.

With the help of federal highway aid after 1916, the state's expenditures on road construction and maintenance rose from an average of roughly $3 million annually during the late 1910s to an average of over $10 million per year in the 1920s. With education receiving only about two-thirds as much as the highway department, such auto-oriented priorities led the president of the State Teachers College at Greeley to complain that, in Colorado, million-dollar highways ran by $500 schoolhouses with $100-a-month teachers.

Although initially called "toys of the rich," automobiles became the everyday transportation of the middle class after Henry Ford began selling Model Ts for as little as $290. By 1928, Coloradans owned one car for every 4.38 residents and had the nation's eighth-highest auto ownership per capita. By the 1950s, even the poorest household usually owned at least an old jalopy. By the 2000s, Colorado motor vehicle registration figures showed approximately one vehicle for every adult.

As late as 1929, the State Highway Commissioner reported, after surveying 1,600 miles of Colorado's highways: "We found bridges we did not dare to cross in a car, encountered mud that stuck us, found grades we managed to crawl up at the speed of a snail, and roads that were not meant for anything but a horse drawn vehicle." Such conditions caused many early vehicles to break down, get mired in mud or snow, or get stranded in bridgeless streams. The vehicles had to be towed by horses or humans into blacksmith shops, which served as early auto repair shops.

The Eisenhower-Johnson Memorial Tunnels take I-70 under the Continental Divide. Their completion in 1979 opened up western Colorado to a population boom centered on winter resort towns that began to thrive year-round. Today, the twin tunnels of the overcrowded interstate become a bottleneck during weekends and holidays, still awaiting a solution. TOM NOEL COLLECTION

As roads became ever more crowded, interstate highways became the prescribed solution. Still, the first transcontinental highway, the Lincoln Highway, again bypassed Colorado in favor of Wyoming. Colorado's first interstate, I-25, was dedicated in 1958, after ten years of construction. While I-25 ran north–south along the Front Range, I-70, the major east–west route through Colorado, took shape more slowly. The staggering cost of building through the Rockies held up construction for years, while 1-80 zoomed through Wyoming and I-40 breezed through New Mexico. Coloradans once again, as in the days of the transcontinental railroad, found themselves bypassed. The first interstate plans terminated I-70 in Denver and steered travelers via I-25 either south to I-40 or north to I-80.

State highway engineer Charles D. Vail expressed alarm as early as the 1940s. Governor Edwin C. Johnson took the state's plight directly to

Streetcars Encore

In the 1870s, larger Colorado cities began building streetcar lines. Originally these street railways were pulled by horses or mules. Like railroads, street railways transformed cities. They shaped the path of development as cities began to sprawl outward. Folks could now move out to streetcar suburbs, assured of cheap, easy transportation into town and schools, workplaces, markets, health care, or entertainment. Denver, Pueblo, Colorado Springs, and other booming urban areas were soon surrounded by streetcar suburbs.

As automobiles began luring away streetcar travelers, city centers became almost ghost towns as suburbia evolved and thrived amid their own shopping centers and workplaces, and there was less need to head downtown. For many years, much of Denver became blighted. In the 1970s, preservation efforts saved many historic Denver residences and commercial buildings from so-called urban renewal.

As nearly everyone switched from street railways to automobiles, the new contraptions began to create problems. Motor vehicles congested many cities and towns and caused air pollution. Planners looked to the past for a solution—streetcars. Metro Denver's Regional Transportation District (RTD) began building a rail system in 1994, and by 2020, rail lines had been completed to many Denver suburbs. Like yesterday's railroads and streetcars, the system is centered on a formerly sleepy Union Station, which is once again reincarnated as both a busy front door to Denver as well as a hub for intraurban streetcar travel. After some hiccups, the A Line starting at Union Station began catering to Denver International Airport passengers.

President Dwight D. Eisenhower, who vacationed in Colorado to fish. Johnson gave the president Colorado Fishing License No. 1 along with an elaborate presentation book that made the case for I-70. Eisenhower smiled and later helped persuade Congress to approve a route through the Rockies, breaching the Continental Divide beneath Loveland Pass with 1.6-mile-long tunnels. While the westbound tunnel was named for President Eisenhower, the second, later bore was named for Governor Johnson.

Breaching the Continental Divide was not the last challenge for I-70. It still had to pass through 12.4 miles of scenic Glenwood Canyon, east of

Glenwood Springs, to complete the four-lane interstate. Suggestions to go around the canyon were soon abandoned. An early proposal to blast the canyon walls and rechannel the Colorado River horrified environmentalists, who protested mightily. Eventually, after $490 million and eleven years of planning and construction, the engineering challenge was met with an array of tunnels and cantilevered roadways flowing with the natural terrain. Finally completed in 1992, it won praise for its sensitive regard for Mother Nature.

The Air Age
Colorado's first recorded engine-powered flight came in 1910 when Louis "Birdman" Paulhan brought his Farman biplane to Denver in a boxcar. Thousands thronged Overland Park to witness the arrival of the air age. This Frenchman, famous for his exhibitions in Paris, had performed at the first US air show, the Los Angeles Aviation Meet, just two weeks earlier. After some tinkering, Paulhan left the ground in a big, boxy contraption wired together and sporting a yellow linen skin. He failed to circle Pikes Peak, as one promoter had promised, but spent three days making skillful, if short, flights—none lasted more than a few minutes. On his sixth flight, he crashed into the crowd, injuring three spectators.

Despite this smashup, Coloradans took to these newfangled flying contraptions. In a large state of long distances and difficult terrain, airplanes became popular. Eventually, Colorado would boast the second-most pilots per capita, behind only Alaska. Still, the high altitude, rarified air, and turbulent weather of the Rockies thwarted early air travel, as planes could not obtain adequate lift to fly over the largely uncharted Continental Divide. Once again, Denver was left off early transcontinental aviation routes in favor of the gentler Rockies of Wyoming. Many who tried Colorado's Rockies failed, especially early mail carriers who took quicker and shorter routes, regardless of the perilous terrain.

"Dead reckoning" was the unfortunately named tool for early mail carriers and those aviators braving the Colorado Rockies. Many crashed into lofty mountainsides and perished. Mountain mail flyer Elroy Borge Jeppesen (1907–1996) pioneered aviation charting with a little "Black Book" of personal observations and detailed charts, which eventually were published to wide acclaim, becoming standard for many pilots. He moved his prospering business to Denver in 1941 and was so successful that Denver International Airport's (DIA) main terminal is named in his honor. With improved

Denver Municipal Airport opened as a consolidation of various small airports scattered around the city. It evolved and became so crowded and noisy that it was moved northeast to become Denver International Airport. The many restaurants there today are descended from the pioneer concessionaire, Mom's Skyline Buffet, shown here. DENVER PUBLIC LIBRARY, WESTERN HISTORY DEPARTMENT

charting, as well as multi-propeller planes, longer runways, and the jet age, the Colorado Rockies were eventually surmounted.

To keep up with other cities, Denver mayor Benjamin Stapleton suggested building a consolidated city airport on the northeastern outskirts of the Mile High City in 1929. The mayor met opposition, shrilly led by the *Denver Post*, which ridiculed the idea as "Stapleton's Folly" and dubbed the Sand Creek airport site "Simpleton's Sand Dunes." Some cynics blasted the project as a taxpayer subsidy for a few rich kids who liked to play with airplanes.

Despite all the flack, Denver Municipal Airport opened in October of 1929, one week before the stock market crashed. To honor the mayor who had braved considerable opposition to build it, Denver Municipal Airport was renamed Stapleton Airport in 1944. The name changed again in 1964, after the Denver Chamber of Commerce suggested that it be renamed Stapleton International Airport. Four years later, it actually became international when Western Airlines inaugurated nonstop flights to Calgary, Canada.

Stapleton soared from the twenty-first-busiest terminal in 1960 to the fifth-busiest in the United States in terms of passengers during the mid-1980s. Two-thirds of these travelers were merely switching planes. They complained that one had to go through the Denver airport even to get to heaven or hell. Jammed flights, growing crowds, and congestion led Denver to ponder a new airport.

Like Mayor Stapleton before him in the 1920s, Mayor Federico Peña was criticized for planning an unneeded airport too far away from the city. Peña's determination climbed after Salt Lake City emerged as a rival in 1986. That year, the Utah capital became a major hub after Delta acquired Western Airlines. This new threat galled Denverites with a full-page ad in the *New York Times* and other national publications: A harried executive arriving late for a meeting apologizes, "Sorry I'm late but I had to fly through Denver." Next time he would fly through Salt Lake City.

Governor Roy Romer and the business community joined Mayor Peña in a crusade to build the world's largest airport, failing to add that the fifty-five-square-mile site was largest only in terms of land. In 1995, DIA opened after four years of construction and more than $5 billion. Some critics called it the start of a colossal disaster movie, featuring a suitcase-swallowing automatic baggage system, stalled "people-mover" trains trapped underground, and terminal passengers smothered by a collapsing fabric roof. That wacky tent roof, cynics promised, would soon be shredded by heavy snow loads, hailstorms, and/or tornados.

To the contrary, DIA has stood up to Colorado's mercurial weather and been acclaimed a technical success by engineers. Tony Robbins, in *Engineering a New Architecture* (New Haven: Yale University Press, 1996), devotes a section to DIA as "confirmation of the practical advantages of tensioned membrane roofs for long span enclosures in cold climates." Architect Curt Fentress says the terminal's snow-white tent roof was inspired by Colorado's soaring mountain peaks.

Denver's urban sprawl soon saw residential, hotel, and commercial buildings boom around DIA. Adams County joined in the eastern expansion. In Denver's northeast, Montbello and Green Valley Ranch are continuously expanding with new subdivisions. Many of these newcomers in the shadows of DIA perhaps forgot that the noise from Stapleton and the surrounding congestion in northeast Denver were leading factors in the airport's relocation.

A more recent light-rail connection and a spectacular new airport Westin Hotel and nearby hotel development have generally made DIA a traveler's treat. Direct travel to Europe and Asia is now available. Still, seemingly

136

endless expansions, construction disputes, and cost overruns have dampened the enthusiasm of many as Denver tries to keep pace with the booming air traffic. The 2020 pandemic wreaked havoc on Colorado's airline industry, likely resulting in long-term shifts in transportation patterns.

THE BOOMING AEROSPACE INDUSTRY: THE SKY IS NO LONGER THE LIMIT

While the Colorado Rockies thwarted most transportation development, its strategic midcontinent location, one mile closer to space, and mid-continental protective mountains have created a booming aerospace industry since the space race began in the 1950s. Martin Marietta built a major and secretive defense plant in 1955 located behind a hogback in Waterton Canyon. It developed and tested the highly successful Titan multistage rockets beginning in the 1950s as launch vehicles for missiles, satellites, exploration,

Martin Marietta's highly successful Titan missile development in the 1950s and 1960s transported astronauts to the moon and beyond. DENVER PUBLIC LIBRARY, WESTERN HISTORY DEPARTMENT

and for lunar landing vehicles. After merging to become Lockheed Martin in 1994, Atlas V booster rockets were developed for both exploring and landing on Mars.

Other aerospace achievements include the US Air Force Academy, air force bases, NORAD, Cheyenne Mountain, Space Command Headquarters, and more than 180 aerospace companies. Colorado's "Aerospace Alley," stretching from Boulder to Colorado Springs, has the second-largest aerospace industry in the country, behind only California.

PRAYING FOR A BUST

For over a century, Coloradans worried about transportation and how to attract people. Nowadays, it is increasingly a question of too many people getting and staying here. Overcrowded Front Range streets and highways are causing horrendous traffic jams. Roads are becoming ever more clogged as a thousand people a day move into Colorado. The I-70 corridor through the mountains has become a nightmare for both residents and tourists alike.

Some are now fleeing the state for less crowded, less expensive places with fewer traffic and transportation problems. But Colorado's population is expected to keep mushrooming. The state's twenty-first-century population boom with its congestion, rising prices, and housing shortage has left some hoping for a bust. Yet the tourist industry, which rode various means of transportation successfully, continues to recruit more visitors. Those greenhorns have a habit of becoming residents.

CHAPTER NINE

Touring the Highest State

THE SKY-HIGH COLORADO ROCKY MOUNTAINS INITIALLY SERVED AS A BARrier to transportation, mineral exploitation, and economic development. Later, the barrier became a boon, as the Rockies became the state's signature attraction, even stamped on Colorado license plates. Once a bust, the mountains began booming with tourists. Health, sightseeing, and winter tourism are just three types of tourism in the booming field that has become Colorado's second-largest employer after the service industry. Even snow, once an impediment, is now a major draw thanks to growing numbers of skiers, snowboarders, snowshoers, and snowmobilers.

Sightseers come to see the literally breathtaking highest and most rugged link in the mountain chain stretching from Mexico to Canada. The Colorado Rockies include 54 "fourteeners" over 14,000 feet and 600 peaks over 13,000. The Rockies are headwaters of seven major rivers which water the entire Southwest. Besides the mountains and the waterways, other attractions are numerous natural hot springs, twelve national monuments, and more than forty state parks. Among the state's four national parks, Rocky Mountain National Park has become the nation's third most visited.

National forests, with their many recreational offerings, occupy 22 percent of Colorado's land area (the third-largest percentage in the United States). Outdoor recreation has made the state a national playground. Today, Colorado has graduated from primarily summer tourism to four-season recreational activities. Environmental as well as economic benefits have come from the outdoor sports industry as it has championed environmental protection, thus softening the impact of extractive industries, past and present, which have scarred the state.

Since the gold rush days, tourism has been less boom and bust than a consistent growth industry, even in slow times. It even helped buoy the state's economy following the Panic of 1893 and the Great Depression. Some, such as health tourists, came and decided to stay. Others returned, taking up permanent residence after beholding its wonders.

As of 2019, Colorado ranked eighth nationally for leisure travelers. This audience had continuously grown. In 2015, it was ranked thirteenth and in 2016 was ranked ninth. The hospitality industry directly supports 171,000 jobs earning $6.3 billion as of 2018. Those figures would experience a disastrous decline as a result of the 2020 COVID-19 pandemic.

As one the strongest drivers of the state's economy, tourism in 2017 lured 84.7 million US-based travelers plus 1 million international visitors. Collectively, they spent $20.9 billion and filled the state and local tax coffers with $1.28 billion. Denver alone attracts 31.7 million visitors and accounts for over half of all in-state tourist spending. The industry has been promoted by the Colorado Tourism Office, which has a relatively constant annual budget of about $20 million.

NATURAL MINERAL HOT SPRINGS

Native Americans, of course, were the first sightseers in what they called the "land of the long look." They, like others to come later, were intrigued by the mountains and the plains, the canyons and the waterways. Some of the most treasured, sacred, and comforting attractions were the state's ninety-three natural hot springs. The largest and one of the hottest, the 136-degree Great Pagosa, bears the Ute name for "healing water."

Ute legends speak of a plague that fell upon the tribe. Hoping for a cure, the Utes danced and prayed deep into the night around a huge bonfire until, exhausted, they slept. Upon awakening in morning sunshine, the tribe found, in place of the bonfire, the hot waters of the Great Pagosa. After bathing in and drinking from the waters, the Utes were healed.

White tourists also fancied hot springs, as "taking the waters" was known to be most healthful. Geothermally warmed waters, rich in minerals and often enclosed as elaborate bathhouses, had been popular for their healing and cleansing qualities since ancient times.

The Indian Hot Springs in Idaho Springs claims to be Colorado's first commercial tourist attraction, dating to the early gold rush days. Many other visitors, more concerned about health than finding gold, came to cure their bodies. The 1881 discovery of the miracle mineral radium in Soda Creek gave Idaho Springs another magnet. The Radium Hot Springs Hotel sprang up

The still-bubbling Hot Springs Resort established in 1863 at Idaho Springs has since been renamed the Indian Hot Springs for its original patrons. TOM NOEL COLLECTION

over the magic waters, and the proprietors declared that due to the supposedly curative radium waters, "the stretcher is carried in only one direction."

Other hot springs, mineral springs, and vapor cave resorts soon followed in such places as Glenwood Springs, dubbed the "Spa in the Mountains." William Jackson Palmer, hoping to elevate his railroad stop to a resort community, founded Colorado Springs, even though the closest hot springs were in Manitou Springs, about six miles away, which he later hyped as the "Saratoga of the West."

The World's Sanitarium

Early settlers had noted the frequent mildness of many Colorado winters and reported that picnics and outdoor activities could often be enjoyed even in winter. Furthermore, the state's pure and exhilarating air and its high, sunny dryness, said physicians, helped cure diseases of the lungs, particularly tuberculosis, then called consumption. As the leading cause of death in America, consumption was also referred to as the "White Death" for the pallor caused by the disease. "Invalids," "lungers," and "hackers" soon swarmed Colorado "chasing the cure."

Lady Isabella Bird, one of Colorado's first world-traveling tourists, had observed that "Colorado is the most remarkable sanitarium in the world." The notion stuck and railroads, promotors, and even government officials soon dubbed Colorado "The World's Sanitarium."

In 1884, Denver physician Charles Denison helped organize the American Climatological Association. Over the next two decades, its *Transactions* presented scientific discussion of Colorado's climate cure by Denison and his fellow physicians. Dr. Edwin Solly praised the benefits of Manitou Springs' mineral waters for the blood and the digestive system. The *Transactions* noted that Colorado benefited consumptives through the abundance of sunshine and the clear atmosphere free of moisture and grit. The *Boulder Camera* affirmed that the "tuberculosis bacilli will not develop at a greater altitude than 4,500 feet above sea level and a dry atmosphere where the development of the bacilli will be arrested and the progress of the disease checked in all cases."

So many health seekers arrived at Manitou Springs, a resort town a few miles west of Colorado Springs, that a common greeting between strangers became "What is your complaint, sir?" Physicians promoted the springs as curative for any number of nebulous Victorian illnesses, including gout, stiffness, flatulence, chronic dyspepsia, uterine complaints, and even alcoholism. Colorado's "champagne air" was touted as a tonic for any and all ailments.

Residence at high elevation, claimed Denver's Dr. Frederick J. Bancroft, caused "the narrow in chest to become broad, the relaxed in muscle to grow strong, the thin in flesh to gain weight, and [it] thoroughly regenerates those suffering from the bilious diseases caused by prolonged residence in malarial districts." Healthy food, fresh air, the outdoor life, and cool nights combined to ensure restful sleep. The result, according to Dr. Bancroft, was "cheerfulness and a contented frame of mind—the true requisites of good health."

Governor Frederick Pitkin's claim that "we can almost bring a dead man to life" can be dismissed as boosterism, but many experts agreed that living in the state quickened and strengthened the functioning of any healthy organism. "There is a wealth of life stored up in the dry, sunny climate of this State," wrote Dr. Samuel Fisk, "more precious than the hidden treasures which the mountains contain." Coloradans boasted that invalids coming to the state to die would be disappointed.

Desperately ill people flocked in to test these promises. Physicians back east readily sent their sickest and hopeless patients west. Many could afford to try the climate cure because Colorado lay only $40 away by rail from midwestern cities. Every year, a wave of asthmatics and consumptives fled the cold, dreary winters of the East. Thumbing their copies of Dr. Denison's *Rocky Mountain Health Resort* or Dr. Solly's *Health Resorts of Colorado Springs and Manitou*, hopeful people filled Colorado hotels and boardinghouses. Poorer invalids sometimes made do with makeshift accommodations, including tent encampments. The more advanced cases were provided with one-way tickets and often died en route or shortly after arrival.

From the 1870s to the early 1900s, the common estimate was that one-third of the state's population was composed of health seekers. Historians later quoted that guess, but its validity is impossible to verify. It is also difficult to prove claims that Denver's "one-lung army" totaled 30,000 in 1890. Certainly, in Colorado Springs, there were enough invalids living on outside incomes to buffer the shock of the 1893 depression and to help the town through the hard times without a bank failure. Some historians have also suggested that tuberculosis specifically, and health generally, drew more people to Colorado by the early twentieth century than mining and ranching combined. Similarly, many of Colorado's early physicians came to Colorado not to treat others but to heal themselves.

Another survey in 1926 found that 60 percent of Denver's population came to Denver because they or someone they knew had tuberculosis. Statistics for the first decade of the twentieth century, however, show that nearly one-quarter of all deaths in Denver resulted from tuberculosis—far above the national average. "For years," proclaimed the *Boulder-Colorado Sanitarium Bulletin* 1 (January 1902), "Colorado has been considered the Mecca of the poor consumptive, and justly so. Thousands are living the enjoyment of excellent health who, had they not left their homes in the east, would today be filling untimely graves."

What the promotional literature did not say was that the large-scale migration of tuberculars was already ebbing when these statistics were gathered. Physicians began to advise institutionalization near the victim's home

The vast Woodmen of the World Sanatorium in Colorado Springs, with 200 tent homes as well as hospital buildings, helps illustrate how more people probably came to Colorado for their health than for gold and silver. BILL HANSEN COLLECTION

rather than travel across a continent. At the same time, the proof that tuberculosis was a contagious disease raised fears throughout the West. By 1900, Coloradans were blaming the flow of health seekers on overblown publicity put out by "selfish interests engaged in transportation and inn-keeping." Dread replaced sympathy for the consumptives, and some people suggested quarantining dangerous cases. Landlords rejected their applications, and employers refused to hire them. Some urged putting bells on the "lungers" to warn folks to stay clear. "No Spitting!" signs went up on walls and down on sidewalks, as promiscuous expectoration was thought to be a major means of spreading the dread disease.

Unfortunately, the curative powers of Colorado's climate were a bust. The health hype was a hoax. At best, Colorado's climate was a distracting placebo, a scenic gilded pill. Tuberculosis was incurable and would remain so until the advent of antibiotics in the 1940s.

Still, tubercular sanatoriums offered hope and provided the foundation for Colorado's booming health industry. Colorado Springs boasted the high-end Glockner (1890) and the Cragmoor (1914). The Cragmoor was rumored to encourage nude heliotherapy on its sundecks. Denver housed major institutions such as the Agnes Memorial Sanatorium (1904), the National Jewish Hospital (1899), the Jewish Consumptives' Relief Society (1904), the Swedish National Sanitarium (1905), and the Evangelical Lutheran Sanitarium (1905). National Jewish thrives to this day and boasts of being the nation's best respiratory care institution. Swedish and Lutheran have become full-service hospitals.

By 1911, Colorado ranked first in the West and fifth in the United States in the number of sanatorium beds, with 1,695 in twenty-one institutions. This early start laid a foundation for Colorado's extensive health-care network, with nationally ranked National Jewish, Children's Hospital Colorado, and the University of Colorado Health Sciences Center on the Anschutz Medical Campus. Health care and the flourishing bioscience industry are a continually expanding mainstay of the Colorado economy. Health care is one part of the Colorado economy that never gets sick.

SIGHTSEEING AND TRAIN TOURISM

Along with hot springs aficionados, thousands of gold rushers pouring into Colorado wrote books and letters that attracted tourists. William H. Larimer, who helped his father found Denver City November 22, 1858, wrote in *Larimer Reminiscences* (Lancaster, PA: New Era Publishing Company, 1918) that "everyone would soon be flocking to Denver for the most picturesque country in the world, with fine air, good water and everything to make a man happy and live to a good, old age."

In 1869, the federal government commissioned the Ferdinand V. Hayden Survey to map Colorado. Accompanying the survey was noted photographer William Henry Jackson and renowned artist Thomas Moran. Their awesome and romantic images of Colorado's scenery were widely disseminated by the state's boosters to plug Colorado tourism. Moran's painting *Mount of the Holy Cross* became a particularly popular subject, as did paintings by such renowned western landscape artists as Albert Bierstadt.

Such magnificent mountain landscapes had largely eluded the early prospectors and miners, who viewed the lofty peaks, craggy gulches, and swift-flowing rivers and streams as hindrances to their mad quest for gold and silver. The mineral rushes despoiled the landscape with dredged-up riverbeds, denuded forests, mounds of mountain side tailings, and befouled air. By 1920, hard rock mining had largely faded and many of the gold and silver

145

Puffing its Switzerland-like alpine scenery as well as honoring Switzerland's globally pacesetting tourist promotion, Colorado boosters adopted the "Switzerland of America" slogan. BILL HANSEN COLLECTION

mining camps had been abandoned. Yet even ghost towns attracted visitors. In 1940, Harold Arthur Hoffmeister, in his multivolume treatise *Economic Geography* (New York: Doubleday, 1940), made the following observations, which remain true today:

> *The hustle and excitement of the mining town has passed, but the glamor and personality of the former periods will not die. The rugged beauty of the region and the romantic history of the camps that is written in every mine dump and in every weather-beaten structure now act as a magnet to draw thousands of tourists and resorters each year. The gold which was sent out in earlier periods to enrich the East is returning to the mountains to be spent by tourists.*

Massachusetts journalist Samuel Bowles visited Colorado in 1869 and soon became an ardent booster. He trumpeted the Rocky Mountains as adorned with glacial lakes, meadows, and forests, with its pure, dry, stimulating mountain air the New World's answer to Europe's Alps. Bowles enticed city slickers from the polluted eastern industrial areas to make Colorado a dream destination in his guidebook *The Switzerland of America: A Summer's Vacation in the Parks and Mountains of Colorado* (Springfield, MA: S. Bowles and Co., 1869). The title of his book soon stuck.

Switzerland, as the first country to develop an international tourist industry, set the pace globally. This role model inspired Coloradans to use their state's alpine scenery to puff Colorado as the "Switzerland of America." The town of Ouray officially adopted that slogan, as did the Denver, Boulder & Western Railroad, which dubbed its route the Switzerland Trail to capture sightseers. Some Colorado boosters quipped that Switzerland should return the favor with boasting the Swiss Alps in "Colorado of Europe" campaigns.

Railroads dominated the tourist trade from the arrival of the first lines in 1870 until the 1950s. The Denver and Rio Grande (D&RG), the largest Colorado-based railroad, had a department of photographers, poets, and promoters who enticed people from all over the globe to head for Colorado. By 1890, the D&RG was spending $60,000 a year for such advertising, complete with poems, booklets, and newspapers stories, accompanied by photographs by the West's premier camera artist, William Henry Jackson. The railroad's *Rhymes of the Rockies*, with fifty pages of verse and photographs, went through seventeen editions and 425,000 copies.

Another favorite from the D&RG's promotional crew was "A Honeymoon Letter from a Bride to Her Chum Discovering the Beauty of Colorado." Blushing newlyweds boarded cliff-crawling trains for spectacular alpine honeymoons. To preserve their and the railroads' reputations, they pinned their marriage licenses outside their berths before retiring.

Other railroads soon emulated the D&RG. The Colorado Central, later bought by the Union Pacific, promoted "Doing the Loop" between Georgetown and Silver Plume. David Moffat's ambitiously named Denver, Northwest & Pacific Railroad soon became known as the Moffat Road, which chugged up snowy and treacherous 12,660-foot Rollins Pass before the Moffat Tunnel was opened in 1928. In 1905, the railroad promised the "greatest one day scenic trip in the world over the Divide," marketed as both "To the Crest of the Continent" and "To the Top o' the World."

Pullman Palace Cars and other amenities of railroad travel converted armchair travelers into actual tourists. A typical railway ad boasted:

The sleeping cars are fitted up with oiled walnut, etched and stained plate glass, silver plated metals, seats cushioned with thick plushes, washstands of marble and walnut, damask curtains and massive mirrors in frames of gilded walnut. The floors are draped with the costliest Brussels carpets, and the roof beautifully frescoed in mosaics of gold, emerald-green, crimson and sky-blue.

Railroads provided Victorian parlor cars on wheels as an inviting transition between comfortable eastern homes and roughing it out west. One early rail rider, the Earl of Dunraven, came to Colorado in 1872 to hunt. The train, he wrote in his autobiographical *Past Times and Pastimes* (London, 1922), was "like a slice out of one of the Eastern cities set down bodily in the midst of a perfect wilderness. When we stepped off the platform, we plunged suddenly into the wild and woolly West."

Railroads would often create their own specially chosen and developed stops at exotically named natural features and vistas offering refreshments, dance pavilions, picnic tables, boating facilities, hiking trails, and scenic overlooks. Anglers on certain "Trout Routes" or "Fish Trains" could be let off along streams that had been stocked with fish by the railroads. At day's end, railroads would pick up fisherpersons for the ride back home. Some lines cooperated with Colorado dude ranch operators to offer "rail to ranch"

The Denver & Rio Grande originally strove to reach mining towns, then shifted to mining tourists as a potentially more lucrative business model. TOM NOEL COLLECTION

"Wish You Were Here."

By 1900, tourist postcards became popular as both souvenirs and to send short messages to family and friends about tourist sites and travels with the common message of "wish you were here." Postcards' 1-cent postage and collectible nature heightened their popularity. If a picture is worth a thousand words, a postcard was even better. Postcards were offered in large display racks at virtually all visitor centers, tourist attractions, curio shops, and resort hotels and motels.

By the 1930s, color photographic postcards were introduced, many with foldouts showing pictures of surrounding sites. Postcards offered better quality, perfect weather, and creative angle photos superior to what most travelers could capture with their own cameras. By the 1950s and 1960s, they also became advertising mediums for even more modest motels and restaurants. Their use and popularity quickly waned with the advent of the digital age with all its photographic possibilities, including stick-held "selfies" with exotic backgrounds.

vacations. This allowed greenhorns to become real westerners, or at least wear boots and a cowboy hat, and to "rough it" by horseback riding, hayrides, calf roping, square dancing, and sampling bunkhouse grub. Especially for ladies, railroads offered summertime wildflower excursions and a chance to pick their favorite blossoms.

After the 1880s, dining cars became common and offered much better meals and service than the depot eateries where guests had to mingle with western ruffians. Before or after feasting in the dining car, gentleman travelers could drink and smoke in the lounge car.

At the urban ends of their excursions, tourists looked for the same sort of elegance and comfort. The Mile High City responded by building luxurious hotels such as the Windsor, the Oxford, and the Brown Palace. Such hotels' concierges would help visitors plan their trips into the mountains. "Seeing Denver" was a highly popular omnibus tour of the Queen City and its surroundings, with ticketing offices in the Brown Palace.

LINCOLN HILLS: A RESORT FOR AFRICAN AMERICANS
During its heyday from 1922 to 1965, Lincoln Hills claimed to be the largest African American resort community west of the Mississippi. Many Black

Coloradans had leisure time and good incomes, especially those working on railroads as Pullman car porters, maids, and waiters. A substantial and thriving African American community developed in Denver's Five Points neighborhood. No matter how financially well off, Black people were not welcome at white resorts, especially during the KKK-infested 1920s.

Vacationing proved difficult for African Americans who were denied access to restaurants, overnight accommodations, gas stations, or even restrooms. Addressing this problem, in 1922, two Denver entrepreneurs from Five Points, E. C. Regnier and Roger Ewalt, purchased about a hundred acres of scenic hills along South Boulder Creek and the Moffat Railroad, in Gilpin County between Pinecliffe and Nederland. They named the park Lincoln Hills, after the great liberator. It offered forested mountain scenery, a stream for swimming and fishing, hiking paths, horseback riding, and most

City girls frolic in South Boulder Creek at Camp Nizhoni, a summer camp at Lincoln Hills, the state's only resort for African Americans. DENVER PUBLIC LIBRARY, WESTERN HISTORY DEPARTMENT

importantly, an oasis of relaxed freedom and congenial company along with meals and lodging.

In 1925, the land was subdivided into long, narrow lots of twenty-five feet by one hundred feet and offered at affordable prices of $50 to $100, with easy financing of $5 down and $5 per month. Promoted across the country, about 600 lots were eventually sold, with about half to families from Denver.

Lincoln Hills was transformed into a full-service resort in 1928 when Oliver Wendell "Winks" Hamlet and his wife Naomi opened Winks Lodge. This three-story hotel offered six rooms in the main building and additional accommodations in nearby cabins, including a honeymoon cabin. Winks Lodge offered Naomi's tasty home-cooked meals. Prominent guests included such musical luminaries as Count Basie, Duke Ellington, Lena Horne, and Billy Eckstine, who relaxed at Winks before or after performing in Denver's Five Points' jazz venues. Readings were also offered akin to those literary salons that were flourishing in New York's Harlem Renaissance.

Denver's YMCA and YWCA, both segregated, likewise offered a Blacks-only retreat at Lincoln Hills. From 1927 to 1945, the all-Black Alice Wheatley Chapter of the segregated YMCA operated Camp Nizhoni as a girl's camp. *Nizhoni* is Navajo for "beautiful," and the camp's mission was to enhance the city girls' self-esteem. A two-story creekside dormitory and dining facility supported fifty girls each summer at the two-week summer camp of outdoor education, skills, and recreation, including horseback riding, swimming, hiking, and classes in biology and astronomy.

With the advent of auto tourism, Winks Lodge was prominently promoted in *The Negro Motorist's Green Book*, the "bible" for Black travelers. Published annually from 1936 to 1964, it provided a city-by-city guide to numerous Black-friendly guest accommodations and services. With Winks's death and the enactment of the Civil Rights Act of 1964, Lincoln Hills declined in both need and popularity. Winks Lodge is now on the National Register of Historic Places, and a nonprofit called Lincoln Hills Cares has resurrected the area for inner-city youths, offering outdoor activities, including the Nizhoni Equestrian Program.

AUTOMOBILE TOURISM

During the early twentieth century, Colorado tourism was drastically changed with the rise of the automobile. Motoring tourists were given the freedom to go anywhere roads could take them, whenever they wanted, and

As tourists increasingly abandoned railroads for automobiles, early customized campers evolved to provide all of the amenities and necessities for those wishing to enjoy the great outdoors and avoid the high prices of resort hotels. DENVER PUBLIC LIBRARY

stop at their favorite vistas and tourist destinations. President Theodore Roosevelt praised Colorado as "the playground of the entire Republic." Promotors soon picked up the phrase and boasted Colorado as "the Playground of America," again comparing it to Switzerland, which had long been "the Playground of Europe." Soon, out-of-state license plates began overtaking Colorado plates at many of the prime tourist resorts and destinations.

Auto tourism found its strongest booster in Freelan Oscar Stanley, manufacturer of the Stanley Steamer. Like many before him, Stanley came to Colorado to recover from tuberculosis. His Stanley Steamer soon followed by rail. The roads to Estes Park were barely passable to his hardy steamer, so he put up $5,000 to build a road from the railhead at Lyons to Estes Park, where he invested another fortune in constructing the Stanley Hotel at the gateway to what would soon become Rocky Mountain National Park. The Georgian-style Stanley opened on July 4, 1909, and boasted old-world charm

Mesa Verde, Colorado's first national park, was the first in the nation to primarily celebrate the accomplishments of prehistoric Native Americans. Scenery was second to the amazing cliff dwellings. MESA VERDE NATIONAL PARK

with all of the modern amenities—except steam heat, which the developer of the Stanley Steamer ignored, as the resort was only to be open in the summer.

Most early resort hotels catered primarily to railroad tourists, as did Denver's elegant grand hotels. Hotels were expensive and offered no parking. Denver had to open a number of city parks to accommodate the booming out-of-state automobile tourists. Camping in tents was allowed, as was fishing in the rivers or lakes. Eventually, motor hotels, or motels, began to sprout up at tourist destinations all over Colorado. Kitschy "tourist traps" abounded. Highway 40 (Colfax Avenue) and Highway 85 (Santa Fe Drive) through Denver became long stretches of gaudy motels, restaurants, bars, curio shops, trading posts, and gas stations catering to the overwhelming cross-country tourist traffic. The introduction of the interstate highway system doomed these previously booming lengthy urban corridors to busted, decaying, and seedy sections of the city that are still being revitalized to this day.

NATIONAL PARKS

National parks draw the greatest number of tourists to Colorado. Colorado's popular national parks continue to grow. In the last few decades, two national monuments, Great Sand Dunes and the Black Canyon of the Gunnison, were promoted to national parks. The state's first, Mesa Verde, in the southwest corner of Colorado, was created in 1906. As the first national park to celebrate primarily prehistoric peoples and their architectural achievements, it would later be designated the first World Heritage Site in the United States by the United Nation's Educational, Scientific, and Cultural Organization (UNESCO).

Mesa Verde is also unusual in that it resulted from the work of Colorado's newly empowered women who had been voting since 1893. Lucy Peabody, a Cincinnati native and trained archaeologist, came west with her husband, the brother of Colorado governor James H. Peabody. In Colorado, she became fascinated with Mesa Verde and soon became an expert on it.

Peabody befriended Virginia McClurg, who traveled all over the country with her slideshow on Mesa Verde. McClurg also excelled at organizing women's clubs in Colorado and the nation to help with the campaign to designate Mesa Verde a national park. The ladies persuaded Governor John F. Shafroth and President Theodore Roosevelt to support the idea. Yet these two women do not often receive credit for championing Mesa Verde National Park. They also supported in 1906 the Antiquities Act, which outlawed removal of Native

Enos Mills, the Father of Rocky Mountain National Park, urged Americans in many publications and his popular talks across the country to support the park. As Colorado's foremost tree hugger, he preached against demolishing forests. One of his favorite stunts was climbing high up a tree to "dance with it in the wind." DENVER PUBLIC LIBRARY, WESTERN HISTORY DEPARTMENT

American artifacts from federal lands. This was an early effort to stop pot hunting and other theft and vandalism. Ironically, McClurg nonetheless relocated a cliff dwelling tourist attraction to Manitou Springs, which opened in 1907, largely made up of looted Mesa Verde–area artifacts.

Rocky Mountain National Park, the largest and most popular tourist target in Colorado, was dedicated in 1915. It straddled the Continental Divide with year-round snow that let tourists cool off with snowball fights even in summer. Rocky's greatest champion, Enos Mills, operated the Long's Peak Inn and had long served as nature guide and ardent conservationist. In his many books, articles, and talks, Mills did more than anyone to attract visitors to the Colorado mountains. For years, he crusaded tirelessly for the creation of Rocky Mountain National Park. Mills was duly honored as "The Father of Rocky Mountain National Park" when President Woodrow Wilson designated the park in 1915.

By 2019, Rocky Mountain National Park was drawing over 4.5 million visitors each year as the nation's third-busiest park. It has become so busy that some popular areas now have restricted access due to congested traffic and overflowing parking lots.

OTHER MOUNTAIN PARKS

Federal government park building helped inspire some Colorado cities and counties to do likewise. Trinidad, Pueblo, Denver, Colorado Springs, Boulder, and other tourist-courting communities established mountain parks. Denver led the way by designating some 14,000 acres, included sites in Jefferson, Douglas, and Grand Counties. Attractions included a ski area in Winter Park, Red Rocks Outdoor Amphitheater near Morrison, and buffalo herds in Genesee and Daniels Parks. The Genesee herd was pastured along I-70 near the Lookout Mountain Park grave of the man who gained fame for killing bison. He lies dead in a shrine-like grave, but the buffalo herd thrives.

After William F. "Buffalo Bill" Cody's death in Denver in 1917, the city created a major tourist mecca by burying him atop Lookout Mountain. Army scout, Indian War Congressional Medal of Honor winner, showman, and hunter—he claimed to have killed 4,280 buffalo—Cody was celebrated as the best-known American of his era.

To reach this shrine, Denver boosters promoted construction of the switchback-packed motor road to the top of Lookout Mountain in 1913. Denver then built a much longer and higher road to the top of Mount Evans, the most prominent peak due west of the city. Completion of the highway to the summit of 14,258-foot Mount Evans in 1927 gave Colorado bragging rights to the world's highest paved highway. At its crest, oxygen supplies were available for those overcome by the literally breathtaking views.

THE NATION'S TOP WINTER SPORTS DESTINATION

Until the mid-twentieth century, Colorado tourism flourished only in the summer and ended with the changing of the aspen leaves to gold and the first snow blanketing the mountains. Tourism hibernated until the following spring, which in the high country did not arrive until June.

By the 1950s, Colorado had become a four-season resort destination, with winter sports venues opening in late October and some staying open until July. The state contains twenty-five ski and snowboard resorts, as well as winter carnivals and festivals and backcountry skiing and snowshoeing. *Ski Magazine* reports Colorado having twelve of the country's top thirty ski resorts as the most popular ski destination in North America. Skiing now anchors Colorado tourism and draws over twelve million visitors to winter resorts each year.

Colorado skiing began in the nineteenth century when Scandinavian immigrant miners and loggers introduced eleven-foot-long heavy, clumsy "snow shoes" to their comrades as a way to travel on snow. The Methodist Reverend John L. Dyer carried mail and a Bible over mountain passes to deliver news and the word of God to distant mining communities such as Breckenridge in the 1860s. Over time, skiing also became sport for recreationists. Early ski racing in 1883 at Irwin awarded prizes to those who fell down the fewest times. Carl "The Flying Norwegian" Howelson's daring ski jumping at the Winter Carnival in the ranching and mining community of Steamboat Springs in 1914 began with parades of horse-pulled men and women skiers. Howelson Hill claims to be the oldest still-operating ski hill in North America, with the motto "If at first you don't succeed, then ski jumping is probably not for you."

George Ernest Cranmer, Denver's Manager of Parks and Improvements, began envisioning Denver's mountain parks as winter sports playgrounds in the mid-1930s. With access provided via Berthoud Pass on Highway 40 plowed for motorists, as well as the Denver & Rio Grande's ski train from Denver, Winter Park Ski Area opened in 1940 at the western rail portal of the Moffat Tunnel. A $1 admission gave skiers ascents on a 2,300-foot-long T-bar and a 2,700-foot-long tow rope. Accommodations consisted of only warming sheds and toilets. These primitive facilities have since been replaced by a large village of luxury hotels, fancy restaurants, and tourist boutiques. The

Aspen Mountain was opened in 1946 by several veterans of the Tenth Mountain Division who transformed the busted silver boomtown into Colorado's glitziest ski resort area, with all of the vacant land and crumbling miners' residences shown here being swept up for millions by the wealthy and famous. TOM NOEL COLLECTION

"Mary Jane" ski area was added to Winter Park in 1975 and, contrary to the belief of some, was not named after the notorious weed but for a notorious early twentieth-century madam who entertained railroad workers in the area.

The US Army gave Colorado skiing its greatest push. During World War II, the Tenth Mountain Division was formed as a specialized infantry unit for mountain warfare. To train the division for winter and alpine warfare, Camp Hale opened in January 1943 between Leadville and Red Cliff, on the west side of Tennessee Pass. At its peak, the site included 800 buildings as well as ski runs and a ski lift. Intense training for the 16,000 recruits prepared them to be shipped overseas for service in the Alps and Scandinavia. Following the war, many returned and transformed Colorado's ski industry by founding and staffing Arapahoe Basin, Aspen, Vail, and other ski areas.

Aspen was a sleepy hamlet of 777 residents in 1940, a far cry from its silver-mining boom times of more than 5,000 souls. In 1946, Aspen Mountain was opened by veterans of the Tenth Mountain Division, with the first chairlift in the country. In 1950, it hosted one of the world's first skiing competitions. As Aspen became trendy, old mining cottages were snapped up as second homes. It became one of the nation's favorite playgrounds for the rich and famous, flying in on their private jets, paying millions for anything with four walls and a roof, and resurrecting the downtown area as an upscale shopping district.

Vail opened in a remote mountain valley with a sheep ranch and potato patch after state highway engineer Charles Davis Vail helped create Vail Pass, which became the route for I-70. At the bottom of Vail Pass, Peter Seibert and other Tenth Mountain veterans leased large mountain tracts from the US Forest Service to open Vail Ski Area in 1962. With the completion of I-70 through Eisenhower Tower in 1973, ski area proliferation joined massive real estate development along the interstate corridor to create a boom that outdid the mineral rush a century earlier. European-style Vail Village became car-free and boasted the largest free shuttle system in the country. As Vail became the nation's largest snow resort, further expansion and public land development led to clashes with environmentalists. Eco-radicals torched Two Elks Lodge to protest Vail's expansion into the habitat of the threatened lynx, a rare, cute wildcat with huge feet and tufted ears.

Coloradans eventually determined that they had perhaps enough winter tourists, and protecting the environment became a growing concern. Denver was in the running for the 1976 Winter Olympics but voters, protesting the expense and environmentally damaging development, shot the idea down in 1972. Over a hundred ski areas and resorts had opened in Colorado but fewer than thirty survive, most having succumbed to busted ghost slopes down to vacant, long-overgrown parking areas. Shortage of snow can be a problem, although Utes are brought back to land once theirs to do rain/snow dances.

HERITAGE TOURISM

As populations age with more leisure time and more disposable income, heritage tourism has become especially important in Colorado with its many historic attractions, various heritage railroads, numerous ghost towns, "rails-to-trails" recreation along abandoned railroad lines, and over a hundred house museums. With their educational focus, guided tours and museums are frequent heritage tourism targets. Some 600 Colorado heritage sites are listed in Victor Danilov's book, *Colorado Museums and Historic Sites* (Boulder: University Press of Colorado, 2000).

CHAPTER TEN

The Beeriest State

COLORADO IS THE BEERIEST STATE IN MANY PER CAPITA MEASUREMENTS and in the top five in consumption and production. In 2018, the Brewers Association ranked Chicago first and Denver second in number of breweries: 167 to 158. Besides some 444 craft breweries and brewpubs, Colorado has heavy hitters in the giant plants for Budweiser in Fort Collins and Coors in Golden. Coors claims to be the world's largest brewery under one roof. Even those two giants have not matched the boom in smaller beer makers.

The state's hoppy history goes back over 800 years ago. Long before Europeans landed in the New World, indigenous Pueblo-dwelling Indians of the American Southwest brewed their own style of beer from corn maize.

Denver's Rocky Mountain Brewery started serving suds in 1859. Colorado's "John Barleycorn," John Good, brought the first wagonload of hops across the plains that year to begin brewing after becoming a partner in Rocky Mountain Brewery. To supply the brewery and his general merchandise store, Good made sixteen trips over the prairie freighting with ox teams. Jars of fine white powdered yeast were easily transported with the hops, and by 1863, crops of high-country barley were being grown along the Front Range as well as the San Luis Valley to support the growing beer industry. Good would later put together the Tivoli-Union Brewing Company and, in 1880, sold the Rocky Mountain Brewery to his manager there, Philip Zang, who changed the name to Philip Zang & Company.

Zang, a native of Bavaria, had apprenticed to a brewer in the old country. He came to America in 1853 and, after starting a brewery in Louisville, Kentucky, moved to Colorado in 1869. He found work managing the Rocky Mountain Brewery, which he soon owned. Zang expanded on the old Rocky Mountain Brewery site at Seventh Street and the South Platte River. Production soared to 10,000 barrels per year, helping that brewery grow into one

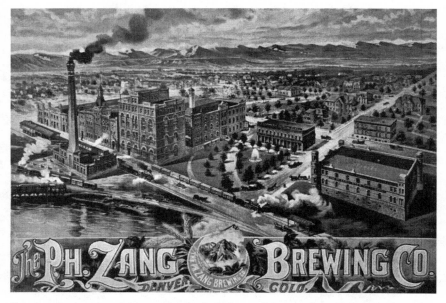

Zang's massive riverside complex included a malt house, ice plant, lager beer vault, a smoke-belching boiler house, large turreted horse stables, and a railroad spur line. Today, only the hillside brewmaster's house and an employees' hotel, both at the upper right, survive. TOM NOEL COLLECTION

of the largest beer producers west of the Missouri River. As his wealth grew, Zang's philanthropy included a bit of promotion as well. When he funded the bells at St. Elizabeth of Hungary Church, he made sure that they were a bit out of tune so as to ring "Zang Zang" instead of "clang clang."

In 1889, Zang sold to an English syndicate, retiring as one of Denver's early millionaires. At the time, there was already fierce competition between German lagers and pilsners and British porters, ales, and stouts. When asked whether the new company would be "English," Zang replied, "While there is considerable English capital in the concern, there is not an Englishman on the premises, but practically the same old force is running it." To allay such concerns, the British firm kept the Zang name, continued brewing lager beer, and had Philip's only son manage the plant.

The Zangs diversified by investing in many fields. They bought 3,600 acres north of Denver, where they established the Elmwood Stock Farm to raise the Percheron draft horses that lugged their beer wagons to customers. The farm and railroad stop there, Zang's Spur, has evolved into the City and County of Broomfield, a mushrooming Front Range community. Ultimately, Zang and every other beer maker in Colorado was overshadowed by a Golden brewery founded by a man named Coors who would create the state's best-known brand.

ADOLPH COORS AND HIS BREWERY

Adolph Coors, an orphan and undocumented stowaway, reached America in 1868. Three years later, the twenty-four-year-old German landed in Colorado. There, he came to appreciate the frontier practice of not questioning a man's past. For a runaway eluding the Prussian army, America provided a chance to start anew. Changing his name from "Kohrs" to a more Americanized "Coors," he joined 55,000 other Germans who immigrated to the United States in 1868.

Swept west by the huge tide of immigration that followed the Civil War, Coors found 1872 Denver to be booming. The poor but hardworking and ambitious young German brewing apprentice found a wealthy partner, confectioner and bottler Jacob Schueler. Along Clear Creek, where others had searched for gold, Coors found the clear, pure waters an ideal source for brewing liquid gold.

In 1873, Coors and Schueler bought the abandoned Golden City Tannery and converted it to a brewery. "A brick brewery of the most modern plan," noted the R. G. Dun credit agent in his May 2, 1874, report. Coors, he added, "is a young man of good character & habits . . . a practical brewer [with] but little means and gets an interest in the business for his services." Coors oversaw the brewery operations and, borrowing from his old-world experience, introduced the latest steam technology.

By 1878, Coors was also using the brewery ponds to produce ice, which he sold out of ice wagons that delivered to customers' doors at five pounds for $2 a month or ten pounds for $3. With both beer and ice selling well, Adolph Coors came up with $90,000 to buy Schueler out in 1878.

By 1880, Denver had sixteen breweries and Coors faced stiff competition, including Joseph E. Bates. In 1869, Bates joined the beer battle by opening the Denver Ale Brewing Company. Bates as well as his English-style ale proved popular; he was elected mayor of Denver in 1872 and again in 1885. He rewarded his supporters with free beer. Bates's brewery was Colorado's second largest behind Zang's until it closed in 1895. Second place then went to John Good's Tivoli Brewery, which in 1901

Central City Breweries, Past and Present

Capitalizing on the swarm of miners, Denver's Rocky Mountain Brewery helped the Mack brothers join up with Denver's John Good to create a Central City brewery in 1862. It came replete with a legendary beer garden that featured a large mural of King Gambrinus, the beer-bellied legendary patron of brewing. The king ruled on the stone walls of the old Mack Brewery on Eureka Gulch midway between the town and its hilltop cemeteries, and mourners would often stop on the way back to town to toast the deceased. The beer garden mural had the king raising a toast to the men and ladies meeting at Mack's while their children swam in the brewery's ponds or, in winter, skated there. Mack's survived until 1898, when it dried up due to competition from the big breweries downstream.

While Mack's is long gone, another sanctuary survives. The Gold Coin Saloon is one of Colorado's least-altered antique saloons. Opened

Central City's now-gone Mack Beer Garden showcased a mural of King Gambrinus, the unofficial patron saint of brewing. BILL HANSEN COLLECTION

Gold Coin Saloon interior circa 1915. The saloon has been diligently preserved to look now as then, except for the addition of bar stools and the removal of the spittoons. DENVER PUBLIC LIBRARY, WESTERN HISTORY DEPARTMENT

in 1897, its interior has been designated as a landmark by the Central City Historic Preservation Commission. An original "Alcohol Futures Board" hangs on the wall where patrons can prepay their friends' drinks, which are then chalked up until redeemed. This saloon remains undefiled by slot machines and other gaming devices. While many buildings have ordinances preserving their exterior, the Gold Coin boasts one of the few designated interiors.

A few doors down from the Coin is the Dostal Alley Brew Pub & Casino, the only brewery now serving Gilpin County. The allegedly haunted former brothel was opened as one of Central City's first casinos in 1991 and began brewing in 1993. Buddy Schmaltz, a third-generation Central City resident, is as popular as his brewpub. He has been elected mayor and then county commissioner. One of his brews is Jacob Mack Mild Ale, named for the former Mack Brewery owner. Schmaltz feeds his tiny, two-barrel pub with the wild hops that grow around this mountain town and are gathered each fall by locals. Buddy boasts that his is the only brewpub in Colorado with slot machines. His slogan: "No crap on tap."

Beer Is Good for You

Tivoli claimed its product improved customers' health. Many other breweries also promoted their products as health aids. Alcohol was a key ingredient in many nineteenth-century patent medicines. Mayor Bates advertised "Invalids seeking health and strength are recommended by all physicians to drink Denver Ale Brewing Co's Ale and Porter." Other medical advice came from Neef Brothers Brewery, which touted their Neef's Red Cross Malt Tonic. The idea of alcohol as medicine had become institutionalized in drugstore liquor licenses sanctioned by Colorado's earliest laws.

Such health drinks were safer than Denver's early drinking water, which came out of the waste-filled South Platte River and Cherry Creek, from wells often adjacent to outhouses, and from irrigation ditches that guttered city streets. Brewing beer often made polluted local stream water safe because it required boiling as part of the brewing process. Beer was also far safer than Colorado's early Taos Lightning and other fiery and often rotgut swills passed off as whiskey. Then as now, beer was the most popular drink in the world after water and tea.

merged with the Union Brewery to become the Tivoli-Union. Good had already acquired Max Melsheimer's Milwaukee Brewery, whose 1880 mansard tower became the dominant landmark of the still-standing Tivoli complex.

To quench the thirst of Coloradans, more than 120 different breweries opened in 44 Colorado towns in pre-Prohibition Colorado. Denver alone had 23. Few survived for more than several years. Many failed to capitalize on inventions that revolutionized the beer business. Pasteurization, replacing corks with gas-tight crown caps, and refrigerated railroad cars made possible long-range shipment in bottles with minimum spoilage. Due to these technological advancements, Colorado breweries began facing growing competition from breweries across the country like Pabst and Schlitz of Milwaukee and Anheuser-Busch of St. Louis. Still, the fiercest competition remained local as Colorado breweries competed mightily. It was often German pilsners versus English pale ales.

In the late 1880s, a British syndicate, the Denver United Breweries, acquired the Zang brewery, followed by Mayor Bates's Denver Ale Brewing

Company. Attempting to monopolize local breweries, beer bottle battles escalated to full keg warfare.

In 1890, the British approached Adolph Coors with an offer. He said no. Subsequently Denver United Breweries, Ltd., put pressure on Coors—and on saloonkeepers who sold Coors—to reconsider. The Golden brewer responded by opening his own saloons around Colorado where only Coors would be served.

Coors not only survived the beer wars but thrived. To market beer beyond the Denver-Golden area, Coors built in 1899 a huge Beer Depot next to Union Station in Denver. He also set up other depots throughout the state. To this day some of those buildings survive with a large porcelain sign over the door: COORS.

These COORS saloons survive from the statewide dry spell that began on New Year's Day 1916, when Coors dumped 561 barrels of Coors Golden

Adolph Coors, in white hat, sitting above his son Grover with son Herman to the right, poses with his dedicated workers in this 1890s image. TOM NOEL COLLECTION

Lager into Clear Creek, turning the waters amber. During Prohibition, Coors hoped the "national madness" would end in but a few short years. He retained his employees and switched to near beer and malted milk, which he sold to Mars Candy for production of sweets. He then mined Golden's clay to produce porcelain and ceramics such as teacups, creamers, and sugar bowls. The company and family name survived Prohibition, but Adolph Coors did not. Having exhausted much of his personal wealth trying to save his company during the dry times, he died by suicide in 1929.

After Prohibition, the company adopted the phrase "Brewed with Rocky Mountain Spring Water" and a waterfall logo. Coors expanded to selling in thirteen western states and developed a mystique and almost cultlike following, as glorified by the 1977 cross-country bootlegging movie *Smokey and the Bandit*. In the 1980 film *Any Which Way You Can*, Clint Eastwood and Ray Charles sang a duet praising Coors called "Beers to You." Even presidents Dwight Eisenhower and Gerald Ford were said to have smuggled Coors beer back east aboard Air Force One.

Ahead of all competitors, Coors introduced beer in an aluminum can in 1957 and introduced the press-top tab in 1970. To finance such expansion, the company went public in 1975 after three generations of family ownership. In 1976, Coors was the second-largest private employer in the state with 8,000 in Golden and an annual revenue of $550 million. In 1978, to appeal to a burgeoning market of women drinkers with less calories and lower alcohol content, the brewery introduced Coors Light, which became a top seller among the lights.

In 1985, Coors formed a partnership with Canada's Molson, enabling it to market Coors throughout the United States and Canada. By 1990, Coors had become the third-best-selling US beer behind Budweiser and Miller's. That changed in a complicated series of regulatory-supervised acquisitions, mergers, and restructuring. Molson Coors emerged as one of the largest brewers in the world.

Throughout all these changes Coors kept its own name, brand, and Golden plant, and Coors family members remained involved. In 1995, Coloradans cheered the coming of big-league baseball at Coors Field with the Colorado Rockies. The Rockies compete in other beery National League venues such as Miller Field, home of the Milwaukee Brewers, and Busch Stadium, home of the St. Louis Cardinals. By adding its own Blue Moon label to its Sandlot Brewery, Coors Field outpours its competitors as one of the nation's top baseball parks for craft beer. Much to the chagrin of Coors's many followers as Colorado's iconic historic brewery, the company moved its headquarters to Chicago in 2019.

THE TIVOLI BREWERY

Coors was not the only survivor of the Prohibition dry spell that ended in 1933. The Tivoli Brewing Company squeezed through the drought on a diet of near beer. Despite fifteen different beers, Tivoli neared the bottom of its last barrel during the 1960s. The South Platte River Flood of 1965 swept nine feet of water into the brewery, and its beer never tasted the same again. The brewery closed four years after the flood, with a strike adding to its problems.

A Denver Landmark designation saved Tivoli's castle-like building from being urban renewed with the rest of the old Auraria neighborhood. A 169-acre site was cleared for the Auraria Higher Education Center, a partnership

The Tivoli Brewery survived Prohibition but finally shut its doors on April 25, 1969, only to be reincarnated in 2015 using the original building, some of the brewery apparatus, logo, and even old-time Tivoli beer recipes. TOM NOEL COLLECTION

Pueblo Brews

Pueblo, Colorado's second-largest city from 1890 to the 1950s, harbored one of the state's largest breweries, Walter's. Martin Walter came to Pueblo by way of Wisconsin, where he was the youngest son of a large brewery-owning German clan. With family capital he bought a failing Pueblo brewery and opened Walter's Brewing Company in 1889. By 1902, it was turning out 170 barrels daily. Walter, a staunch union brewer, promoted his product as union made and often led Pueblo's Labor Day parade.

After Prohibition, one of the brewery's prized customers, Gus Masciotra, opened a saloon in his small cottage across the street from his former employer, the CF&I steel plant. Gus's eighteen-ounce schooners and Dutch lunches are a Colorado legend to this day. Buckets of beer to go used to be available through a special window. Beer rushed to the nearby steelworkers helped earn Gus's the 1937, 1939,

To demonstrate its wartime loyalty, Walter's Brewing Company in Pueblo featured bathing beauties atop floats touting that it was "100% Union" and "100% American." TOM NOEL COLLECTION

and 1941 honors as national champion for beer sales per square foot according to *Ripley's Believe It or Not.*

Gus's survives but Walter's waded through Prohibition only to sink in 1975. In 2014, a group of Puebloans reached out to the Walter descendants in Eau Claire, Wisconsin, to acquire the logo, name, and the pre-Prohibition recipe to refloat Walter's Original Pilsner at their new establishment, Walter's Brewery and Taproom.

of the Community College of Denver, Metropolitan State University of Denver, and the University of Colorado Denver. More than 43,000 students on what has become the most popular campus in the state voted to use the old brewery as a student union. Fulfilling a longtime dream, students can now major in beer.

The Tivoli Brewery eventually sprang back to life with the same name. The man behind the resurrected Tivoli is Corey Marshall. A fifth-generation German American, he remembers his grandfather as a devout Tivoli beer drinker. Corey himself is a beefy, beer-drinking, former rugby player for Metro State. After working as a bouncer at the old Tijuana Yacht Club in the Tivoli complex, he joined Coors for seventeen years. Corey reports: "After I graduated to the downtown corporate Molson Coors office on 17th Street, I looked out every day on the old Tivoli building. Light bulbs kept going on in my head. Why not bring back the Tivoli?"

Marshall spent ten years tracking down the trademarks, procuring the original Tivoli recipes, and solving construction puzzles before a grand opening on August 22, 2015. Among its more than fifty brews are some replicas using antique Tivoli formulas. Marshall, his wife, and investors spent more than $8 million to revive and modernize the massive old brewery and then earned a branch at Denver International Airport.

PROHIBITION: THE GREAT BOOZE BUST

After early boom times, beer, liquor, and saloons went bust in the early twentieth century. The dry spell did not affect some Colorado communities born dry. One of the most notable, Greeley, was founded in 1869 as the Union Colony, an experimental Utopian society founded on the principles of "temperance, religion, agriculture, education and family values." Greeley retained Prohibition for a century. Quaker General William Jackson Palmer and his English colleagues established Colorado Springs in 1871 banning alcohol from the outset. It became so Anglophilic that it was soon known as "Little London," where the high-toned teetotalers celebrated not a cocktail hour but high tea.

The mountain mining towns largely retained their hard-drinking Wild West ways. Leadville, the wildest of all, attracted the Irish poet and aesthete Oscar Wilde, who toured Colorado in 1882 lecturing on art. He received rousing applause from an enthusiastic audience in rowdy Leadville, where he

"Hatchetarian" Carrie Nation, lower left, and her stern sisters of sobriety used this anti-liquor propaganda around 1900. The scowling Nation was notorious for smashing up saloons and their barrels of whiskey and beer with her hatchet. BILL HANSEN COLLECTION

shared whiskey with the miners. They fancied Wilde for such quips as "Work is the curse of the drinking classes."

In 1916, Colorado saloonkeepers, brewers, and their patrons were stunned. As of January 1 that year, Colorado went dry four years ahead of national Prohibition. Wets could not comprehend the puzzling change in public attitudes that brought forth the "noble experiment." In retrospect, scholars suspect Prohibition was rooted in ethnic prejudices. White Protestants voted for Prohibition as a way to control Germans with their beer, the Irish with their whiskey, and Italians with their wine.

Brewers, saloonkeepers, and red-nosed tipplers weakened their cause by not taking their blue-nosed opponents seriously. For years the wets scoffed at the dry coalition of the Templars, the Women's Christian Temperance Union (WCTU), the Prohibition Party, the Anti-Saloon League, and other dry crusaders. Bartenders traded free drinks for temperance pledge cards, which they posted on their back bars as trophies. Drinkers jeered at "hatchetarian" Carrie Nation's propaganda and the hatchet she wielded to smash up saloons, making barrels and bottles of booze her special target. Another of her smashing favorites were nude paintings, no matter how lovely the lady or famous the artist. She made forays into Glenwood Springs and Cripple Creek and was jailed in Denver for disturbing the peace. Saloonkeepers mocked her by concocting Carrie Nation cocktails.

Belatedly, drinking men realized their error in not organizing more effectively against women's suffrage, for it was the female vote, many thought, that led to Prohibition. The liquor industry was the only business to campaign against women's suffrage, handing out fliers warning "Women's suffrage is a dangerous experiment." In 1893, Colorado became the second state to give women the vote. "It was a great mistake to give women the ballot," a spokesman for Colorado saloonkeepers told the *Rocky Mountain News* on August 3, 1896, "and now that it has been granted saloon men had better look out or Colorado will be a prohibition state."

Ladies of the WCTU worked night and day to that end. They stationed themselves at saloon doors to record who entered, how long they stayed, and their condition when they left. Some bars retaliated by posting their own guards at the windows to watch the saloon watchers. If one of the ladies tried to enter, customers chanted in union, "WHORE!" One saloonkeeper, finding a horse-drawn gospel wagon full of repentant sinners singing praises to the Lord in front of his beer parlor, turned a hose on the wagon to drown out the evangelists. Gospel wagon worker Rachel Wild Peterson proudly reported after the soaking that "the Christian people of our country are used to water."

Colorado prohibitionists brought in national speakers such as the evangelist Billy Sunday, who taught locals to sing "The Brewers' Big White Horses Can't Run Over Me." Churchgoers worked harder knowing that the houses of alcohol outnumbered the houses of God. In 1890, Denver had 81 churches and 319 saloons but, by 1910, the number of saloons had proliferated to 410. Colorado journalist Ellis Meredith calculated in the WCTU's *Union Signal* publication that Denver's saloons were open 3,540,000 hours a year while the city's 100 churches were only open a total of 26,000 hours a year. The *Union Signal's* message was clear: the godly had to work harder. The WCTU came up with a Little Christian Temperance League, which taught children to sing:

C-O-L-O-R-A-D-O
Who are we? The L.C.T.U.
HO! HO! HO! Watch us grow.
When we vote, saloons will go!

Coloradans grew weary of Prohibition and eagerly rejected it in 1932 by a two-thirds majority vote for repealing national Prohibition. After enough states approved repeal, it became law with the ratification of the 21st Amendment on December 5, 1933. The crowds sang "Happy Days Are Here Again" as John Barleycorn was resurrected from the dead. A half century later, beer would make another huge comeback with the emergence of brewpubs and craft breweries. That comeback began with two astrophysicists, a goat shed, and the national birth of craft beer.

CRAFT BEER

In 1979, Coors was the only brewery left in Colorado and one of only forty-two breweries nationwide. It took two astrophysicists from the University of Colorado in Boulder to figure out how to make craft beer in a microbrewery. Randolph "Stick" Ware and Dave Hummer began messing around with beer ingredients in their basements. Their wives nixed the amateurs' further home-brew efforts due to the strong smell of fermenting hops. Both were banished to a 1,000-square-foot goat shed in nearby Hygiene. With stainless-steel food-processing kettles, they eventually came up with very drinkable, and later award-winning, English-style porters, stouts, and pale ales.

The drinking duo went on to establish the first craft beer microbrewery in Colorado and arguably the first in the nation on September 25, 1979. Once licensed, their Boulder plant became the forty-third brewery in the country and began selling on July 4, 1980. Ware and Hummer hired a professional brewmaster and a staff and in 1984 built a bigger and better brewery in Boulder. They were soon selling 8,000 barrels of beer in twenty-six states and eventually went public as the Boulder Brewing Company.

Successful restaurateur Frank Day purchased the Boulder Brewing Company in 1990, cleaned house, and turned it back into a private enterprise. Production increased dramatically to 20,000 barrels annually in the 1990s. In 2005, it was rechristened as Boulder Beer, Colorado's first craft beer brewery. Unfortunately, with the beer boom going flat by 2019, Boulder Beer cut back on production and did not survive the 2020 pandemic.

In 1990, Frank Day joined the brewpub craze by opening Walnut Brewery, Boulder's first brewpub. That success led to his opening of many Rock Bottom Restaurant & Brewery locations.

Day's success can be credited in part to Colorado's first brewpub creator, John Wright Hickenlooper Jr. Hickenlooper joined forces with a recently unemployed cook, Mark Schiffler, and home brewers Jerry Williams and Russell Scherer, to start Colorado's first brewpub, the Wynkoop Brewing Company on Wynkoop Street across from Denver's Union Station. Mayor Federico Peña cut the ribbon for the grand opening on October 18, 1988. Crowds mobbed the place, standing four-deep at the bar. Over 6,000 plastic cups of 25-cent craft beer were sold—so many that employees had to rummage through the trash cans and recycle the cups after washing them.

After the 1988 grand opening, the Wynkoop Brewing Company became the hottest spot in town. As many as 1,000 people a day flowed through the funky, hardwood-floored, reborn warehouse with its shiny stainless-steel beer-making apparatus. Customers washed down tasty, moderately priced pub food with a full spectrum of brews. Until his death in 1996, Scherer served Wynkoop brews British style, declaring that "warm and flat is where it's at." By 1997, Wynkoop boasted of being the nation's largest brewpub, having served 5,008 barrels over the counter that year.

Hickenlooper started a foamy revolution. At its pre-pandemic 2019 peak, Colorado boasted some 444 craft breweries and brewpubs that produced oceans of beer. New craft beer makers and brewpubs seemed to pop up every week all around the state, even though some fizzled.

John Wright Hickenlooper Jr. introduced Coloradans to brewpubs in 1988. Appreciative admirers helped to subsequently launch his winning political career as mayor of Denver, then governor of Colorado, then a US senator. Here, Hickenlooper is seen around 1990 at the beginning of his Wynkoop Brewing Company career. TOM NOEL COLLECTION

After his spectacular success in the beer business, Hickenlooper began an underdog campaign to become mayor of Denver. In an upset, he won that office in 2002 and again in 2006, becoming the first brewery-owning mayor since Mayor Bates in the 1870s and 1880s. From 2011 to 2019 he served as a popular governor of Colorado. Beer lovers cheered as he rode to his first inauguration in a horse-drawn Wynkoop Brewery beer wagon and then installed a beer tap in the governor's mansion. After term limits took him out of the governor's chair in 2019, Hickenlooper continued to pursue politics on a grander scale and announced a long-shot run for the Democratic nomination for president of the United States. He ran unsuccessfully for president, but was elected to the US Senate in 2020.

In 1988, Fort Collins showed up on the beer map when Anheuser-Busch opened a regional brewery to compete on Coors's home turf. After several expansions on its 130-acre site, the one-million-square-foot facility, working around the clock, turns out rivers of beer in numbers that would make even the sober stagger. Located next to I-25 and a railroad spur, the St. Louis–based brewery ships 225 trucks per day and 30 railcars each week. Thankfully, the famed Budweiser Clydesdales, which make occasional appearances, are no longer burdened with such distribution.

Like Denver's Lower Downtown, Fort Collins's historic downtown center had declined over the years into a shabby vestige of itself. That all changed in May 1989, when brewpub pioneer Hickenlooper and colleagues bought an old grocery store and opened CooperSmith's Pub and Brewery as the anchor of the Old Town Fort Collins Historic District, now rejuvenated and the hottest spot in town.

In 1990, CooperSmith's and the Odell Brewing Company of Fort Collins partnered in starting the Colorado Brewers' Festival in Old Town. Eleven Colorado brewers participated in the inaugural event, which grew by 2019 to forty Colorado brewers offering 150 beers with art and live music. The now fourth-longest-running beer festival in the nation required a larger venue and was moved into the football stadium at Colorado State University (CSU).

Besides hosting a beer festival, CSU also offers a degree in "Fermentation Science and Technology." Two campus brewing labs provide training that can be applied by selling craft beer at the Ramskeller Pub and Grub in

New Belgium Brewing Company emphasizes sustainability and a bicycle culture by each year presenting new employees with limited edition "New Belgium Cruisers" which are proudly parked outside, minimizing employee driving and the company's parking needs. BILL HANSEN COLLECTION

the Lory Student Center. CSU's program is heavily supported by Colorado's largest and best-known craft brewery, New Belgium Brewing Company.

Colorado's most nationally recognized craft brewer, New Belgium Brewing, is marketed in all fifty states and internationally. It had regularly ranked as the fourth-largest craft brewery and is the eighth-largest overall brewery in the nation. It introduced Belgian-style beer in a market long dominated by the German- and English-style brews. Brewing close to one million barrels per year, New Belgium outproduced the rest of the top ten craft breweries in Colorado combined.

Incredibly, New Belgium began and flourished by being 100 percent employee-owned until recently going public. Its cofounder, long-term CEO, and now chairperson of the board, Kim Jordan, has become a virtual legend in trailblazing women's roles in a male-dominated business. Women are now actively involved in ownership, management, and as brewmasters and line workers in many breweries, large and small.

As with most startup craft brewers, New Belgium had humble origins. Jordan was a mother and social worker when her partner, Jeff Lebesch, an electrical engineer and amateur brewer, left home on a business trip to Belgium in 1988. Lebesch began biking the countryside from brewery to brewery, making extensive notes of everything he learned. He also could not help but observe that many breweries had racks of colorful vintage bicycles outside for the thrifty workers. He even worked at a beer café in Bruges in exchange for free beer.

Returning home, Lebesch persuaded Jordan to partner in brewing batches of Belgian-style ale in their basement. They used repurposed dairy equipment, which Jordan bottled with labels printed at Kinkos. She pedaled the suds from door to door and to every liquor store in town. One of her first customers was a watercolorist, Ann Fitch, who designed a colorful label for the bicycle-themed flagship beer Fat Tire Amber Ale. By 1991, New Belgium put out 8.5 barrels per week. Jordan recalled, "Our beers were good, our labels were interesting, and we very quickly had a robust following."

Within a short time, New Belgium graduated to an old train depot before purchasing in 1995 fifty acres of what was once a Great Western Sugar plant. Lebesch left the company in 2008 for other pursuits, but with a severance package that included free beer for life. With Jordan in charge, a variety of new craft labels have been added, including the introduction of Belgian sour beer and the new Voodoo Ranger family of smiling, scary, skull-labeled suds.

New Belgium's accomplishments were all the more startling given its unique business plan that did not prioritize profits. Its mission statement emphasized environmental sustainability and being a pioneer in the greening of the beer industry. It minimizes water use and waste and initially relied on 100 percent wind power before switching to solar energy. It donated millions to charity each year, and one of the company's quirky core values was "having fun."

New Belgium boasted less than a 3 percent annual employee turnover rate. After one year of employment, each new employee was given stock in the company as well as a limited edition "New Belgium Cruiser" bicycle. After five years, employees were further rewarded with a free trip to Belgium. In 2008, *Outdoor Magazine* dubbed it "the best place to work in America." In 2018, it was ranked as one of the fifty most sustainable companies in the world.

New Belgium's bicycle culture led it to help fund Fort Collins's bike paths to lessen the carbon imprint, and each year it sponsors a brightly costumed "Tour de Fat" charity event of bicycles, beer drinking, and music in downtown Fort Collins. Given its national presence, to further lower the energy of a vast transportation network, New Belgium opened a second plant in Asheville, North Carolina, in 2016. Even more dramatic change came three years later.

In November 2019, New Belgium announced its sale to Australian-based Lion Little World Beverages, a subsidiary of the Japanese firm Kirin Holdings Company Limited. New Belgium is Kirin's first full brewery acquisition in the United States. Cofounder and CEO Kim Jordan announced that she and the leadership team will stay.

Mark Tapper, managing director of Lion Little World Beverages, the largest brewery in Australia, claims they will maintain New Belgium's "ethos to be a force for good." New Belgium will lose its craft beer status and no longer be 100 percent employee-owned. Jordan claimed the sale was the best way for the company to raise capital for continued expansion. New Belgium will continue to sponsor the nation's largest brew-ha-ha.

Beer and Now

For decades, post-Prohibition "Beer Wars" had raged with liquor stores attempting to fend off chains of grocery and convenience stores eager to sell full-strength beer. Colorado law relegated chains to selling watered-down

Great American Beer Festival

Charlie Papazian was another Boulderite and former schoolteacher who dabbled early in home brewing as a hoppy hobby. In 1976, he published his first of many editions of *The Joy of Homebrewing* before founding the American Homebrewers Association in 1982. Papazian's pioneering work kick-started the craft beer revolution. He also fostered Denver's Great American Beer Festival (GABF), the nation's largest and oldest craft brew-ha-ha. From modest 1981 origins in Boulder organized by Papazian, the GABF moved to Denver's convention center in 1984. With breweries from both coasts and everywhere in between, beer lovers can gulp their way from sea to foaming sea.

From 1981, when 22 breweries poured their wares, the GABF has fermented into an event attracting as of 2019 more than 800 breweries pouring 4,000 different beers into one-ounce tasters. During the 2019 three-day fest, 60,000 attendees chose from a dizzying array of different beers, earning a *Guinness Book of World Records* acclamation as "the most beers on tap in one place on earth."

3.2 percent beer while liquor stores remained single-owner, one-location outlets that could not sell food and convenience items. That arrangement dramatically changed as of January 2019, when full-strength 5 percent or more alcoholic content beer could finally be sold in grocery stores, creating huge competition for local liquor stores, which fought the change bitterly. It was another fight pitting local, small-business Davids against national Goliaths.

Local mom-and-pop liquor stores claimed that they review twenty new craft beers per week, while grocery stores will get maybe five new beers each six months. Liquor stores and small brewpubs and craft breweries would soon suffer under the new arrangement. "It's another win for corporate America," lamented one Colorado liquor store owner.

Patrick Maroney, Colorado Liquor Enforcement Division director, noted, "These new regulations are some of the largest, sweeping changes to the State's liquor laws since Prohibition. Disallowing full-strength beer in supermarkets and convenience stores and only 3.2 beer was a relic of Prohibition."

Grocery sales may expedite a bust in small local breweries not big enough to capture grocery store attention. Larger craft brewers will see more outlets for distribution. Since 2000, a gold rush in Colorado's craft brewing created a double-digit increase in outlets nearly each year until 2019. Saturation and fierce competition caused many busts, and the boom times seemed to have leveled off. The new law likely doomed antiquated Prohibition-era 3.2 beer. But the ever-innovative industry was staying liquid by turning out low-alcohol near beers, health-conscious gluten-free beers, and even CBD-infused beers combining beer and cannabis. No matter the origin or ingredients, Coloradans are unlikely to ever give up their love of beer.

With some 444 craft breweries and brewpubs as of 2019, Colorado has been among the nation's beeriest states. With consolidation and closures, however, beer has gone flatter, or, as brewers call it, "skunk." As of 2019, Colorado had 174 brewpubs and 270 breweries. Beer sales were tapering off, according to John A. Carlson of the Colorado Brewers Guild. He explained that young people see the caloric content of full-flavored craft beer as bad. The rise of Colorado cannabis is also impacting demand for beer. Millennials born between 1981 and 1996 are flocking to craft spirits, wine, cannabis, and sparkling or flavored alcoholic water with low to no calories.

The 2019 figure of 444 craft breweries and brewpubs may well have been the sizzling crest before the fizzling decline. With the loss of New Belgium as a craft brewery and the shuttering of some other smaller operations, many had declared, "The boom is over."

Even Coors, Colorado's longtime biggest brewery, has seen sales fall in recent years. Adding insult to injury, Molson Coors, the parent company, moved the corporate headquarters from Denver to Chicago in 2019. Yet Coors and beer have experienced ups and downs before and will most likely bubble up again. The name "Coors" persists. Even though the 2020 pandemic saw many smaller breweries sink during that sobering time, the industry somehow remained afloat as it pivoted production to meet new challenges.

Chapter Eleven

Rocky Mountain High

Colorado has literally gone to pot. The Green Rush briefly made it the cannabis capital of the United States. This budding boom resulted from a literal "grassroots" effort to bypass legislative inaction by ballot initiatives. In 2000, voters sanctioned medical marijuana, and in 2012, made Colorado the first state to legalize adult recreational use. While initially booming, pot, like other bonanzas, is now tapering off as other states, such as California and Illinois, as well as Canada, legalize both medicinal and recreational marijuana.

As the first US state to sell both medicinal and recreational marijuana, Colorado has reasserted its highest state bragging rights. But the state has not always embraced this moniker. The nationwide War on Drugs resulted in years of federal and state efforts to eradicate the noxious weed. From its beginnings, the cultural war against marijuana has been closely tied to oppression of the downtrodden, courting reefer fears to inflame racial tensions and the popular prejudices of the day.

Chinese and Mexicans immigrants, then African Americans, and finally countercultural whites, like the Beats and the hippies, were charged with corrupting Americans' core values and morals with dangerous drugs. As the Latino population became the state's largest foreign-born group by far, they were especially targeted with unfavorable stereotypes. Ultimately, Colorado was in the national forefront of both pot prohibition in the 1930s and its eventual legalization in the twenty-first century. The road to legalization was rough, and Colorado still wrestles with growing pains and uncertainties while reaping tax benefits as the nation's pioneer in legalization.

Chinese Opium

Colorado was an early health mecca, primarily for people with lung ailments like tuberculosis. Patent medicines abounded. Some contained

Cannabis indicia, gaining acceptance in medical journals as a sedative and pain reliever. One popular consumption remedy was Eli Lilly & Co.'s sugar-coated, chocolate-flavored "Chlorodyne," which contained *Cannabis indicia*, morphine, and belladonna, a plant also known as "deadly nightshade." Not surprisingly, such concoctions did relieve suffering. So did opium in the 1800s when Denver's Chinatown boasted numerous outlets for the popular substance.

In 1870, the Colorado Territorial Legislature encouraged Chinese immigration to remedy an acute labor shortage. Corporate Colorado demanded cheap, compliant, and competent labor to work the state's mines and build its railroads. Denver's Chinatown became known as Hop Alley for its opium dens. This alley between Market and Blake Streets lay tucked in amid the saloons, gambling halls, and the red-light district of Lower Downtown. The ostracized Chinese population was confined to this vice district, where they "hopped up" on opium.

Opium use, simmering anger over labor competition, and overt racism led to the anti-Chinese riot of October 31, 1880. On that particularly scary Halloween, an unruly mob of thousands converged on Hop Alley, determined to evict the roughly 200 Chinese residents. Their homes and so-called "washee houses" were ransacked and razed. Many were physically assaulted as they fled to the sanctuary of the local brothels. Crowded together in Denver's worst neighborhood, prostitutes allied themselves with the Chinese, whom they relied on for laundry service and for opium. Armed with champagne bottles and high-heeled shoes, the ladies of the evening held the mob at bay. While saving some Chinese from harm, the ladies of Market Street could not rescue one unfortunate laundry worker, Sing Lee, also known as Look Young. He was first lynched with a laundry line and then kicked and beaten to death.

Hop Alley became synonymous with Chinese opium use, containing twelve of Denver's seventeen known opium dens. The rest of the city left the Chinese alone, as long as they kept their vices to themselves. Historical accounts paint a bleak picture of the scene inside these dens, with addicts puffing lethargically on bamboo pipes. Even when sex workers and gamblers from the adjacent brothels, saloons, and gambling halls began partaking of opium, city officials turned a blind eye.

That all changed when curious white middle-class men and women began drifting to Hop Alley to indulge in the mind-altering pleasures of exotic opium. Eventually, even the upper classes of Denver's elite society, primarily women, occasionally took to the pipe. As opium's popularity peaked in

In Denver's 1880 anti-Chinese race riot, working-class whites sought to evict Chinese immigrants and their opium dens from Hop Alley. Ironically, those attacked as "filthy heathens" and "dirty Chinese" were doing much of Denver's laundry service. DENVER PUBLIC LIBRARY, WESTERN HISTORY DEPARTMENT

the 1890s, over 60 percent of opium addicts were white, many being women. False reports of opium-addicted Chinese men preying upon these so-called virtuous young white women, including exchanging drugs for sex, inflamed societal demands that something had to be done to curb this insidious vice.

To regulate narcotics, primarily opium, state and federal governments began passing laws in the early 1900s. The federal Harrison Narcotics Act of 1914 banned the sale of opium and other narcotics except when prescribed by a physician for legitimate medical usage. The laws were silent on cannabis, which would arrive from south of the Mexican border.

MEXICAN MARIJUANA

The bloody Mexican Revolution raged from 1910 to 1920 and brought social and economic chaos to Mexico. Hundreds of thousands of Mexicans fled for the United States, not only as war refugees but for economic opportunity. Colorado's booming sugar beet industry was in desperate need of reliable workers to perform backbreaking labor to plant, cultivate, and harvest Colorado's number one crop during the early 1900s. Strong, sturdy, and reliable Mexican immigrants, used to toiling all day in the sun, were actively recruited.

Mexican field-workers brought their local customs, culture, and habits with them. After long hours in the fields, the euphoria of marijuana eased their troubled minds and allowed them some relief from the oppression they suffered daily. Marijuana also provided some pain relief to overworked bodies. The drug was accessible, as immigrants could grow it in nearby fields or even in their backyards and sell their harvests to supplement their meager wages.

The language of cannabis changed with the new arrivals. "Marijuana" was originally Mexican slang for *Cannabis sativa*, which, unlike *Cannabis indica*, created an exhilarating high. Besides the original *marihuana* being anglicized as "marijuana," terms such as "weed" or "loco weed" emerged. The word "pot" became widespread, derived from *potiguaya*, a wine in which marijuana buds were immersed. "Mary Jane," or *Maria Juana*, became another popular name for marijuana.

Many Coloradans did not welcome their new Mexican neighbors, who were stereotyped as illiterate pot smokers. The rise of the Ku Klux Klan in the 1920s and its control over Denver and Colorado politics made the situation even worse, promoting racist attitudes toward minority groups including Mexican immigrants. Segregationist signs began to appear in store windows warning "No Dogs or Mexicans!"

A federal agent was quoted in the November 28, 1921, *Denver Post* as attributing a shoot-out between two Mexican immigrants to marijuana. He claimed that marijuana usage caused "slight exhilaration to downright ugliness" and declared that "when Mexicans fight each other they are apt to be full of marijuana. It is far more deadly in its effects than either cocaine or morphine." This report typifies the mainstream mindset at the time—that immigrants and marijuana were trouble.

Newspapers in Colorado and across the country began a constant barrage of yellow journalism, blaming Mexican immigrants and their marijuana for murder, mayhem, and madness. Such themes raised Colorado to a feverish anti-Hispanic pitch in the late 1920s. The February 18, 1927, *Denver Post* claimed that smuggled Mexican marijuana had been introduced into the Pueblo city schools and was "weakening high school morals." By December 30, 1928, *Denver Post* headlines screamed "A Homegrown New Drug That Drives Its Victims Mad!" The article demonized marijuana as "leading to violence and a fiendish desire to mutilate and kill." "When a peon has smoked a pipeful of it, he runs completely insane, runs amuck—kills!"

The December 30, 1928, *Denver Post* demonized marijuana as causing murder, mayhem, and madness among Latinos and ominously portrayed its degrading effects on the morals of young white women. BILL HANSEN COLLECTION

"Insanity is worse in the primitive brains of Mexicans. . . . It is the most deadly narcotic in the U.S." The general public readily embraced these racist views, with fears that white society was somehow imperiled.

In 1922, Denver passed an ordinance banning the possession, sale, or use of marijuana. A statewide ban followed in 1928 making such acts a felony. Colorado's Mexican population began disguising marijuana cultivation in fields of well-watered corn, whose tall stalks concealed the shorter cannabis. In 1933, two-thirds of Denver's drug arrests had Spanish surnames and, by 1935, that number had increased to 80 percent.

"REEFER MADNESS" AND THE MARIJUANA TAX ACT OF 1937

The Wall Street crash of 1929 led to the country's worst depression. The economy collapsed. Unemployment surged. Racial tensions grew. Nativism soared. Cracking down on immigrant Mexicans and their marijuana usage provided both a ready scapegoat and a defenseless target. As enthusiasm for alcohol prohibition waned, the Federal Bureau of Narcotics (FBN) was created in 1930, predecessor to today's Drug Enforcement Agency. Because of Colorado's large Mexican population and drug use, it became a focus of attention for the FBN.

The September 16, 1934, *New York Times* claimed that marijuana appeared to be "unchecked in Colorado and other western states" and its use was "spreading to all classes." Anxiety over immigrants and marijuana entering the state made fertile ground for drastic measures. In 1936, Colorado governor Edwin "Big Ed" Johnson declared martial law and sent the National Guard to New Mexico border to bar the "hordes" of Mexican migrant workers supposedly invading Colorado.

Not to be outdone by the *Times*, a 1936 *Rocky Mountain News* headlined "Habit-Forming Marijuana Grown in Great Quantities in Colorado." This article claimed that three and a half tons of pot had been seized by local authorities in the previous nine months and that morphine abusers were switching to weed because it was cheaper. From August to September 1936, the *Alamosa Daily Courier* pled for federal intervention when a young girl was brutally assaulted by a criminal supposedly under the influence of marijuana. The paper reported that the drug problem was particularly acute among "degenerate Spanish-speaking residents."

The FBN responded and urged the states to pass uniform bans, which Colorado did. The Marijuana Tax Act of 1937 was then hastily passed, based

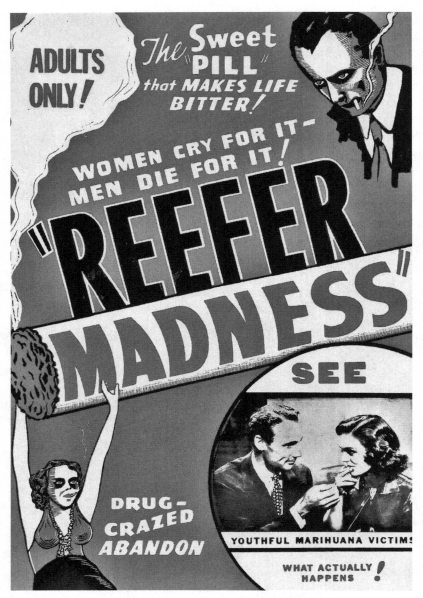

The 1936 film *Reefer Madness* was billed as educational but was really a federally inspired propaganda piece to showcase the evils of marijuana to white youth. BILL HANSEN COLLECTION

largely on the Colorado experience and newspaper hysteria stoked nation-wide. It essentially made individual possession and sale of marijuana a federal crime. There were no medical exceptions. Yet the American Medical Association (AMA) opposed the law because it prevented physicians and pharmacists from using cannabis for medicinal purposes. The AMA was ignored. Legions of G-men who had become superfluous with the end of alcohol prohibition in 1933 once again were unleashed on a new mission. Many saw this 1937 act as a second era of Prohibition. The law was not stricken until the 1960s.

Even before the Marijuana Tax Act became effective on October 1, 1937, the feds made it clear that Colorado would be the focus of early enforcement. Splashy busts were expected. In the wee hours of October 3, 1937, Mexican American Moses Baca, age twenty-three, was arrested for drunk and disorderly conduct after beating his wife in his third-floor rooming house at 2625 California Street in Denver's Five Points neighborhood. He was found to have a quarter ounce of marijuana in his possession. A day later, former bootlegger, career criminal, and small-time dealer Samuel Caldwell, age fifty-seven, sold three joints to an undercover agent. Four pounds of marijuana were found in the Denver flophouse where he was staying.

Justice was swift. Convictions followed a few days after their arrests. US District Court Judge J. Foster Symes declared at their sentencing hearing:

I consider marijuana the worst of all narcotics, far worse than the use of morphine or coca. Under its influence, men become beasts. Marijuana destroys life itself. I have no sympathy for those who sell the weed. The Government is going to enforce the law to the letter.

Baca was sentenced to eighteen months at Leavenworth Penitentiary. For dealing, Caldwell received four years.

In the weeks following Baca's and Caldwell's sentencing, undocumented Mexican immigrants were rounded up, and Judge Symes urged that all those found to be in possession of marijuana should be deported.

In the winter of 1940–41, federal agents in Denver struck what they thought was the mother lode. After purchasing $4,000 worth of marijuana over a three-week period, undercover agents traced the drugs back to their source, a fifty-three-year-old Mexican immigrant named Melitone Garcia. From his farm of cultivated marijuana east of Fort Collins, Garcia operated

Colorado's pioneer pot purveyor, Samuel Caldwell, was one of the first two men arrested under the Marijuana Tax Act of 1937. He would later become the pro-cannabis crowd's poster child as the first POW in the nation's war on cannabis.
DENVER PUBLIC LIBRARY, WESTERN HISTORY DEPARTMENT

a sophisticated ring of pot pushers in Denver, a hashish parlor where the goods could be sampled, and an abandoned quarry in Windsor where he would take the blindfolded customers to complete deals. Narcotics agents crowned Garcia the "Marijuana King of America." The January 12, 1941, *Rocky Mountain News* crowed "17 Held as U.S. Agents Claim Smashing of Dope Ring That Preyed on Boys, Girls." As he was handcuffed and led away, Garcia reportedly (and prophetically) told one of the agents that "there was a fortune to be made in the sale of weed in Colorado."

To further crack down on the perceived threat of marijuana nationwide, the FBN also focused on Black jazz musicians. On October 23, 1950, Denver's top FBN official was quoted in the *Rocky Mountain News* as saying that "marijuana was sold mostly in small, dark 'dine and dance dives' where racial lines frequently meet and overlap," referring to Denver's Five Points area, which had gained a reputation as the Harlem of the West. At its heart was the triangular brick, three-story Rossonian Hotel and Lounge at 2650 Welton Street, hailed as the most important jazz club between Kansas City and Los Angeles. The country's greatest jazz musicians played there, often after completing more formal, better-paying gigs downtown. At its peak in the 1940s and early 1950s, the Rossonian attracted more white patrons than Black because the surrounding African American community could not afford the price of admission.

During the post–World War II Red Scare of Communism and rabid McCarthyism, as well as a nascent but growing civil rights movement, the FBN did a complete about-face. Evidence of marijuana fueling ax-wielding Mexican madmen had been elusive from the outset. The public was losing interest. A new crisis was perpetrated to refocus attention to other claimed

The Rossonian Hotel and Lounge, shown here around 1949, was at the time a hot spot where both Black and white patrons freely intermingled to enjoy jazz, dancing, and pot. BLACK AMERICAN WEST MUSEUM

threats to white American morals and values. Infiltration of the white youth was the new perceived problem. Abandoning cries of murder, mayhem, and madness, the FBN proclaimed "marijuana leads to pacifism and communist brain-washing."

The 1950 *Denver Post* bellowed "War on Dope—U.S. Rates Marijuana America's Greatest Menace." Federally, the Boggs Act of 1952 and the Narcotics Control Act of 1956 imposed draconian increases in penalties, with mandatory prison sentences and even the death penalty for marijuana crimes. Colorado laws were generally in lockstep with the federal legislation. Soon white pot users would join people of color as targets but would ultimately soften the stigma against marijuana.

THE COUNTERCULTURE, BEATS, AND HIPPIES

In the 1950s, a bohemian culture of aesthetes, writers, and musicians concentrated in Greenwich Village launched the Beat generation. Led by such disillusioned hipsters as the novelist Jack Kerouac and poet Allen Ginsberg, the Beats eschewed traditional American values, norms, militarism, and materialism. They also turned to pot for their inspiration. Denver's Neal Cassady became Kerouac's and Ginsberg's muse.

Cassady grew up in the skid row, fleabag flophouses of Denver. A serial car thief, street hustler, and overall ne'er-do-well, the wild and charismatic Cassady took to the road with Kerouac in 1947 in an alcohol-and-drug-fueled trip from New York to San Francisco. In Denver, they hooked up with Ginsberg. The three drank beer at the still-standing My Brother's Bar at 2376 15th Street, partied in Central City, and moved to the beat of jazz music at the Rossonian Hotel. Their cross-country escapade would later be memorialized in Kerouac's best-selling novel, *On the Road* (New York: Viking, 1957), encouraging a whole generation to do likewise.

In the 1960s, the Beat generation gave way to the hippies. A 1967 Denver Police Department publicity sheet described hippies as "long-haired, vagrant, anti-social, psychopathic, dangerous drug users who refer to themselves as the hippie subculture." It was claimed that crime was rampant among these social misfits and that marijuana was the cause.

Many true hippies dropped out of society and lived as so-called street people—stereotyped as shaggy-maned vagrants, transients, and shiftless panhandlers, who sat on street corners strumming guitars with glazed eyes from getting high all day on marijuana or various psychedelics. They were society "dropouts."

But many young people were not dropouts. They attended colleges and universities while embracing the lifestyle, dress, and music of the hippies. After studying all day, they would retire to their dorm rooms and squeeze wet towels under the doors so they could clandestinely smoke doobies or pipe-like bongs. Boulder became the hippie capital of the Rocky Mountain West, with the University of Colorado singled out at congressional hearings for its marijuana usage as early as 1965. Even at liberal Colorado College in conservative Colorado Springs, a 1968 study found that 41 percent of students had smoked pot and 67 percent favored legalization. These students did not view their activities as criminal. Strangely, many middle-class parents agreed, and many student hippies managed to get high while maintaining good grades and retaining good-kid status.

This generation of pot-smokers was far more politically active than previous generations. Facing direct involvement in the unpopular Viet Nam War, pacifist hippies and rebellious college students took to the streets in

Some hippies fled the city and sought sanctuary in self-sustaining communes in the vast, remote Colorado countryside. Here a resident of the hippie commune called Libre in Huerfano County is harvesting a crop of marijuana. TOM NOEL COLLECTION

active protest chanting "make love, not war." They also rallied to the then-burgeoning civil rights movement.

The rise of the white counterculture youth of Beats and hippies startled, even scared, many establishment Americans, who in 1969 elected law and order president Richard M. Nixon. He sought a scapegoat and distraction from the failing Viet Nam War and the rising civil rights movement to help mobilize what he called the silent majority against the so-called noisy minority. On June 18, 1971, Nixon declared his War on Drugs, proclaiming marijuana "Public Enemy Number One."

The Controlled Substances Act of 1970 scheduled various narcotics. Marijuana was placed at the highest level, a Schedule I Narcotic, meaning that it had a high potential for abuse, a high potential for dependence, and no known acceptable medical benefit. It was scheduled the same as heroin and cocaine. The Drug Enforcement Agency (DEA) was created in 1973 to enforce such laws. A decade later, President Ronald Reagan declared marijuana "the most dangerous drug in America." First Lady Nancy Reagan implored American youths to "Just Say No."

The War on Drugs caused many casualties and imprisoned hundreds of thousands, if not millions, of low-level users as prisoners of war. Disproportionally, those prisoners were Black or Hispanic. An estimated one in five African Americans would spend time behind bars for drug arrests. Still, hundreds of thousands of whites were also swept up in the war and were saddled with criminal records, primarily for possession or use. The term "War on Drugs" was used until 2009, when the war was deemed a failure.

DECRIMINALIZATION AND THE ROAD TO LEGALIZATION

By the 1970s, Colorado began retreating from the federal war on pot. In 1975, Colorado joined ten other states in decriminalizing marijuana from a felony to a misdemeanor for possession of one to eight ounces and a petty offense for an ounce or less with a fine of $100. Colorado also removed cannabis from the State Narcotics Act and downgraded it to merely a dangerous drug.

In 1979 and again in 1981, Colorado tried to pass medical marijuana acts. Both laws depended on federal approval. None came. With or without the feds, the times were changing. The weed-loving young baby boomers of the '60s and '70s inevitably grew up and become the middle-aged establishment. As of 2018, almost two-thirds of Americans favor recreational legalization

194

with a whopping 94 percent favoring medical pot, while research confirming various medical benefits continues to stack up.

Since 1910, reform-minded Coloradans have had a constitutional right to bypass legislature and establishment politicians and pass laws by ballot initiatives and referendums. That process enabled marijuana to gain legalization through a true "grassroots" campaign.

In 1996, California became the first state to adopt a medical marijuana use law by ballot initiative. Colorado and seven other states soon followed. On November 7, 2000, 54 percent of Colorado voters approved the legalization of medical marijuana under a statewide referendum. It soon became apparent that these laws were going to be complicated to adopt, apply, and maintain, given the continuing federal ban. In 2006, the United States Supreme Court held that federal laws trumped California's medical marijuana law, leaving state laws in a constant state of tension with federal law.

In Colorado, medical marijuana patients have to be eighteen years or older and obtain a "red card" from the Colorado Department of Public Health and Environment and be listed on a patient registry. They have to be diagnosed with a qualified medical condition, which initially was limited to conditions such as chronic pain, glaucoma, cancer, HIV/AIDS, nausea, and PTSD. Physicians, whose prescribing licenses are issued by the DEA, could not prescribe marijuana. They could only recommend it and assure that a qualified medical condition was involved. Colorado medical dispensaries proliferated, bearing the neon-lit green cross emblem.

On November 6, 2012, 57.13 percent of Colorado voters passed Amendment 64, another ballot initiative, to legalize recreational use of marijuana. Washington State also legalized recreational pot in the same election cycle. Both states claim bragging rights as to which was first, but in terms of the actual sale of marijuana, Colorado whipped Washington by beginning recreational sales on January 1, 2014, narrowly winning the pot race.

Colorado's law approved adult recreational use for those twenty-one years or older. The new law limited sales to one ounce per transaction—half of what medical users could procure. Proof of Colorado residency was required, with nonresidents being limited to one-half ounce.

BOOM IN SALES AND DISPENSARIES

Every phase of the new marijuana industry is heavily licensed, regulated, and taxed. The actual hybridization, growing, cultivation, harvesting, and marketing of both medical and recreational pot have evolved into an extremely high science of industrialized proportions, all monitored by government regulations, with Colorado initially leading the way in marijuana horticulture.

Not all Colorado residents were thrilled by either medical or recreational legalization despite the potential economic benefits it might bring local economies. Many were outraged and wanted nothing to do with pot, still viewing it as a social evil. The key to Colorado's law was emphasizing complete local control. Each county and municipality could determine locally whether it would allow or limit the various kinds of dispensaries and grow houses, hours of operation, zoning issues, local taxes, etc. Colorado was divided between the opt-ins and the opt-outs, or, as some have referred to it, the "highs" and "drys," harkening back to the days of alcohol prohibition.

Eventually three-fourths of Colorado's 271 municipalities and over half of Colorado's 64 counties banned retail sales, although some allowed medical dispensaries. A virtual patchwork of differing decisions and restrictions dotted the state and remain ever-changing.

Denver, of course, allowed everything, as did Boulder. Colorado Springs and Lakewood allowed medical shops only. Aurora limited the numbers of recreational dispensaries. The former temperance town of Greeley prohibited all marijuana sales. Mesa County and its county seat, Grand Junction, banned all pot sales. When a new ballot initiative was again attempted in 2013, defiant local officials in Grand Junction rejected it for insufficient staples on the paperwork.

Despite the rejection from certain areas of the state, Colorado's marijuana industry boomed from the start. The state's marijuana economy flourished from the get-go. By year's end in 2019, over $8.2 billion worth of weed had been sold in Colorado since 2014, including $1.72 billion in 2019 alone. There were almost 3,000 marijuana-related businesses employing over 41,000 licensed individuals. Dispensaries—medical, recreational, or both—have budded profusely throughout the state's opt-in locales. Retail storefronts have sprouted up on many major thoroughfares, strip malls, and entertainment districts. Alluring business names beckon customers, such as Denver's Cherry Peak, Glendale's Emerald Fields, Boulder's Green Room, Aurora's Euflora, Fort Collins's Flower Power Botanica, and Carbondale's Tumbleweed.

Some dispensaries offer novel marketing gimmicks. Glendale's Smokin' Gun Apothecary pushed the iconic, ongoing Shotgun Willie's strip club to the back of the busy corner property at Colorado Boulevard and Virginia

Avenue in 2016. The Apothecary then moved into its new building on the more prominent corner site. Primarily a women-owned dispensary, the Smokin' Gun claims to be the first stand-alone dispensary built in the state. Inside, a mini museum includes an antique 1870 bank cage where pot is actually sold through teller windows. An original mural by artist Daniel Chavez chronicles the legacy of the first arrests of Samuel Caldwell, Black jazz musicians, and Willie Nelson. Just beyond a sign reading "For what you are about to buy, you'd get life in prison" lies a re-created 1941 prison cell in this dopey museum.

Nowadays, many pot shops and grow houses are connected in seed-to-sell chains. Warehouse space was grabbed up all over the Denver metro area, quickly driving up real estate prices. Almost any empty building could be retrofitted to accommodate cultivation.

Many such indoor nurseries moved to the corridor of warehouses straddling I-70 north of downtown Denver, which already had a distribution infrastructure of railroad sidings, truck ramps, and loading docks. Formerly cheap spaces in the old buildings along I-25 and the railroad tracks of the South Platte River Valley were also quickly snatched up.

Huge amounts of energy and water are needed to support indoor urban agriculture. Four percent of Denver's electricity became devoted to marijuana cultivation, and increased hydrocarbon emissions have resulted. The added strain on Denver's already precious water supply was unexpected. By May 2016, Denver had to cap its number of cultivation facilities.

This caused some of the larger grow facilities to go green in another way. The old tried-and-true glass greenhouses were far more energy efficient than fully roofed warehouses. Solar-powered sustainable greenhouses emerged as a green alternative to indoor energy-grabbing warehouses.

COLORADO'S COMPLAINING NEIGHBORS

Outside the Denver metro area, many dispensaries congregate along the interstate corridors of I-25 and I-70. Colorado is a virtually isolated green oasis among a desert of prohibition states, including Nebraska, Kansas, Oklahoma, Wyoming, and Texas, while medical-only use is tolerated in New Mexico, Arizona, and Utah. Communities on Colorado's fringes seek to capitalize on cross-border green tourists.

While Grand Junction and Mesa County have bans, the Mesa County town of Palisade grabbed the eastbound market of I-70 and beckons tourists from Utah with more than wine and peaches. It has somewhat usurped Parachute some miles farther to the east, which offered the state's first drive-through dispensary. After a busted oil boom left its economy crumbling, cannabis sales buoyed Parachute's local taxes from a low of $831,000 in 2015 to a 2018 high of $16 million.

The pot bonanza lifted even tiny Sedgwick, comprising one-third of a square mile with a population of less than 200 within prohibition Sedgwick County. This northeast Colorado hamlet caters to I-76 traffic from Nebraska and Kansas. In the southwest corner of Colorado, Cortez serves travelers from the other three of the four corners states—New Mexico, Arizona, and Utah—which have all resisted the siren call of recreational marijuana so far.

Needless to say, adjacent prohibition states do not view Colorado as a good neighbor. It has been estimated that 12 percent of Colorado's legal marijuana sales have somehow drifted out of state to feed a black market elsewhere, where Colorado pot can be resold at a 300 percent profit. With skyrocketing numbers of busts across the borders and the need for heightened law enforcement, tensions have escalated to interstate litigation.

Trinidad is the most notorious of the border pot towns. With over twenty dispensaries just across the state line from New Mexico in Las Animas County, it has become a booming marijuana mecca. The *Colorado Springs Gazette* claimed Trinidad should be called the pot capital of the Rockies.

Denver's 420: From Protest to Celebration

The worldwide roots of 420 are hazy and debated. In Denver, the reference dates back to the 1990s when pro-pot protesters first began rallying in Civic Center Park to publicly toke up at 4:20 p.m. on April 20th.

Denver's unofficial Stoners' Holiday, now called the Mile High 420 Festival, draws as many as 50,000 to Denver's Civic Center Park. Originally, before the state legalized recreational use, it was a protest of civil disobedience, activism, and advocacy that became so massive that Denver police were bewildered as to how to respond. The crowd was peaceful and mellow but openly defying state and federal marijuana bans. With legalization, it has transformed from a massive activist rally to a festive celebration. Pot smoking is still illegal in public, and especially in public parks, but Denver officials have largely given up on trying to forcibly ban it.

Given the amount of recreational sales, the *Gazette* estimated that, if sold only for local consumption, $300 per month was being spent for every man, woman, and child in Las Animas County. Per capita, Trinidad boasts eighteen times more sales than Boulder County.

Trinidad dispensaries such as Freedom Road are primarily peddling pot south to travelers from New Mexico and, especially, Texas. There, vigilant Lone Star State Highway Patrol officers lurk along the side of the highway, pulling over vehicles arriving from Colorado for minor speeding, defective taillights, and any other potential infraction as a pretext to stop and search out the locally banned substance.

Boom in State and Local Tax Revenue

As the pioneer in a nascent industry of legal adult recreational use, Colorado has devised a constantly changing scheme of what to tax, at what level, by what entity, and at what rate. Distribution of these taxes is also constantly being tweaked as state and local coffers are filled beyond expectations. Colorado served as a national guinea pig in how best to regulate and tax this lucrative new industry. Still, by year's end of 2019, over $1.2 billion has been reaped in tax revenue since record keeping began in 2014 following the legalization of recreational pot. State pot revenues seem to keep rising, with $302 million in 2019, up 12 percent from the $266.5 million collected in 2018. Pot revenue easily dominates all of the other "sin taxes" for tobacco, alcohol, and gaming combined.

Currently, every licensed cultivator pays a 15 percent state excise tax for each sale to a retailer. The retail dispensary pays another 15 percent state sales tax on all recreational sales and 2.9 percent sales tax for all medical pot sales. Each local opt-in community adds its own layers of licensing fees and sales and excise taxes.

Amendment 64 legalizing recreational marijuana was sold to voters as a way to enhance Colorado's low education funding using pot taxes. Help was desperately needed because penny-pinching taxpayers keep Colorado among the lowest states in terms of support of public education. Hopes were high when recreational marijuana sales began in 2014, generating hundreds of millions of dollars each year in taxes for Colorado. The major recipient has been the "BEST" program, or Building Excellent Schools Today. Those funds are limited to the construction of new K through 12 public schools and repairing existing educational facilities. Nothing is designated for chronically

Antonito: Pot to the Rescue

Antonito, a one-stoplight town of about 780 huddled along US 285 just north of the New Mexico border, narrowly voted in medical and recreational pot by a five-vote margin in 2013. Back in 2005, this financially struggling town had to fire its entire police department and cut back on many town services because of a dwindling tax base. Legalization brought three pot shops hoping to cash in on New Mexican customers. The taxes from the quickly booming marijuana tourist industry enabled the town to purchase the Warshauer Mansion and also helped pay for a major water project and a new police cruiser to replace the one totaled in a chase at the lone stoplight in town.

Antonito townspeople have used their pot taxes to proudly restore and repurpose the Warshauer Mansion as the new town hall, police station, and a museum. BILL HANSEN COLLECTION

low teachers' salaries, aging school buses, or the shortage of supplies, books, and computers, especially in the poorer districts. In reality, funds collected are a mere drop in the bucket for needed capital improvements. As a cure-all for education, the hyped boom has largely been a bust.

Opt-in communities can assess their own sales and excise taxes, on top of their regular sales taxes, as well as special taxes for particular programs or needs such as fixing roads and building recreation centers. With bulging tax coffers, opt-in communities have widely varying agendas. Aurora, Colorado's third-largest city, focuses on homelessness, while Pueblo awards college scholarships to underprivileged public school children. Denver's funds go to park improvements, affordable housing, and opioid abuse prevention. Tiny Ridgway bought a much-needed snowplow to clear its annual average of seven feet.

HAZY HORIZONS

As an embryonic industry matures through adolescence, growing pains still abound. Most problematic is that the booming green economy can function solely on green as a medium of exchange, as in cash-only. Federally regulated banks and credit unions deny marijuana businesses access to their most basic financial services such as checking accounts, credit cards, lines of credit, and ATMs, fearing the wrath of federal prosecution for money laundering and participation in racketeering. Every transaction must be in cash. Larger pot chains hire armed guards or retain specialty armored car services. Employees are paid in cash, rent and utilities bills are satisfied in cash, all vendors are reimbursed in cash, and even the state and local monthly taxes are discharged in cash. In recent years, some local Colorado financial institutions have cautiously extended services to a highly scrutinized clientele while Washington politicos endlessly debate the issue.

A recurring, regularly tested issue is what constitutes open and public use of marijuana, which remains banned under Colorado law. Pot smoking is prohibited in public parks and other open areas where cigarette smoking is allowed. City and statewide efforts to allow licensed pot-smoking social venues have been hampered by the extensive regulatory red tape involved. In 2020, locally licensed marijuana "hospitality establishments" were authorized, including tasting rooms and pot party buses.

One particularly active organization has been the International Church of Cannabis. In 2015, its founders purchased a 1904 Gothic Revival former Lutheran church at 400 South Logan Street in Denver. Ironically, in the 1920s, the house of worship was used by the Pillar of Fire Church to preach against the evils of alcohol. This fiery past was ignored by Los Angeles street artist Kenny Scharf, who adorned the exterior with his colorful murals. The church boasts no religious dogma and encourages each member to discover their own spiritual pathway. Referring to themselves as "elevationists," members call marijuana the "Sacred Flower." The only regular service, celebrating the Sacrament of Cannabis, is held weekly, when the members-only

Cofounder Lee Molloy of Denver's International Church of Cannabis, shown here with historian Tom Noel, leads "elevationists" who smoke the "Sacred Flower" in a former Pillar of Fire church, whose interior walls and ceilings have been brightly adorned by acclaimed Spanish chapel artist Okuda San Miguel, hailed as the Michelangelo of Cannabis. BILL HANSEN COLLECTION

congregation can puff and pray to get what some have referred to as high and holy.

The inaugural service of the church was held on April 20, 2017, and attracted an undercover Denver cop, who somehow gained entrance to the members-only event. Cofounder Steve Berke was cited for open and public consumption, as well as violation of the Colorado Clean Indoor Air Act. He vowed to fight the charges in what became one of the most prolonged and complicated litigations in Denver Municipal Court history. After two years of expensive court proceedings by both Berke and the Denver City Attorney's Office, including a mistrial and a jury trial, Berke was eventually found guilty and fined $50. Cofounder Lee Molloy was later acquitted of the same charges in a separate trial. The issue of what constitutes public consumption remains unresolved.

So long as marijuana remains illegal under federal law, problems continue in the area of employment. In 2015, the Colorado Supreme Court confronted a claim by Brandon Coats, a quadriplegic who used medical marijuana to treat his painful muscle spasms. After failing a random drug test, he was fired by his employer. The court held that the employer did not have to accommodate medical use and could adopt a zero-tolerance policy for marijuana even if it was smoked outside of work and in no way affected work performance.

Another difficulty is how to deal with the thousands of pre-legalization low-level convictions for possession and use that were disproportionately African American and Hispanic. The stigma of such convictions for what is now legal creates hurdles to obtaining basic necessities such as employment opportunities, home rentals, or access to credit. In 2018, Denver joined Boulder in adopting a law allowing the expungement of over 10,000 such convictions. In 2020, Governor Jared Polis took executive action to pardon many of that same population.

While the medical benefits continue to be studied, medical side effects and societal harms are becoming better known. Some level of dependence has been established, and admissions to hospitals and calls to poison control centers are on the rise. Crime, an increase in traffic fatalities, and the effects of usage among youths continue to be studied. Limits on potency have been proposed. Most importantly, the black market continues to thrive in illegal grow houses that do not have to conform to extensive regulation or collect taxes, allowing them to easily undercut the prices of legitimate dealers. Active state and federal busts continue of such scofflaws.

Colorado's boom period had leveled off after 46 percent growth from 2014 to 2015. It was 15 percent from 2016 to 2107, but only 2 percent from 2017 to 2018. California and Illinois both legalized recreational marijuana in 2018, as did the entire country of Canada. As they see the tax revenues, other states are following suit. With ever-growing competition, Colorado has seen the need to continually innovate. But, with a decline in sales and a shrinking number of grow houses and pot purveyors projected for 2020, many claimed that Colorado's boom was over.

The threats of Big Pharma, Big Tobacco, and even Big Beer raised the specter of overwhelming local businesses, both big and small, in massive consolidation and vertical integration. As other venues legalized and potential saturation seemed imminent, it was feared that Colorado's giddy pot boom might wilt from sizzle to fizzle and go up in smoke. Instead, the 2020 pandemic closures saw Colorado's pot industry boom with sky-high demand, record sales, and more-than-welcome tax revenues to relieve desperate state and local budgets. It was one of the latest industries in Colorado's diversified economy and perhaps the one that fared the best during the 2020 bust.

CHAPTER TWELVE

Colorado's 2020 COVID-19 Bust:
History Repeated

THE YEAR 2020 SAW A NEAR-TOTAL BUST. BEFORE COVID-19, COLORADO'S economy was booming, recovering from a deep recession in 2008. Unemployment among its population of 5.8 million was less than 2.5 percent, the lowest in its history. Then came Colorado's sharpest and swiftest economic crash in its history. Its booming industries collapsed, businesses closed, and jobs disappeared. Racial and social unrest flared during the turmoil.

The novel coronavirus swept across the Pacific, hitting the West Coast in late January and breaching the Colorado Rockies a month later. Like 1918, the country was ill-prepared for a new pandemic. As before, the country was at war—this time, with itself. It was a highly contentious election year. Ugly political, cultural, and social divisiveness already reigned. Deeply polarized political parties and their adherents simply attacked each other and refused to compromise. The media was under assault. Science was questioned and often denied. Public health officials were under attack—sometimes ignored or vilified and often overruled by squabbling politicians.

At the forefront was the clash over economic survival and perceived overreach by the government on the liberty interests of its citizens versus protecting the public health needs of those same citizens. It was personal individual freedom opposing self-sacrifice and collective actions for the common good. Discordant views abounded on too rash versus too slow, too extreme versus too casual, and opening up versus shutting down.

Colorado had turned "purple" and deeply divided against itself within its own borders. Progressive Democrat governor Jared Polis had the support of a blue General Assembly. Denver's mayor was Democrat Michael Hancock, with many of the surrounding metropolitan cities and towns along the Front Range also a liberal dark or light blue. The rural eastern plains and Western Slope communities were primarily die-hard red conservatives, often feeling ignored by the big-city politicians and used to an independent frontier fortitude of "toughing it out" without government help, intervention, or interference.

THE FIRST WAVE—EARLY LOCKDOWN

The Colorado Springs Bridge Center held a five-day bridge tournament of mostly elderly players from February 27 to March 3. Someone dealt a bad hand of infected cards as they moved from table to table. Colorado's first presumptive case was diagnosed on March 5. Within days, dozens were hospitalized. Colorado's first death was likely an eighty-three-year-old player who perished on March 13. Four more would soon succumb, all traced to an unlucky game of cards.

On March 10, Governor Polis declared a "Disaster Emergency." After quickly reaching one hundred cases within a week, he urged that this was "one of the greatest public health disasters of our lifetime." By mid-March, executive orders began pouring forth, closing most businesses and retail stores, schools, ski resorts, bars, restaurants, nightclubs, entertainment venues, theaters, and gyms. All St. Patrick's Day celebrations were canceled.

Similar preventatives used in the 1918 pandemic were reintroduced, including mask-wearing, social distancing, and thorough handwashing. Well-ventilated work, shopping, and home environments were actively promoted.

On March 23, Denver issued a "Stay at Home" order, followed two days later by Governor Polis covering the entire state. Colorado was to be locked down. All nonessential travel was banned. An extensive list of excluded "critical businesses" and "essential services" accompanied the orders. Grocery stores, convenience stores, gas stations, and hardware stores, along with health care, news media, construction, many government services, and some financial and professional services, could remain open. Restaurants were all closed to inside dining but could offer takeout and delivery. Bars, theaters, gyms, spas, salons, retailers, and all places of indoor amusement and recreation were shuttered. Somehow, gun stores were deemed "critical," but houses of worship were not.

A mad rush of panicky and desperate potheads and imbibers lined up at marijuana dispensaries and liquor stores, causing chaos. Within a few hours, the "Stay at Home" order was quickly modified. Both became "critical" businesses. If Coloradans were going to be stuck at home, it was apparently best they be stoned, drunk, and well-armed rather than be allowed to attend their churches, synagogues, and mosques to pray for hope and salvation from this new plague.

Closing houses of worship and restricting religious practices proved especially thorny and became a lightning rod for many. To protect their flocks and their communities, most religious leaders strove to comply with public health orders to preserve and nurture their congregations without congregating. They resorted to livestreaming holy days and holidays; Zoom confessionals, prayer sessions, and individual counseling; holding outdoor services in parking lots or grassy lawns with social distancing and masks; offering drive-through communions; and worshipping with unmasked soloist music in lieu of choirs. A few churches protested and some sued, decrying that they were being treated differently than many commercial enterprises deemed "critical."

Nudged by an earlier decision of the United States Supreme Court, Colorado lifted most such restrictions on December 9, finally declaring houses of worship as being "essential." To prevent any change of mind by Colorado, the United States Supreme Court sided with the 150-seat High Plains Harvest Church in Greeley on December 15, striking any restrictions on capacity or in-person attendance. Colorado houses of worship would be open for the holidays.

When the "Stay at Home" order was initially mandated, a terrified populace rushed to grocery stores to clear the shelves of anything they thought necessary to stockpile and hoard during the lockdown. What seemed most necessary to many was toilet paper, as shelves were quickly wiped clean. Hand sanitizers, disinfectant wipes, paper towels, liquid soap, and other personal hygiene products disappeared in hours, with masks and gloves long gone. With most businesses and restaurants closed, increased home meal preparation created a rush on any fresh produce, canned goods, frozen dinners, pasta and rice, and meat products. With people hunkered down at their computers and TVs, frozen pizzas, snacks, and other comfort foods seemed their best solace. As stores replenished, prices soared and limits were placed on how much people could buy.

Still, outbreaks abounded. The most severely hit were nursing homes and assisted living facilities, where the elderly at-risk residents were confined and clustered. Visitors were immediately banished. The lonely, isolated, fearful, and often debilitated residents could only peer out their windows and touch hands against the glass panes as children and grandchildren rushed to

Empty store shelves were a common sight during the weeks following the COVID-19 lockdown as folks hoarded personal products such as toilet paper. BILL HANSEN COLLECTION

visit, often for the last time. Large chains fruitlessly played "musical beds," transferring sick patients to one facility or ward and still-healthy residents to another and then back and forth as their status quickly changed. Many care providers refused to come to work, fearing for their own families. Those who did were praised as heroes. Unfortunately, many of those heroic staff, usually underpaid, worked at several different facilities to make a living and inadvertently helped spread the disease.

Hospitals were similarly overwhelmed and faced the same shortages of both staff and personal protective equipment (PPE). Ambulances were sanitized and fumigated after each run. General wards were transformed into isolation wards, and hospital capacity concerns became desperate. Ad hoc emergency hospitals were set up in the Colorado Convention Center and the Larimer County Fairgrounds, awaiting a deluge.

As ICUs filled, a severe shortage of mechanical ventilators arose. Numerous experimental therapeutics were tried, but none were curative. Health-care providers were overwhelmed, overworked, and exhausted, as they moved quickly from patient to patient after changing all hospital PPE between each visit. Fearful for their own health and that of their families, many self-isolated when finally returning home after long shifts. Some became ill and could not return to work, further depleting health-care resources.

April to May was the peak of the first wave. Colorado's economy had gone bust by the end of April. In less than a month, Colorado's unemployment rate skyrocketed from a pre-pandemic level of about 2.5 percent to about 12.2 percent in April—the greatest hit since the Great Depression. Metro Denver hit 12.7 percent, while some of the mountain communities saw rates of well over 20 percent. The working classes were especially hard hit, with 60 percent of all unemployment claims being filed by those making $20,000 a year or less. By December, 25 percent of the state's active workforce

Over Easter weekend, April 11–12, Denver street artist Austin Zucchini-Fowler painted this iconic mural in an alley at East Colfax Avenue and Williams Street as a public art tribute to all frontline health workers. BILL HANSEN COLLECTION

had filed for some form of unemployment benefits and the unemployment rate still hovered at about 6.4 percent.

Lifelines were cast too short, and safety nets unraveled. The state's unemployment office was soon overwhelmed as desperate and frustrated jobless applicants inundated an antiquated computer system and call system, hoping and praying that benefits would soon arrive. With such crushing numbers, the head of the Colorado Department of Labor and Employment later admitted, "Yes, we've learned our systems are put together with duct tape and chicken wire," and announced a new system for 2021.

Those who remained employed were encouraged to work from home via telecommunication and the internet. Most small businesses and mom-and-pop brick-and-mortar retailers were devastated. They legitimately complained that big-box stores like Walmart and Target were still flourishing as "grocery stores" yet could sell all manner of retail goods, while small businesses offering just retail goods were biting the dust. Some retailers permanently closed their doors, while others went online to scrape by.

Attempts at website marketing and e-commerce had to somehow compete with big-time online retailers such as Amazon, which prospered as one of the few businesses offering employment opportunities at expanded distribution centers. Delivery services for all kinds of goods, from food to parcels of consumer products purchased over the internet, provided other scarce job openings. Big business was thriving while small businesses were going bust.

Those people not desperately struggling to survive often became resigned to a new "normal." There were few places to go and little to do. Staying in replaced going out. Many learned to work remotely from home. With kids not physically in school, families united around the kitchen table with homework and home-cooked meals, studied, watched TV, played computer games, and reconnected with friends and family by FaceTime, Skype, or Zoom instead of less personal texting, emailing, or social media. Those venturing out for groceries or supplies found streets, arterials, and even expressways empty of traffic. As silence descended on the city, one Denver neighborhood blogger wrote, "Denver is now what it was like 40 years ago: no traffic, no pollution, no noise. You can actually hear the birds sing."

For some Coloradans, anger, fear, fatigue, and frustration soon boiled over after a month of shutdown. Many believed the arbitrary restrictions were destroying their livelihoods and the economy. On April 19, a cavalcade of vehicles, together with one horse-riding cowboy, surrounded the state capitol in a protest dubbed "Operation Gridlock." Hundreds also gathered on the capitol grounds, maskless and tightly packed, waving flags and brandishing signs proclaiming "Everything We Do Is Essential!," "Lay Off Polis!," "Freedom over Fear!," "Quarantine = Tyranny, Constitution = Liberty!," and "Your Health Does Not Supersede My Rights!"

Denver officials called the protest "wholly irresponsible." Other citizens publicly objected in print. In a letter to the editor of the *Denver Post* on April 21, one disgruntled Coloradan argued against the "doomsday politicians and pundits" and the "siege mentality of cowering at home." The writer urged, "Get out, get it, get over it, get a life, and let's get back to work."

GRADUAL REOPENING AND "SAFER AT HOME"

With cases, hospitalizations, and deaths trending downward slightly, Governor Polis announced a gradual and phased reopening called "Safer at Home," to begin April 26. He emphasized that it was "a marathon, not a sprint" and "we are going to have to live with coronavirus for a while."

Some previously closed shops and businesses could reopen at limited capacities and with social distancing and masking. Opening personal services allowed hair to once again be cut, dyed, and braided; teeth cleaned, filled, or pulled; bunionectomies performed; and even shaggy dogs groomed. Bars, nightclubs, gyms, theaters, libraries, and playgrounds remained closed. With schools emptied and most childcare services shuttered, working parents, and especially single mothers, faced an overwhelming dilemma of struggling to somehow survive with children at home and work at whatever jobs they had. Many single moms put their children first and dropped out of the workforce altogether, artificially lowering the unemployment rate.

Local counties and communities could mandate stricter but not more lenient measures. Many counties remained locked down under the "Stay at Home" mandate, including Denver, Jefferson, Broomfield, Boulder, Adams, Arapahoe, and Pitkin.

As Colorado slowly reopened, extraordinary measures were taken by many businesses trying to comply. Stores offered curbside pickup, and home deliveries for the elderly and infirm or anyone asking for it. Dirty paper bills and a coin shortage resulted in most businesses demanding cashless, touch-free payments. With closed bank lobbies, lines of vehicles snaked around the blocks. Grocery stores sported warning signs and placards, and decals on the floor and outside at six-foot intervals. Masked workers counted customers coming and going to limit capacity, tried to enforce masking rules, and regularly sanitized shopping carts. Plexiglas screens were erected around masked and gloved cashiers, aisles were made one-way to control traffic, and special hours were implemented.

Even with some retail stores reopening, would-be shoppers remained concerned about venturing out. Of the 175 retailers in Cherry Creek North, Denver's densest business district, only 20 percent reopened on May 10. Despite balloons, sale signs, and inviting smiles through masked faces, few customers responded. Park Meadows in Douglas County, the state's largest shopping mall, reopened on May 24 in fits and starts but remained only 10 percent operational until August.

Before Memorial Day, hurting restaurants were finally reopened for indoor dining with strict rules. At limited capacity, spontaneous dining was often thwarted by necessary reservations or restricted hours. Masked customers were often met by masked and gloved hostesses pointing guns—infrared thermometer guns—to screen for fevers. Small parties were seated at alternating or distantly spaced tables. Menu items were restricted to keep food fresh and usually offered digitally with QR codes for cellphones, posted on boards, or provided on sanitized plastic or throwaway paper menus. Communal tables, salad bars, and buffets were banned. There was no more "Pass the salt, please," as single-serve condiments were provided only on request. As groups departed, all tables, counters, and surfaces were religiously sanitized, and servers had to vigorously wash their hands at regular intervals.

Restaurant owner Christine Parisi told the *Denver Post* on May 27: "Rules, masks, side eyes from other customers watching everyone's moves, constant sanitizing sessions . . . all make for a tangled web of very uncomfortable scenarios for a small business and my staff."

Many people still remained reluctant to venture out. Dozens of restaurants had already closed during the two-month takeout and delivery restrictions, and, with limited capacities to dwindling crowds, more shut down. After twenty-three years in business as a famed farm-to-table eatery, Vesta, in Denver's previously popular Blake Street dining district, closed in July. Owner Josh Wolken told the *Denver Post*, "There's no office traffic, no business travel, no tourism and no hotels and most of the local clientele unfortunately seem to be avoiding downtown."

The restaurant closures confirmed the fears of many that Denver's downtown core was decaying and becoming a busted and deserted ghost town. Some compared it to the 1950s, when the automobile had freed workers to escape to the suburbs. The pandemic and forced reliance on telecommunication and the internet in business, retail, education, and entertainment created a similar phenomenon. Small businesses soon sprouted "Closed" signs on their permanently padlocked doors and posted "Going Out of Business" sales as lights were turned off and windows boarded up. Office workers and inner-city residents were again fleeing to the suburbs or mountains to work remotely and to escape the high rents, density, violence, crime, boarded-up buildings, the homeless, and the noise, traffic, and parking problems. With the closure of bars, restaurants, entertainment venues, and retail stores that had lured them in the first place, Denver's previously booming urban center had lost its allure.

Valid concerns remained in an increasingly socially distant society. Joseph M. Lemma of Parker eloquently expressed this view in a letter to the editor of the *Denver Post* on May 29. His wife had not been able to accompany their young child to the dentist, he couldn't be with his wife when she endured a painful orthopedic injection, and he still couldn't visit his ninety-two-year-old father in a senior care facility. "In our Grail-like quest to save human lives, we have completely forgotten about humanity. We have forgotten what makes human life important. Yes, wear a mask. Yes, keep social distancing. But *please* let us not forget that it is human contact that makes us human."

Protest and Unrest

Even with the gradual reopening, most restaurants remained shuttered to all but curbside service and home delivery. Employing almost 300,000 workers, restaurants made up 10 percent of the state's workforce. During the first month of the state's closure order, 37 percent of the claims for jobless benefits were in the restaurant industry. Most restaurants were small businesses getting by on slim profit margins, and many of the workers were young, women, and minorities, already barely enduring day by day.

Perhaps nothing better illustrated the political, economic, and social chasm that had befallen Colorado than the so-called Spring Restaurant Rebellion of 2020. It also garnered national attention in its defiance over compliance. While there were others, one stood out.

In early May, Shooters Grill, a gun-themed restaurant aptly located in Rifle, brazenly defied the "Safer at Home" policies by opening for indoor dining despite cease-and-desist orders issued by Garfield County. The popular eatery on the Western Slope was already renowned for its well-armed staff serving hot food with holstered heat and inviting customers to similarly display their "open carry" firearms. Its website boasted upholding "personal freedom, citizen's rights, and the Constitution of the United States."

The owner, Lauren Boebert, soon garnered national attention by using the closure as a launchpad to make a rookie run for Congress in the Third Congressional District, covering over one-third of Colorado's landmass and stretching from Grand Junction to Pueblo, including mostly rural and western Colorado. "I support opening all businesses. Our response has been ridiculous. The cure is worse than the disease itself." The diminutive neophyte politician and gun-toting millennial mother surprisingly beat the incumbent Republican Scott Tipton in the primaries and went on the road on her "Freedom Cruise Campaign" at numerous large flag-waving rallies in small towns across the district. Preceded by a heavy metal rendition of "The Star-Spangled Banner," Boebert used a bullhorn to attack the media, science, and public health officials, and urged the recall of the governor and the support of President Donald Trump. "Not wearing a mask is patriotic!" she exclaimed. Boebert easily won the November election. Colorado was deeply divided.

Just as Colorado was trying to slowly reopen, events in Minnesota added to the chaos and divisiveness. George Floyd, an unarmed Black man, was killed by Minneapolis police during an arrest for passing a $20 counterfeit bill. On May 28, thousands poured into the streets of downtown Denver around the capitol and Civic Center Park, locking arms and carrying signs protesting "No Justice, No Peace!" and "Respect Our Existence or Expect Our Resistance" under the general rallying banner of "Black Lives Matter!"

Police responded in bulletproof vests and riot gear, filling the air with teargas, pepper spray, flash bangs, and rubber bullets as water bottles and rocks were hurled at them, barricades were upended, and dumpsters set afire. Four days of protests and riots ensued. A curfew was largely ignored. During the day, peaceful Black and white sign-carrying marchers continued protesting. As dark fell, young, often white, anarchists rioted, spread graffiti, vandalized, and looted late into the evening, effectively drowning out and hijacking the underlying message of the protesters. Destruction of both government and private businesses extended down the 16th Street Mall, Broadway, and East Colfax.

By early June, the violent protests largely settled down in Denver, with many businesses and government buildings damaged and boarded up. Other protests had occurred statewide, some small and some large, blocking expressways and downtown business districts. Colorado, like the rest of the country, was forced to confront pent-up frustration over racial inequality.

A grim demographic theme was highlighted during the 2020 COVID-19 pandemic in Colorado. Black people and Latinos made up much of the "essential" state workforce keeping the barebones economy running. They worked for low wages in close-quarter jobs in food processing plants, construction sites, road crews, food preparation, grocery stores, warehouses, and hospitals trying to eke out a living. Many others were laid off from jobs in hotels and motels, restaurants and bars, airlines, office buildings, schools, and other service industries. They tended to have larger families in overcrowded households in densely populated neighborhoods, be reliant on public transportation, and often have preexisting conditions but a lack of health insurance or trust in the medical profession. Many were disproportionately incarcerated in overcrowded correctional facilities, where numerous outbreaks occurred. Few had the luxury to work from home with fancy high-tech computers or adapt to online schooling. Housing, food, and medical insecurity became more apparent during the pandemic. The rich seemed to be getting richer, the poor poorer, and the economic, social, and racial gap widened.

Black people made up almost 6.5 percent of the coronavirus deaths and 10 percent of the hospitalizations, despite being only 4 percent of Colorado's population. Hispanics similarly showed a disproportionate number of cases, hospitalizations, and deaths. Governor Polis declared this disparity a "public health crisis" and a "result of the long tail of systemic racism." On August 27, the governor signed an executive order on "Equality, Diversity, and Inclusion." Colorado still had a long way to go to assure racial and social equality among its diverse population.

THE SECOND AND THIRD WAVES

A second wave hit Colorado in mid-June to early July, due to pandemic fatigue and Memorial Day and July Fourth celebrations. Young people socialized, partied, protested, and began playing contact sports. Testing increased. The second wave primarily infected healthy youths, who endured mostly minor illnesses with just a slight surge in hospitalizations and deaths. It was a mere blip compared to the first wave. By July 4, the death toll had only increased to a little over 1,500.

Denver and many of the surrounding counties had imposed mandatory masking on May 1. Governor Polis urged masking but was hesitant to impose a statewide mandate. By July 10, half of Colorado had face-covering orders. Governor Polis desperately urged "Wear a damn mask!" When Tri-County public health officials ordered universal masking for Adams, Arapaho, and Douglas Counties, Douglas County threatened to withdraw from the pact because there was no statewide requirement. On July 16, the governor relented and issued an executive order requiring masks, stating, "Look, in Colorado, it's no shirt, no shoes, no mask, no service. Very simple."

Still, confusion reigned as to when and where masking was required, what types were most effective, how to minimize the inconvenience, and how they were to be worn. Some complained that masks fogged up glasses, muffled speech, hid facial expressions, and diminished breathing. In the November 1 *Denver Post*, one comment offered more lighthearted reasons for facial coverings: they could be made fashion statements, were warm in winter, and you could talk to yourself without anyone knowing, avoid shaving, and save money on mouthwash. Misuse was common. Some wore them only as chinstraps or handkerchiefs around their neck, while many more became "nosers" for covering their mouth only. Some derided them as "face diapers."

Compliance varied from county to county and among age, sex, cultural, and sociopolitical groups. As late as November, a grocery store worker in Montrose complained that there was only about 50 percent compliance, with the others claiming some "phony medical excuse." In early December, Dr. Kurt Papenfus, the only ER physician in tiny Cheyenne Wells by the Kansas border, who had just recently recovered from a prolonged bout of COVID, frustratedly told Colorado Public Radio, "The western prairie isn't mask country. People don't wear masks out there. Bank robbers wear masks out there." In other parts of the state, those who wore masks were contemptuously referred to as "maskers" or "one of those." Masking became a flashpoint for many with dirty looks, derogatory words, and hostile finger gestures.

Masking had unfortunately become a political issue, locally and nationally. From the outset, Weld County, despite one of the highest case counts and death rates in the state, defied the governor's mask mandates. On April 22, Dr. Mark Wallace, director of Weld County's Department of Public Health for twenty years, had warned, "I have serious heartburn looking at our data in Weld County." On April 27, the Weld County Commissioners ignored his advice and the governor's statewide public health orders and released a set of guidelines allowing virtually all businesses to reopen whenever they chose to and allowing most gatherings. Dr. Wallace joined the growing number of beleaguered, overworked, underpaid, and unappreciated public health officials in the state and resigned two weeks later.

When the state's masking order went into effect in July, Weld County sheriffs refused to enforce it. On July 26, one of the county commissioners stated: "We believe in our citizens' right to make that determination."

When the third wave hit in November, Weld County had only three ICU beds left and no other hospital beds available as its infection rates, hospital rates, and deaths soared and eclipsed those of all the surrounding counties. The state ordered it into a "red" "Stay at Home" category of restrictions, the same as all of its neighboring and nearby counties. The Weld County Commissioners again refused and deferred to its individual citizens and businesses to "take individual responsibility and make their own decisions to protect themselves, their family, their community and their businesses." When the commissioners downplayed its hospital's woes because nearby Longmont still had sufficient bed capacity in its two large hospitals, Longmont's mayor threatened an ordinance banning any admission to its hospitals of any resident from a county that was not enforcing state public health orders, especially those from Weld.

Over Thanksgiving weekend, restaurants and bars that relaxed their vigil due to lack of county enforcement were initially warned, and one liquor license was suspended by state officials. In response, one Weld County commissioner posted on Facebook that businesses should "do what you choose is right." Weld County was not going to intervene.

STAY AT HOME FOR THE HOLIDAYS

Fear of a winter surge grew as more people headed indoors for large family gatherings over the upcoming holidays and public fatigue had reached its limits. By Halloween, fears were real as trick-or-treaters were told to stay home as the scary third wave began. In early November, Denver and over twenty counties, mostly along the Front Range, went "red" and closed up, with cases tripling and hospitals filling up and quickly and exponentially surpassing the April records. Restaurants were again closed to indoors dining, further challenging the entire already struggling industry.

Counties had to report their data to the state and then negotiate which level of restrictions they would fall into. Again, health officials came under attack. As Leon Kelly, the El Paso Public Coroner, complained on December 1, "Somehow you've trusted me for more than a decade to offer you the truth about why people are dying and now suddenly, me, the hospitals, the public health officials are all of us in cahoots and lying to you about this."

Thanksgiving proved a major benchmark. On November 24, just after cellphones blared an emergency "Red Alert" in Denver, Governor Polis held a news conference reporting that there had been almost 2,800 dead in the state, over 230,000 infected, and about 13,000 hospitalized since March. One in forty-one Coloradans were now actively infected and contagious. With these grim statistics, Polis urged Coloradans to cancel Thanksgiving plans with anyone outside their immediate households.

On the Western Slope, pistol-packing Congresswoman-Elect Boebert expressed moral outrage over what many also believed: "No government has the right to tell anyone that they can't celebrate Thanksgiving." Denver's Mayor Hancock disagreed, texting "We need everyone to stay home—Pass the Potatoes, not COVID!" He then quietly flew off to spend Thanksgiving with his family in Mississippi, drawing national scorn for his hypocrisy. Despite a public apology, Hancock was demonized for not leading by example. In a further twist of events, two days after Thanksgiving and after heeding his own advice, Governor Polis and First Gentleman Martin Reiss both tested positive and, while Polis quarantined, Reiss was hospitalized. "No family is immune to the virus," the governor emphasized.

Colorado had been below all of the national averages for similar-sized states through the summer, then surged well past them in the late fall. It then somehow avoided the post-Thanksgiving surge and fell back below the national average in December. Denver, like most of the Front Range urban areas that had gone to level red and shut down, had peaked in early November and then fallen by November 20. However, Colorado's rural areas fared worse and continued to surge into December but began slightly falling off by December 5. No other states had seen this unique phenomenon.

By mid-December, Colorado approached 4,000 COVID-related deaths, with almost a thousand from mid-November to early December. Pueblo, with one of the worst death rates in the state, deployed refrigerated semitrailers as makeshift morgues for the upcoming wave of mortality. Some hospitals double-bunked infected patients to make more room.

New Year's Eve 2020 finally brought joyous holiday news, as Governor Polis had announced that Denver and surrounding communities could stumble out of the "red" shutdown and open up into the less-restrictive "orange" the first week of January.

Salvation was already under way. The first vaccines arrived in Colorado on December 15 and the first Coloradan vaccinated was Kevin Londrigan, a respiratory therapist at UCHealth Medical Center of the Rockies in

Loveland. Health-care providers and at-risk residents of nursing homes were to be the first groups inoculated.

Despite such much-needed holiday hope for the new year, Colorado had approached nearly 5,000 deaths by year's end, when the national fatalities passed 500,000. As vaccines were hastily rolled out in early 2021, Colorado began cautiously loosening more restrictions. By mid-March, the first anniversary of the pandemic in Colorado, there had been almost 450,000 cases reported and over 6,000 dead from COVID. Colorado's experience would be fertile autopsy work for medical historians dissecting the 2020 pandemic to evaluate the Centennial State's preventive approaches.

Boom and Bust 2020

Colorado's previously booming industries were all impacted by the 2020 bust. Some fared better than others. Many seemingly went bust, confronting a long road to recovery with likely long-term changes. Others that seemed to have hit a plateau suddenly boomed again. Most struggled to reinvent themselves in a new world "normal" with hopes of continued prosperity in new boom times to come.

On November 12, 2020, Colorado Secretary of State Jena Marie Griswold best summed up Colorado's faith in the future: "Colorado's diverse economy has proven resilient in the past and we are positioned to recover faster than other states, provided that we properly manage the COVID-19 pandemic." Still, economists at the University of Colorado more cautiously predicted that it would likely be 2023 before employment counts recovered and a potentially robust economy might once again be realized.

Agriculture—Where's the Beef?

Colorado's beef industry had seen booming times but in 2020 was suddenly confronted with a self-created vulnerability. Meatpacking plants had over-consolidated and monopolized 80 percent of the industry, creating a huge potential bottleneck in the distribution chain if production was disrupted. It soon was.

The JBS USA meatpacking plant in Greeley, one of the biggest in the country, was the largest employer in Weld County. It saw one of Colorado's earliest, severest, and most deadly outbreaks. Working shoulder to shoulder and elbow to elbow in workstations along production lines, the packed packers saw 292 workers infected and over a dozen hospitalized through early

April. Some soon died. Saul Sanchez, at seventy-eight and who had worked there for decades, succumbed on April 7. The plant shut down on April 14 to put up barriers between workstations, clean and sanitize the facility, add a new ventilation system and UV lights, and stagger shifts before reopening on April 24 at 60 percent capacity. Many still called in sick out of fear, and the union still complained. Eventually, seven died by mid-May, the largest death toll of any meatpacking facility in the country. OSHA citations were issued, but a second outbreak in late November again slowed production.

Similar outbreaks occurred at Leprino Foods in Fort Morgan and Greeley and at the Cargill meatpacking plant in Fort Morgan, where sixty-eight cases and three deaths had occurred by late March. Both giants curtailed production.

The disruption caused economic disaster spiraling up and down the supply chain. Cattle ranchers faced ruin as feed lots quickly overfilled with fattened cattle awaiting processing. Costs soared and prices for calves and beef bulls plummeted. Semitrailers filled with cattle traversed the state searching for processing plants. An article in the May 10 *Denver Post* quoted Keith Belk, the head of the Department of Animal Services at CSU: "I don't see them coming back to full production for a long time. . . . When you have a supply chain shock like this, its going to have a big impact. People in the industry are saying the last time there was anything like this was World War II."

On the other end of the food chain, over half the sales had been to restaurants, hotels, caterers, and schools, all of which had been closed. Grocery stores had typically sold the other half but overnight shot up to 90 percent of the demand as Coloradans ate at home. Many meat products soon sold out, prices rose, and limits were placed on how much meat shoppers could purchase. None of the increased prices made it back to the ranchers.

The Greeley Stampede never opened that summer. The Colorado State Fair, usually drawing over 450,000 in late August, offered no concerts, rodeos, and carnivals but a small smattering of Junior 4-Hers still competed without spectators as they proudly displayed their cows, goats, sheep, and pigs. Colorado's National Western Stock Show canceled its 2021 event for the first time since 1922, when it had been upended due to an outbreak of hoof-and-mouth disease.

Restaurant Survival and Revival

Throughout the pandemic, restaurants remained the hardest-hit businesses in the state and a leading indicator of the state of the economy. Federal and state bailout money had long been exhausted. There were ever-changing restrictions transitioning back and forth from takeout and delivery, reopening at 50 percent capacity and then 25 percent capacity, and banning indoor versus outdoor dining, with tweaks in hours and "last calls." Eateries were hemorrhaging funds as expenses for staffing, food products, and customer delivery services skyrocketed.

Restaurant remodeling was a constant struggle. During the warm spring, summer, and autumn months, restaurants throughout the state tried desperately to overcome indoor restrictions and to increase their capacity for "dining out"—literally. Many cities and resorts encouraged alfresco dining with permits to expand patios and extend tented seating into parking lots and adjacent sidewalks. Denver approved over 250 such applications by mid-July, with the average expansion costing over $18,000. Some streets around Larimer Square, the Denver Pavilions, and parts of Capitol Hill were cordoned off to vehicle traffic to accommodate increased pedestrian usage and outdoor open-air dining.

As cool weather set in, intrepid and innovative restaurateurs across the state added even more costly changes—glassed-in greenhouses, pavilions, domes, igloos, gazebos, cabanas, and even villages of $4,000 yurts for single parties of six to eight. Most were heated by electric fireplaces, stoves, and oscillating space heaters, with exhaust fans to avoid carbon monoxide poisonings. Furnishings included electric lights or lanterns, area rugs, call buttons, and plenty of warm blankets. After each group left, the entire compartment had to be totally cleaned and sanitized.

High-end dining trailers were introduced in Fort Collins. In Mountain Village near Telluride, refurbished colorful old gondola cars created twenty cabins for winter dining. A converted and heated vintage bus was added to Olde Town Arvada. Anything was tried to keep the industry alive. When indoor dining was again banned, restaurateurs' pricy efforts were again frustrated as many such added outdoor enclosures were cited as not being truly open-air dining.

A lack of full consumer confidence thwarted recovery. Many restaurants closed. Ripples swept down the supply chains like a domino effect of economic ruin to small farms, bakeries, butchers, winemakers, florists, linen companies, delivery services to restaurants, and others.

Denver's usually vibrant Larimer Square dining district lay empty and abandoned on a warm April afternoon, as the restaurants were shut down and Denver's downtown became hauntingly quiet and potentially doomed to ghost town status. By the December holidays, Larimer Square was resurrected as the street was closed off and restaurants reopened with large tents and outside seating to expensively expand their capacity in the face of ongoing restrictions. BILL HANSEN COLLECTION

Entertainment—Lights Dimmed, Curtains Closed, and No More Showtime!

From the Gilded Age on, the "Queen City of the Plains" had become a mecca for live music and entertainment. Virtually everything was canceled with the onset of the pandemic. Through July 31 alone, Denver's creative industries lost 29,848 jobs and $1.4 billion. The music industry alone in Colorado suffered 8,327 lost musicians, sound and light technicians, and stagehands at a loss of almost $345 million during the same time frame. The Denver Center for the Performing Arts postponed all performances indefinitely, with the loss of the ever-popular *Lion King* and *Book of Mormon*, and the long-awaited *Hamilton* at the Buell Theatre. *Tosca* never played at the Ellie Caulkins Opera House. Concerts by Journey and the Pretenders were lost at the Pepsi Center, while Cirque du Soleil's *Volta* in the big top never opened. Red Rocks was roped off and its usual 150 concerts per year were scrapped except for a single concert by the Denver Symphony Orchestra to a sold-out "crowd" of 250.

Denver's smaller local music scene also went silent. Popular venues such as Live at Jack's closed permanently in May, after twenty years. After being shut down for eight months, the Lion's Lair on East Colfax, the oldest concert venue in Denver, raised $16,000 on a GoFundMe campaign in December hoping to reopen. Local musicians tried to entertain their fans by going digital or livestreaming, rather than busking with tip jars on the malls. The popular indie rock band Wildermiss rented a flatbed trailer for mobile, on-demand concerts. The Sunnyside Music Festival switched from stages in a crowded park to transporting musicians through the streets in pedicabs.

Movie theaters went dark, with some, like the artsy Esquire, closing permanently and put up for sale. However, the Denver Mart Drive-in sold out on Memorial Day, as did Film on the Rocks on Colorado's largest inflatable screen in the parking lot at Red Rocks on August 13. Watching movies from the safety of one's car seemed like the 1960s again.

One enterprising group of performing artists stubbornly tried to avoid closures. When Denver initially locked up, La Bohème Gentlemen's Cabaret, located in an old building near the former Curtis Street theater district and the current Denver Center for the Performing Arts, sadly announced on its marquis "Sorry, We Are Clothed Until We Can be Unclothed." Another strip club, Shotgun Willie's, sometimes known as the "Glendale Ballet," immediately transformed itself into a "restaurant" overnight and offered drive-through food and drink service by scantily clad carhops.

When indoor dining resumed, any club with a refrigerated beer cooler, as well as a microwave, grill-top, or deep fat fryer, reopened as a "restaurant" offering "dine-in" service. None had regular cooks. Nobody came for the food. Strippers, never known for their social distancing skills nor for wearing any kind of covering anywhere, still attempted to keep the stages and poles sanitized and occasionally sported exotic masks for their erotic dances. Still, at most clubs, it was business as usual until risqué became too risky. Many were "clothed" for public health and liquor law violations.

Mainstream ballet, symphonies, and concerts tried to remain viable and visible through livestreaming their performances. Celebrating Beethoven's 250th birthday anniversary, the Colorado Symphony livestreamed his "Ode to Joy," trying to lift everyone's spirits. On Thanksgiving evening, Rocky Mountain PBS offered a free, publicly available, live televised holiday presentation by the Colorado Ballet of the annual seasonal favorite *Nutcracker*.

Gambling—Lady Luck Winces, Then Sighs in Relief

Dame Fortune shuddered on March 17 as Colorado's casinos were shuttered. Silence descended as slot machines ceased whirring and dinging and crap tables crapped out. Gilpin County's unemployment rate soared to one of the highest in the state at 23 percent. The *Wall Street Journal* reported that Gilpin County saw the greatest percentage of its economy shattered than any other county in Colorado and was one of the worst in the country. The reincarnated old mining camps again went bust and became near-deserted ghost towns.

But May 1 saw another part of the gambling industry take off with a boom! Online sports gambling launched and, like many other Colorado businesses and industries, the internet was the new vehicle of prosperity. Most Coloradans were hunkered down at home and running out of Netflix movies to watch. One problem remained, though—there were few sports to gamble on. All the major professional leagues and college sports seasons had been cut, if not suspended. Bettors were undeterred. Rousing matches of Eastern European Ping-Pong, cross-ocean Korean baseball games, and bloody UFC and MMA fighting and wrestling matches saved the day. Over $25.6 million was wagered the first month.

After twelve weeks of silence, Colorado's cavernous casinos slowly began to reopen in June, but with limited capacities. Every other "one-armed bandit" was turned back on and regularly sanitized, but limited-stakes table games remained off-limits. When gaming tables were reintroduced, only the dealers could touch the disinfected cards behind Plexiglas screens, and dice, loaded with sterilizing spray, were thrown by gamblers heavily masked to hide their glee or disappointment. By fiscal year-end in late July, revenues were down 26.5 percent from 2019 at the casinos, but continued to increase through the calendar year-end, closing the gap with 2019.

The old gold rush towns still begged for help, and Coloradans overwhelming obliged. Amendment 77 readily passed in the November elections to provide relief to the beleaguered industry by allowing each gambling town to decide for itself the games, betting limits, and hours. Black Hawk, Central City, and Cripple Creek were now going to try to compete with Las Vegas. Somewhat dubiously, Lady Luck smiled.

Transportation—Grounded and Pounded

The pandemic side-railed and grounded Colorado's previously strong transportation industry. With "Stay at Home" orders in place and the state locked down, there were few places to go and few ways to get there. People were simply afraid to travel, even as Colorado began to open up.

Commercial aviation saw the largest smackdown in its history. By early April, DIA became literally a busted ghost town as air travel was down 95 percent. Planes were parked wingtip to wingtip on the tarmac, parking lot shuttles were discontinued, security gates were clear, and trains to the terminals and concourses ran empty. Scheduled flights were canceled and airlines began laying off and furloughing their pilots, flight and gate attendants, and administrative personnel.

It took months for airlines to obtain sufficient lift to even get off the ground. By August, airline traffic out of DIA was still down 75 percent. At year's end, it was expected that DIA would still only see thirty million passengers pass through, compared to sixty-nine million the previous year. Ironically, with the loss of most international travel and DIA being in the center of transcontinental flights, at times DIA leaped from the nation's fifth-busiest airport to first or second. When DIA offered to resume its first nonstop international flight to Europe in late October, Americans were no longer welcome because of Europeans' own fears over America's terrible infection rates and highest death toll in the world.

Airlines had a difficult time luring back leery customers, fearful of flying amid the pandemic in confining closed cabins. Social distancing was impossible inside planes. Would-be fliers had no shuttles from the distant parking lots to even get to the terminal. Planes were regularly fogged with disinfectant, special HEPA filters were added, food and beverage services were discontinued, and masks were required on all flights. Masking was strictly enforced on a zero-tolerance basis to make passengers feel safe.

On December 13, national attention was given a young family from Breckenridge when United Airlines staff escorted them off an outbound flight. Despite the parents' best efforts, they could not get their fussy and crying two-year-old to wear a mask. United claimed the child "failed to comply" with the masking mandate. During the family's later press interviews, they stated that they were "traumatized," "humiliated," and "confused" and that "it was really, really weird." Some felt that Denver's airlines were not exactly helping their image of safety or welcome.

It was expected that there would be long-term consequences to commercial aviation. The extremely lucrative business traveler could now readily conduct business via Zoom and the internet and no longer had a need for face-to-face meetings. Airports like DIA might see the same decay as the inner cities as workers grow used to conducting business from home.

Public ground transportation also crashed hard. Buses and trains faced passenger limits and routes and schedules were cut back as few people wanted to travel or commute in what once was standing room only and packed shoulder to shoulder during rush hours. Downtown travel was also being reduced, and RTD soon began layoffs and braced itself for revenue shortfalls and budget limitations in a busted industry.

Elsewhere on the ground, an older and proven reliable form of transportation saw a booming resurrection. Health-minded Coloradans caused what many called a "bicycle renaissance" as bike shops quickly sold out of bicycles and could not keep up with the demand. Cars and public transportation were abandoned as a renewed cycling craze provided exercise in the fresh air and seemed safer and healthier when commuting and shopping.

Another booming business was in campers and recreation vehicles. Those venturing out were fearful of closed or unsafe motels and overcrowded campgrounds and sought to travel independently on their vacations and outings as in-state tourists. An upset tourist industry had changed transportation patterns.

Tourism and Recreation—Front Rangers to the Rescue!
As Denver closed up early, city tourism dried up overnight. Conventions were nowhere to be seen. Museums, tourist sites, and Denver's previously

vibrant restaurant, bar, music, and nightlife cratered. Downtown hotels saw occupancy dwindle, and they began shutting their doors and laying off staff. The venerable ritzy Brown Palace shut down for the first time in its 117-year history on April 17 not to reopen until June 1, with only a small fraction of its rooms booked.

Colorado Springs' five-star Broadmoor closed earlier on March 19, after cancellation of the huge 36th Annual Space Symposium, expected to bring 14,000 to the Springs and pump millions into the local economy. It would eventually reopen on June 29, with reduced bookings and a diminished staff, while offering substantial discounts.

In the mountains, Gunnison tried to replicate its success during the 1918 pandemic by ordering stricter measures than the state required. Hotels and motels closed early. Visitors and tourists were banned and told to stay out, including part-time residents having second homes. Those residents who left had to quarantine for seven days upon return. Before bars and restaurants closed, guests were carded—not to prevent underage drinking but to keep out all patrons over age sixty-five. Violators faced jail for eighteen months and a $15,000 fine. Gunnison's attempts to close down early failed to work this time. It had five deaths by April 7 and saw one of the highest infection rates in the state.

Pitkin County also saw an early and severe onslaught of COVID. As Aspen closed up, its unemployment rate shot up to 23.1 percent, the highest in the state. Summer saw a reprieve, not by out-of-staters or international travelers but by Front Range urbanites, eager to "shelter in resorts." Masks were required in the outside pedestrian malls and shopping districts and even extended to some popular hiking and cycling trails, preventing enjoyment of the fresh mountain air. By September, Aspen Lodge was doing better than the same time the year before, as Front Rangers booked last-minute occupancies in their scramble to see the foliage change.

Colorado's urban Front Rangers seemed to largely save the day to keep the Centennial State's tourist and recreation industry afloat. As isolation grew into cabin fever, many urban dwellers flocked to the mountains as "day-trippers" and "stay-cationers" to enjoy hiking, cycling, fishing, boating, rafting, hunting, and bird-watching. International tourists, who stayed longer and spent far more money, vanished. There were few foreign accents noticeable, fewer out-of-state license plates, and the usual Texas drawls and "y'alls" were nowhere to be heard.

Colorado's state and national parks saw booming times. The urban shutdown brought a flood of visitors, with campgrounds overwhelmed, parking lots filled, and illegally parked cars spilling over onto the shoulders of choked roadways. In their wake, the crowds left vandalism, graffiti, and overflowing trash as understaffed parks tried to resolve user conflicts and curb illegal campsites.

After a ten-week shutdown, Rocky Mountain National Park opened on May 27 with limited parking and timed reservations only. Some Coloradans were protective of their parks for their own use. Adding to the state's pandemic woes, Colorado saw the worst wildfires in its history, darkening the sky, jumping the Continental Divide, and closing RMNP for weeks. Smoke also descended upon the Front Range, providing another reason for urbanites to mask.

Colorado's ski areas were shut down on March 14. There would be no spring skiing. The ski industry was one of the most important economic drivers in Colorado. As it went through black diamond times in a virtual wipeout, many seasonal ski bums became real bums as they joined the cadres of the unemployed. When ski areas began to reopen around Thanksgiving, most required passes and online reservations for lifts, gondolas, and even parking areas. Masks were required over ski goggles, distancing signs were stuck in the snow by lift lines, and lift and gondola capacities were restricted. The entire Silverton Mountain could be rented out by wealthy diehard powderhounds for $9,990 per day. One study suggested that one in three Coloradans intended to sit out the ski season due to safety concerns.

To allay such concerns, Aspen attempted extreme measures. Effective December 14, visitors planning to stay overnight from outside Pitkin, Eagle, and Garfield Counties were required to fill out an online affidavit affirming that they had tested negative in the last five days before arrival or agreeing to quarantine for two weeks. A spate of cancellations due to the confusion, inconvenience, and reluctance soon made it clear that Aspen had to improve on its safety messaging efforts. It was a bust. Overall, Colorado's winter skiing season would see an almost 50 percent decline in business.

Beer Remains Liquid

There was no green craft beer served on St. Patrick's Day 2020. Sales of Colorado's famous craft beers plummeted with the closure of bars, restaurants, brewpubs, brewery taprooms, and ski resorts. While liquor stores remained open and overall alcohol sales went up, those with tightened budgets returned to budget beers such as Coors and Bud, as well as liquor and wine. The craft beer industry had thrived on customers socializing face to face and paying premium prices for their favorite local beers. Almost 70 percent of Colorado's craft breweries catered to taprooms, brewpubs, and bars.

Many breweries soon closed, including Colorado's oldest, Boulder Beer, as well as C.B. & Potts Restaurant and Brewery in Fort Collins. Some breweries diversified by selling hard seltzer and even nonalcoholic beer. Odell Brewing began selling canned wine.

Many brewers soon turned to packaging beer-to-go, delivered on-site in sealed containers. Online curbside libations were generally sold in "crowlers," thirty-two-ounce large aluminum cans, tediously filled from the tap and then sealed airtight for early home consumption. Unfortunately, the pandemic had also created a "candemic"—a nationwide shortage of aluminum cans and canning supplies. Mobile canning companies plied the rounds, keeping many smaller breweries alive. Some larger craft brewers purchased their own canning equipment to package and sell their regular twelve-ounce six-packs with distinctive colorful labels.

After restaurants were able to open up, brewpubs and taprooms soon followed, so long as food appeared on the same bill. Bars eventually opened their doors to an eager public, anxious to get out of the house to party and socialize. Governor Polis minced no words in discouraging too much drink among the younger generation: "The state of inebriation in a public place is inconsistent with social distancing."

Despite a fiercely competitive market among craft brewers, many collaborated to promote the industry. In May, 125 brewers organized by the Colorado Brewers Guild banded together to sell Colorado Strong Pale Ale, a benefit beer where 20 percent of the sales would go to assist small businesses in the hospitality and service industries, as well as to keep some of the smaller breweries alive. Ingredients were provided free for the same recipe, but each brewery could add their own twists and unique spins. When the East Troublesome wildfire, the second worst in Colorado history, incinerating 200,000 acres, swept through Grand County late in the year, six local breweries offered East Troublesome Pale Ale, with 100 percent of the receipts going to relief efforts.

Like everything else, the Great American Beer Festival moved online, offering virtual competitions and discounts available at local breweries. As usual, Colorado's craft beers won in several categories.

Still, some good news came out in December when *Smart Asset* ranked Denver as the sixth best in the country for beer drinkers and the second highest in breweries per capita. Fort Collins, Colorado Springs, Boulder, and Loveland also all placed in the top fifty. While at least twenty breweries had closed, eight new ones were still scheduled to open in 2021. It was a sobering year, but Colorado's craft beer industry had remained liquid and afloat.

Marijuana—A Heady High in Low Times
One Colorado industry saw huge boom times during the pandemic. Following the initial scramble before dispensaries were deemed "essential," Coloradans rushed to enjoy the benefits of a Rocky Mountain high. With the state in lockdown, many spent their couch-locked days in a haze, blunting the stress, anxiety, boredom, and uncertainty of the times.

Many in the industry expected a decline in business with the loss of tourism, tightened wallets from high unemployment, and venturing out being discouraged. They were wrong. All expectations for 2020 were shattered. Buyers used their stimulus checks to stimulate demand. Edibles and smokables were grabbed up as if they were toilet paper. Prices rose as supply could not keep up with demand.

The yearly stoner's festival of April 20 was canceled but went virtual. Denver tweeted a "Stoned at Home" video playlist urging tokers to "Roll a fatty. Consume responsibly. Enjoy all afternoon." Trinidad's cross-state tourist trade flourished as it also became a haven for Front Range artists fleeing the cities and adding to the smoky haze to enhance their creative talents.

Marketing and sales were also altered by technology and automation. Weed could be purchased online and sold to-go. Self-service kiosks with electronic ordering and payment stations in dispensary lobbies sped up sales, reduced time indoors, and kept outside lines to a minimum.

When monthly numbers started rolling in, they were increasingly record-breaking. June 2020 was the first month in Colorado history to exceed $150 million in sales and grew to almost $200 million by August, with over $1 billion in revenue since the outset of the pandemic alone. By October, pot sales far exceeded all of 2019. Increased tax revenues were the only good news for many financially strapped counties and municipalities and made a small but welcome dent in the state's budget problems.

What made this heady high even more remarkable was that the industry was still deemed "illegal" by the feds and all of Colorado's dispensaries, grow farms, and the various security, cleaning, and professional services that supported them were denied federal stimulus packages, SBA loans, and other benefits. This included all of the employees and staff who were similarly disqualified from stimulus checks and the prospects of enhanced federal unemployment benefits.

Old businesses expanded operations, new businesses entered the field, and new products were introduced. In October, Governor Polis remarked that Colorado's pioneering industry still offered "strong growth potential."

DOWN TIME

Colorado has always been a land of ups and down, of booms and busts. Politicians, pundits, and business leaders continually predict that good times will keep on rolling. If they are not and times are hard, optimists switch the tune to "Good Times Are Just Around the Corner."

The latest bust, the 2020 pandemic, may end the typical boom-bust pattern. A full recovery to the previous "normal" seems unlikely as Coloradans, like other Americans, grow accustomed to working from home and reliant on the internet and telecommunications for their daily needs. Transportation, social cohesion, education, entertainment, and urban life will likely be forever transformed. Downtown office buildings now largely empty may never fill up as businesses and individuals rely on technology to work remotely and avoid expensive rents, costly parking, wasted commuter time, and the daily ritual of dressing up for work. Not only workplaces but school places may forever change as many parents, teachers, and students eventually find distance learning easier and cheaper—although at the cost of social and learning interactions as part of the previous educational experience.

For the first time, the rising generation of Coloradans will not be as well off as their parents. For the most part, they cannot afford the single-family homes that many of them grew up in. The current bust has left more Denverites as renters than homeowners for the first time. This seems unlikely to change as salaries decrease or disappear and the cost of home ownership soars.

For the next generation, many believe that booms seem less likely, or at least less promising. Others remain more hopeful. Will the shuttered small businesses put out of business by online commerce, empty tourist targets, silent stadiums, moribund live entertainment, non-congregating churches, and deserted downtowns growing into homeless encampments ever come back to robust life? Will Coloradans ever resolve their social, cultural, racial, economic, and political differences? One way or the other, the 2020 pandemic bust will be life-altering and transformative.

On the brighter side, while most of the booms discussed in this book have busted, two areas thrive: beer and pot. These tonics offer some comfort while Coloradans adjust and await the next roller-coaster ride.

Sources

Besides those books cited in the text, the authors relied upon the following key additional sources.

Abbott, Carl, Stephen J. Leonard, and Thomas J. Noel. *Colorado: A History of the Centennial State.* Fifth edition. Niwot: University Press of Colorado, 2012.

Baca, Vincent C. de, ed. *La Gente: Hispano History and Life in Colorado.* Niwot: University Press of Colorado and Colorado Historical Society, 1999.

Beaton, Gail M. *Colorado Women: A History.* Foreword by Thomas J. Noel. Boulder: University Press of Colorado, 2012.

Ellis, Anne. *The Life of an Ordinary Woman.* Introduction by Lucy Fitch Perkins. Boston: Houghton Mifflin, 1929. Reprinted in 1981, with an introduction by Elliot West, by University of Nebraska Press (Lincoln).

Escalante, Silvestre Vélez de. *The Dominguez-Escalante Journal: Their Expedition Through Colorado, Utah, Arizona, and New Mexico in 1776.* Translated by Fray Angelico Chavez. Provo, UT: Brigham Young University Press, 1976.

Fell, James Edward, Jr. *Ores to Metals: The Rocky Mountain Smelting Industry.* Lincoln: University of Nebraska Press, 1979. Reprinted in 2009, with an introduction by S. J. Leonard, by University Press of Colorado (Boulder).

Goldberg, Robert Alan. *Hooded Empire: The Ku Klux Klan in Colorado.* Urbana: University of Illinois Press, 1981.

Haywood, William Dudley. *Bill Haywood's Book: The Autobiography of William D. Haywood.* New York: International Publishers, 1929, 1969.

Hoig, Stanley Warlick. *The Sand Creek Massacre.* Norman: University of Oklahoma Press, 1958, 1961.

Hosokawa, William. *Thunder in the Rockies: The Incredible Denver Post.* New York: William Morrow, 1976.

Johnson, Nick. *Grass Roots: A History of Cannabis in the American West.* Corvallis: Oregon State University Press, 2017.

Leonard, Stephen J. "The 1918 Influenza Epidemic in Denver and Colorado." In *Essays and Monographs in Colorado History*, no. 9. Denver: Colorado State Historical Society, 1989.

————. *Trials and Triumphs: A Colorado Portrait of the Great Depression, with FSA Photographs.* Niwot: University Press of Colorado, 1993.

Leonard, Stephen J., and Thomas J. Noel. *Denver: From Mining Camp to Metropolis.* Niwot: University Press of Colorado, 1990 / 1994 paperback edition.

Lindsey, Benjamin Barr, and Harvey J. O'Higgins. *The Beast.* New York: Doubleday, Page, 1910. Reprinted in 2009, with an introduction by Stephen J. Leonard, by University Press of Colorado (Boulder).

McGovern, George S., and Leonard F. Guttridge. *The Great Coalfield War*. Boston: Houghton Mifflin, 1972. Reprinted in 1996 by University Press of Colorado (Boulder).

Noel, Thomas J. *Buildings of Colorado*. New York: Oxford University Press, 1997. Online revised 2020 edition from the Society of Architectural Historians.

Noel, Thomas J., and Debra B. Faulkner. *Mile High Tourism: Denver's Convention and Visitor History*. Denver: Visit Denver, 2010.

Noel, Thomas J., and Cathleen M. Norman. *A Pikes Peak Partnership: The Penroses and the Tutts*. Niwot: University Press of Colorado, 2000.

Noel, Thomas J., and Carol and Zuber-Mallison. *Colorado: A Historical Atlas*. Norman: University of Oklahoma Press, 2015.

Norgren, Barbara J., and Thomas J. Noel. *Denver: The City Beautiful and Its Architects*. Denver: Historic Denver, 1987 / 1993 paperback reprint.

Perkin, Robert L. *The First Hundred Years, 1859–1959: An Informal History of Denver and the Rocky Mountain News*. Foreword by Gene Fowler. Garden City, NY: Doubleday, 1959.

Philpott, William. *Vacationland: Tourist and Environment in the Colorado High Country*. Foreword by William Cronon. Seattle: University of Washington Press, 2013.

Smith, Duane Allan. *The Trail of Gold and Silver: Mining In Colorado, 1859–2009*. Foreword by Thomas J. Noel. Boulder: University Press of Colorado, 2009.

Sprague, Marshall. *Newport in the Rockies: The Life and Good Times of Colorado Springs*. Denver: Sage Books, 1961. Revised edition published in 1987 by Swallow Press (Athens, OH).

Steinel, Alvin T. *History of Agriculture in Colorado, 1858–1926*. Fort Collins, CO: State Agricultural College, 1926.

Stokowski, Patricia. *Riches and Regrets: Betting on Gambling in Two Colorado Mountain Towns*. Niwot: University Press of Colorado, 1996.

Thomas, Dave. *Of Mines and Beer: 150 Years of Brewing History in Gilpin County and Beyond*. Central City, CO: Gilpin County Historical County, 2012.

Wei, William. *Asians in Colorado: A History of Persecution and Perseverance in the Centennial State*. Seattle: University of Washington Press, 2016.

West, Elliott. *The Contested Plains: Indians, Goldseekers and the Rush to Colorado*. Topeka: University Press of Kansas, 1998 / 2000 paperback reprint.

Whiteside, Harry O. *Menace in the West: Colorado and the American Experience with Drugs*. Denver: Colorado Historical Society, 1997.

Wilkins, Tivis E. *Colorado Railroads: Chronological Development*. Boulder, CO: Pruett Publishing, 1974.

Zhu, Liping. *The Road to Chinese Exclusion: The Denver Riot, 1880 Election, and Rise of the West*. Lawrence: University Press of Kansas, 2013.

Index

A

aerospace industry, 137–38
Agnes Memorial Sanatorium, 145
agriculture. *See* farming
Alamosa Daily Courier, 187
Allen, Billy, 109
Alpine Tunnel. *See* Denver, South
    Park & Pacific Railway
    (DSP&P)
American Climatological
    Association. *See* Denison, Dr.
    Charles
American Smelting and Refining
    Co., 13, 54
Ameristar Casino Resort and
    Spa, 116
Amethyst Mine. *See* Creede,
    Nicholas C.
Amtrak, 127
Anheuser-Busch brewery, 166, 176
Anthony, Susan B., 36, 57
Antiquities Act, 1906, 155, 156
Anti-Saloon League, 173
Antonito (CO), 200
Any Which Way You Can (film), 168
Arapahoe Park (racetrack), 112
Argo Smelter. *See* Hill, Nathaniel
    P.
Arizona, and marijuana, 198

Arkansas River, viii
Arkansas Valley, cantaloupes in, 71
Arnett, Anthony, 14
Arthur, Pres. Chester, 35
Aspen (CO), 38–39, 41, 159–60
    impact of pandemic on, 228
    Panic of 1893 in, 48
    Wheeler Opera House in, 83
Aspen Mountain, 159–60
Astor, Mrs. John Jacob, 83
Atchison, Topeka & Santa Fe
    Railroad, 127
Auraria Higher Education Center,
    169, 171
Aurora (CO), 196, 200–201
automobile tourism, 128–34
aviation, development of, 134–37

B

*Baby Doe Tabor: The Madwoman in
    the Cabin* (Temple), 50
Baca, Moses, 189
Baker, Charles, 41
Bancroft, Caroline, 60
Bancroft, Dr. Frederick J., 142
Basie, Count, 152
Bass, Loisa, 97
Bates, Mayor Joseph E., 163,
    166, 176

235

Beaumont Hotel, 83
Belk, Keith, 220
Belmont Lode. *See* silver mining
Berke, Steve, 202
Bernhardt, Sarah, 83
bicycles, 57, 127–28
Bierstadt, Albert, 145
Bigelow, Mary, 17
bingo, popularity of, 112
Bird, Lady Isabella, 27, 142
Black Canyon of the Gunnison
    National Park, 155
Black Hawk (CO), 11
    gambling in, 113, 115–17,
    118, 225
Bland-Allison Act, 24, 45
Boebert, Lauren, 214, 218
Boettcher, Charles, 36, 71–73, 74,
    75–76, 77
Boettcher, Claude, 73, 76
    and Coal War, 77–78
Boettcher, Fannie, 73
Boettcher, Frederick, 71
Boettcher, Herman, 71
Boggs Act, 1952, 191
Boulderado Hotel, 83
Boulder Beer, 175, 229
Boulder Brewing Company, 175
Boulder (CO)
    marijuana in, 192, 196
    mining camps in county, 14
    1918 pandemic in, 90, 91
    Boulder Daily Camera, on
        tuberculosis, 142
Bowles, Samuel, 147

Breckenridge (CO), 17–19, 126
Breckinridge, John C., 17
Breed. Abel, 29, 30
breweries, 161–81
    craft beer in, 174–79
    impact of pandemic on, 228–30
Broadmoor Casino, 104
Broadmoor Resort and Hotel, 83,
    104, 227
Broomfield (CO), 163
    See also Zang, Philip
Brown, Aunt Clara, 12–13
Brown, George, 12
Brown, James, 60, 61
Brown, Margaret "Molly,"
    60–61, 131
Brown Palace (hotel), 76, 83,
    150, 173
Brown's Saloon, 101–2
Brunot Treaty. *See* Utes
Brunton, David W., 128
Bryan, William Jennings, 86
Budweiser Brewery, 161
Buena Vista (CO), 46
Burlington Northern Santa
    Fe, 127
Busch Stadium, 168
Byers, Elizabeth, 62
Byers, William, 62, 70, 122

C
Calamity Jane, 42
Caldwell, Daniel, 197
Caldwell, Samuel, 189, 190
California

gold rush in, 1, 2
medical marijuana in, 195
California Gulch camp, 16–17
California Zephyr, 127
Camp Funston. *See* Influenza
Pandemic, 1918
Camp Hale, 159
Camp Nizhoni. *See* Lincoln Hills
cannabis. *See* marijuana industry
Cannary, Martha Jane, 42
Capitol Life Insurance Co. *See*
Boettcher, Charles
Cargil meatpacking plant, 220
Caribou (CO), 28–30
Caribou Mine. *See* Breed, Abel
Carlson, John A., 181
Carnegie, Andrew, 64
Carnegie Foundation, 64
"Casey's Table d'Hote" (poem), 14
casinos, 224–25
Cassady, Neal, 192
C.B. & Potts Restaurant and
Brewery, 229
Centennial Racetrack, 111–12
Central City (CO), 11, 29
breweries in, 164
gambling in, 110–11, 113, 115,
117, 118, 225
opera house in, 83
Central City Colorado Times, on
Golden (CO), 123
Central Overland California
& Pike's Peak Express
(COC&PP), 120
Chaffee, Jerome, 29–30

Charles, Ray, 168
Chase, Edward, 61, 107–9
Chase, Florence, 109
Chavez, Daniel, 197
Cheesman, Walter, 122, 125
Cheyenne Daily Leader, 122
Cheyenne Mountain, 138
Cheyenne (WY), and Union
Pacific, 122
Chicago, Burlington & Quincy
Railroad, 127
Chicago, Rock Island & Pacific
Railroad, 127
Children's Hospital Colorado, 145
Chrysolite Mine, 38
City Hall War. *See* Smith, Jefferson
Randolph, II
Civic Center Park. *See* Speer,
Mayor Robert W.
Clayton Trust, 61
Clear Creek, 10, 24
Cleveland, Pres. Grover, 45–46, 47
Coal War of 1913-14, 79–81
See also Colorado Fuel & Iron
Co (CF&I)
Coats, Brandon, 203
Cody, William F. "Buffalo
Bill," 157
Colorado, vii–xi
aerospace industry in, 137–38
agricultural festivals in, 71
2020 and COVID-19 in, vii, x–
xi, 205–32
breweries in, 161–81, 232

cattle ranching and sheepherders in, 66–70

East Troublesome wildfire, 229

ethnic diversity in, 74–75

farming and agriculture in, 70–73

Ferdinand V. Hayden Survey of, 145

gambling in, 101–18

Gilded Age in, ix, 64, 82–87

gold in, vii–viii, 1–3, 4, 5–7, 10–11, 14–15, 16–23, 119

Hispanic exploration of, 3–4

1918 Influenza Pandemic in, 87–100

labor war in, 54

marijuana and counter culture in, ix–x, 182, 185–204, 230–31

opium in, 182–85

Panic of 1893 in, 45–48, 55, 66

Populist Party and suffragettes in, 55–59

Prohibition in, 173–74

Rocky Mountains, vii–viii

silver mining in, viii, 24–39, 41–44

smelters in, 13

sugar beets in, 73, 75, 185

tourism in, 139–60

transportation history, 119–37

tuberculosis sanitariums in, 142–45

Ute Indians in, 8–9

women's charities and clubs in, 61–65

women's suffrage in, viii–ix

See also specific locations, individuals

Colorado Ballet, 224

Colorado Brewers' Festival, 177

Colorado Central (CC), 122, 124, 125, 127, 148

Colorado Coal and Iron, 78

Colorado College, 192

Colorado Fuel and Iron Co. (CF& I), 75, 76, 78–81

Colorado History Museum, 86

Colorado Museums and Historic Sites (Danilov), 160

Colorado Parks and Wildlife, 113

Colorado Rockies (baseball team), 168

Colorado Rocky Mountains, vii–viii, 139

See also Colorado

Colorado Springs (CO), 126, 141, 171–72

COVID-19 in, vii, x–xi, 206, 227

marijuana in, 196

1918 pandemic in, 90, 91

tuberculosis in, 143, 144–45

Colorado Springs Gazette, 115, 198, 199

Colorado State Fair, 220

Colorado State University (CSU), 177–78

Colorado Strong Pale Ale, 229

Colorado Symphony, 224
Colorado Territory. *See* Colorado
Colorado Tourism Office, 140
Community College of
    Denver, 171
Conger, Sam, 28, 29
Contassot, Marie, 43
Controlled Substances Act,
    1970, 194
Coors, Adolph, 163, 167–68
Coors, Grover, 167
Coors, Herman, 167
Coors Brewery, 161, 163,
    168–69, 181
    See also Coors, Adolph
Coors Field, 168
CopperSmith's Pub and
    Brewery, 177
Coronado, Gen. Francisco Vázquez
    de, 3
Cortez (CO), marijuana in, 198
Cosmopolitan Saloon. *See*
    Telluride (CO)
Cowell, George, 15
Coxey's Army, 47
Cragmoor (sanatorium), 144–45
Cranmer, George Ernest, 158
Creede, Nicholas C., 42
Creede Candle, on masks, 96
Creede (CO), 42–44
Creede Lil, 43
Cresson Mine, 21–22, 23
Cripple Creek (CO), 19, 20–23
    gambling in, 113–14, 117,
    118, 225

gold in, 48
    See also Womack, "Crazy Bob"
Cripple Creek & Victor Mining
    Co. (CC&V), 22–23

D

D. V. Burnell Seed Co., 71
Daniels Park, 157
Danilov, Victor, 160
Davis, Richard Harding, 42
Day, Frank, 175
Deadwood (SD), gambling in, 113
Dearfield (CO). *See* Jackson,
    Oliver Toussaint
Denison, Dr. Charles, 142, 143
Denver, Boulder & Western
    Railroad, 147
Denver, Northwest & Pacific
    Railroad, 148
    See also Moffat, David
Denver, South Park & Pacific
    Railway (DSP&P), 125,
    126, 127
Denver Ale Brewing Company,
    163, 166–67
Denver and Rio Grande (D&RG)
    railroad, 41, 124, 126,
    147–48, 149
Denver Art Museum, 86
Denver Center for the Performing
    Arts, 223
Denver Children's Home, 62
Denver (CO), ix, 82–83, 230
    Cherry Creek North, 212

COVID-19 in, x, 211, 221, 222–24
Five Points neighborhood, 151
gambling saloons in, 102
Great American Beer Festival (GABF), 180, 229
Hop Alley in, 183, 184
hotels in, 150
Larimer Square, 222
marijuana in, 196, 198
1918 pandemic in, 91, 92–94, 96
Panic of 1893 in, 47–49
professional sports in, 118
2020 protests in, 214
rail hub, 124
smelting in, 13
Speer's improvements in, 84–87
tuberculosis in, 143–44
Wells Fargo stage stop in, 121
women's charities and clubs in, 61–65
Zoological Gardens, 87
See also Colorado
Denver Country Club, 84
Denver House, 102, 103
Denver International Airport, 134, 135, 136–37
impact of pandemic, 225–26
Denver Mart Drive-in, 223
Denver Municipal Airport, 135
Denver Pacific Railway (DP), 122, 123, 124, 127
Denver Polo Club, 84
Denver Post
Belk quote, 220
on marijuana, 186–87, 191
on Stapleton's airport, 135
Denver Public Library, 86
Denver Republican, on Holliday, 109
Denver & Rio Grande (D&RG), 41, 124, 126, 127, 147, 149
ski train, 158
Denver & Rio Grande Western Railway (D&RGW), 126–27
Denver Tramway Co. See Boettcher, Charles
Denver United Breweries, LTD, 166, 167
Denver U.S. Bank. See Boettcher, Charles
Denver Women's Club, 62
Dickens Opera House, 83
Dillon (CO), 126
Dixon, William Hepworth, 102
Dodge, Grenville M., 122
Dominguez, Father Francisco Atanasio, 3
Dostal Alley Brew Pub & Casino, 165
Drug Enforcement Agency (DEA), 194
Dun, Robert G., 30, 73
Dunraven, Earl of, 148
Durango (CO), 42, 126
1918 pandemic in, 97–98
Dyer, Rev. John L., 158

E
Earp, Wyatt, 109

Eastwood, Clint, 168
Eckstine, Billy, 152
Economic Geography
    (Hoffmeister), 147
Edison, Thomas Alva, 83
Eisenhower, Pres. Dwight D.,
    133, 168
Eisenhower-Johnson Memorial
    Tunnels, 132
Eli Lilly & Co., 183
Ellie Caulkins Opera House,
    86, 223
Ellington, Duke, 152
Elmwood Stock Farm, 162
Emma Mine, 39
Engineering a New Architecture
    (Robbins), 136
Esquire (theater), 223
Evangelical Lutheran
    Sanitarium, 145
Evans, John, 62, 122, 123, 125
Evans, Linda, 96
Evans, Margaret Gray, 62
Ewalt, Roger, 151

F
Fairplay (CO), 126
farming, 70–73
Fassett, Mrs. Lillian, 64
Fat Tire Amber Ale, 178
Federal Bureau of Narcotics
    (FBN), 187, 190
Fentress, Curt, 136
Ferril, Thomas Hornsby, 86
Field, Eugene, poem by, 14

Fisk, Dr. Samuel, 143
Fitch, Ann, 178
Floyd, George, 214
Ford, Bob, 42
Ford, Dr. Justina, 59
Ford, Henry, 131
Ford, Pres. Gerald, 168
Fort Collins (CO), 90, 176–77
Fort Mary B. *See* Bigelow, Mary
Fowler, Gene, 60
Foy, Eddie, 106
Fremont, John Charles, 122
Fritchle, Oliver P., 130–31

G
Gallagher, Charles, 33
Gallagher, John, 33
Gallagher, Mrs. Patrick, 33
Gallagher, Patrick, 33
gambling, 101–18
Garcia, Melitone, 189–90
Genesee Park, 157
Georgetown (CO), 24–28, 48
    railroad in, 125
Georgetown Courier, on the
    Palace, 107
Gilpin, Gov. William, 41
Gilpin County, impact of
    COVID-19 on, 114, 224
Ginsberg, Allen, 192
Glenwood Springs (CO), 71, 141
Globe and Grant smelters, 13
Globe Smelting and Refining
    Works, 53
Globeville (CO), 53–54

Glockner (sanatorium), 144
gold, viii, 1–7, 10–11, 119
   dredge boat mining, 18–19
   prices of, 21
   See also specific locations
Gold Coin Saloon, 164–65
Golden City Tannery. *See* Coors,
   Adolph
Golden (CO), railroad in, 122–23,
   124–25
Gold Hill (CO), 14–15
gold rush, 1–7, 10–11
Good, John, 161, 163, 164, 166
Goodnight, Charles, 67
Grand Junction (CO), marijuana
   in, 196
Grant, Gov. James B., 13
Grant, Pres. Ulysses S., 29
Greater Outdoors Colorado, 113
Great Sand Dunes National
   Park, 155
Great Western Sugar Beet Co.
   (GW), 73, 75, 77
Greeley, Horace, 70, 102–3
Greeley (CO), 70, 171, 196
   Greeley Stampede, 220
   High Plains Harvest
      Church, 207
   Potato Days in, 71
Gregory, John H., 11, 24
Gregory Gulch, 10
Gregory Lode, 11
Griffith, Emily, 59
Griffith, George, 25, 26
   See also Georgetown (CO)

Guggenheim, Meyer, 13, 36
Guggenheim, Simon, 13,
   64–65, 73
Gunnison (CO), 88, 227
   1918 pandemic in, 98–99
Gunter, Gov. Julius C., 90

H

Hagus, Pastor Charles H., 112
Hamlet, Naomi, 152
Hamlet, Oliver Wendell, 152
Hancock, Mayor Michael,
   205, 218
Haywood, William Dudley, 52–54
Hickenlooper, John Wright, Jr.,
   175–76, 177
High Plains Harvest Church, 207
Hill, Louise Sneed, 83, 84
Hill, Nathaniel P., 11, 13, 64–65
History of Denver (Smiley), 3
Hoffmeister, Harold Arthur, 147
Holladay, Ben, 120–21
Holliday, John "Doc," 37, 109
Holy Moses Mine. *See* Creede,
   Nicholas C.
Hook, George, 34
Horne, Lena, 152
Horsfal, David, 14
Hotel Colorado, 83
Howelson, Carl, 158
Hummer, Dave, 174–75

I

Ideal Basic Cement. *See* Boettcher,
   Charles

Iliff, Elizabeth Sarah Fraser,
    67–68, 69
Iliff, John Wesley, 66–67, 68, 69
Immaculate Conception
    Cathedral. *See* Mullen, John
    Kernan
Impressions of America (Wilde), 33,
    35–36
Indian Gaming Regulatory
    Act, 113
Indian Hot Springs, 140, 141
Influenza Pandemic, 1918, 87–100
International Church of Cannabis,
    201–2
Iverson, Kristen, 60

J
Jackson, George, 24
Jackson, Helen Hunt, 31
Jackson, Oliver Toussaint, 71
Jackson, William Henry, 145, 147
JBS USA meatpacking, 219–20
Jeppesen, Elroy Borge, 134
Jerome Hotel, 83
Jewish Consumptives' Relief
    Society, 145
Johnson, Gov. Edwin C.,
    132–33, 187
Jordan, Kim, 178, 179
Joy of Homebrewing, The
    (Papazion), 180

K
Kansas Pacific (KP), 70, 123,
    124, 127

Kansas Territory, 1
Kelly, Leon, 217
Kennedy, Blanche, 90
Kennedy, Charles, 90
Kennedy, Robert F., x
Kennedy, William, 90
Kerouac, Jack, 192
Keystone (CO), 126
Killarney Kate, 42–43
Kirin Holdings Company
    Limited, 179
Kreck, Dick, 110
Ku Klux Klan, 185

L
La Bohème Gentlemen's
    Cabaret, 223
Ladies Union Aid Society. *See*
    Byers, Elizabeth
Lady's Life in the Rocky Mountains,
    A (Bird), 27
Lakewood (CO), marijuana in, 196
Laratta, Judy, 117
Larimer, William H., 145
Larimer, William H., Jr., 6
Lathrop, Mary, 61
Leadville (CO), 16, 17, 26, 31–33,
    36–38, 41
    Boettcher in, 73
    drinking in, 172–73
    gambling in, 106
    hospital in, 62–63
    ice palace in, 49
    miners union and strike in, 38,
        49, 52

Panic of 1893 in, 48
  silver in, 126
Leadville Daily Chronicle, 37
Leavenworth and Pike's Peak
  Express, 120
Lebesch, Jeff, 178
Lee, Abe, 15, 16
Lemma, Joseph M., 213
Leprino Foods, 220
libraries, public, 63–64
Libre (commune), 193
Lincoln Hills (resort), 150–52
Lion Little World Beverages, 179
Lion's Lair, 223
Live at Jack's, 223
Londoner, Wolfe, 107
Londrigan, Kevin, 218–19
Long, Maj. Stephen, 1, 70
Longmont (CO), opera house
  in, 83
Lookout Mountain, road to, 157
Look Young. *See* Sing Lee
Los Angeles Aviation Meet, 134
  See also Paulhan, Louis
lotteries, state-run, 112–13
Loveland, William Austin
  Hamilton, 123
Lovell, Lillis, 43
Ludlow Massacre. *See* Coal War of
  1913-14
lynx, habitat of, 160
Lytle, George, 28

M
Mack, Jacob, 164, 165

Manitou Springs (CO), 141, 142
marijuana industry, ix–x, 185–204
  impact of pandemic on, 230–31
  Mexican marijuana, 185–87
Marijuana Tax Act, 1937, 187,
  189, 190
Maroney, Patrick, 180
Marshall, Corey, 171
Martin, Donna, 115
Martin, William, 28
Martin Marietta Corp., 137
Masciotra, Gus, 170–71
Masterson, William Barclay "Bat,"
  42, 109
Matchless Mine, 50
May, David, 36
McCaslin, Matthew, 14
McClurg, Virginia, 155, 157
McCourt, Elizabeth, 35
McGrath, Sister Marceline, 62–63
Meeker, Nathan, 9, 70
Melsheimer, Max, 166
Mercy Hospital, 63
Meredith, Ellis, 174
Mesa Verde National Park,
  154, 155
Metropolitan State University of
  Denver, 171
Mexican Diggings (settlement),
  3–4
Miera y Pacheco, Capt. Don
  Bernardo, 3
Mile High City. *See* Denver (CO)
Mile-High Kennel Club, 111
Mills, Enos, 156, 157

Mills, Mayor William Fitz Randolph, 90, 94
Milwaukee Brewers (team), 168
Milwaukee Brewery, 166
Miners Hotel, 14
Missouri Pacific Railroad, 127
Moffat, David, 29–30, 42, 122, 125, 148
Molloy, Lee, 202
Molly Brown: Unraveling the Myth (Iverson), 60
Molson Coors, 168, 181
Mom's Skyline Buffet, 135
Moran, Thomas, 145
Morning Star Mine. *See* Routt, Gov. John L.
Mountain Village, 221
Mount Evans, road to, 157–58
Mount of the Holy Cross (Moran painting), 145
Mount Olivet Cemetery. *See* Mullen, John Kernan
Mullen, John Kernan, 74, 76–77
My Brother's Bar, 192

N
Narcotic Control Act, 1956, 191
Nation, Carrie, 172, 173
National Fuse and Powder Company, 73
National Jewish Hospital, 145
National Labor Relations Act, 1935, 81
National Western Stock Show, 68, 220

Native Americans, and gambling, 101, 102
Neef Brothers Brewery, 166
Negro Motorist's Green Book, The, 152
Nelson, Willie, 197
New Belgium Brewing Company, 177, 178–79, 181
New Mexico
  cattle and sheep wars in, 70
  and marijuana, 198
  settlement of, 4
New York Times, on marijuana, 187
Nixon, Pres. Richard M., 21, 194
Noel, Tom, 202
NORAD, 138

O
Obama, Pres. Barack, vii, 86
Ochinee (Lone Bear), 68
Odell Brewing Company, 177
Okuda San Miguel, 202
Okuda San Miguel San, 202
Old Town Arvada, 221
On the Road (Kerouac), 192
opera houses, 83
opium, 182–85
Oro City (CO), 15, 16, 17, 31
Osgood, John C., 78, 79
Ouray (CO), 147
Oxford Hotel, 83, 150
Oxford Palace, 83

P
Packer, Alfred, 40, 41

Palace (theater), 107
Pale Horse, Pale Rider (Porter),
    95, 100
Palisade (CO)
    marijuana in, 197–98
    Peach Festival, 71
Palisade Tribune, on 1918
    pandemic, 90
Palmer, William Jackson, 78, 126,
    141, 171–72
Papazian, Charlie, 180
Papenfus, Dr. Kurt, 216
Parachute (CO), marijuana in, 198
Parisi, Christine, 212
Park Meadows (CO), shopping
    mall in, 212
Past Times and Pastimes
    (Dunraven), 148
Paulhan, Louis, 134
Peabody, Gov. James H., 54, 155
Peabody, Lucy, 155
Peña, Mayor Federico, 136, 175
Penrose, Spencer, 129
Pepsi Center, 223
Peterson, Rachel Wild, 173–74
Philip Zang & Company. *See*
    Zang, Philip
Phipps, Lawrence C., Sr., 129
Pikes Peak Hill Climb. *See*
    Penrose, Spencer
Pikes Peak Meadows
    (racetrack), 112
Pillar of Fire Church, 201
Pitkin, Gov. Frederick W., 52,
    142–43

Pitkin County, COVID-19 in, 227
Polis, Gov. Jared, 203, 205
    and COVID-19, 206, 211,
        215–16, 218, 229
    on marijuana industry, 231
Populist Party, 55–56
Porter, Katherine Anne, 95, 100
postcards, tourist, 150
Pourtales, James, 104
Progressive (gambling hall). *See*
    Chase, Edward
Prohibition Party, 173
Prowers, John Wesley, 68–69
Pueblo (CO), 81, 201
    brewery in, 170–71
    Chile and Frijoles Festival, 71
    COVID-19 in, 218
    1918 pandemic in, 91

R
Radium Hot Springs Hotel,
    140–41
railroads, 122–27
    boom of, 69
    and tourism, 145–50
ranching industry, 65–69
Reagan, Nancy, 194
Reagan, Pres. Ronald, 194
Red Rocks, 223
Red Rocks Outdoor
    Amphitheater, 157, 223
Redstone (CO). *See* Osgood, John
    C.
Reefer Madness (film), 188
Regnier, E. C., 151

Reiss, Martin, 218
restaurant industry, in
    pandemic, 221
Revett, Ben Stanley, 18
Rhymes of the Rockies. See Denver
    and Rio Grande (D&RG)
    railroad
Richardson, Albert D., 102
Ridgway (CO), 201
Rische, August, 34
Rivera, Don Juan María de, 3
Robbins, Tony, 136
Robinson, Helen Ring, 58
Rock Bottom Restaurant &
    Brewery, 175
Rockefeller, John D., Jr., 79, 81
Rocky Mountain Brewery,
    161, 164
Rocky Mountain National Park,
    139, 156, 157, 228
    Stanley Hotel, 153
Rocky Mountain News, 6, 122
    on Caribou, 28–29
    on marijuana, 187, 190
    on Palace, 107
    on 1918 pandemic, 90, 92
    on women's clubs, 61
Romer, Gov. Roy, 114, 136
Roosevelt, Pres. Theodore, 153, 155
Rossonian Hotel and Lounge, 190,
    191, 192
Routt, Gov. John L., 13, 36
Russell, William Greeneberry, 10
    and gold rush, 3, 4, 5, 6, 7, 11, 24

S

Salida (CO), 1918 pandemic in,
    96, 98
Sanchez, Saul, 220
San Juans (mountains), 41–42
San Luis (CO), 3
San Miguel. *See* Okuda San
    Miguel
Scharf, Kenny, 201
Scherer, Russell, 175
Schiffler, Mark, 175
Schmaltz, Buddy, 165
Schueler, Jacob, 163
Sedgwick (CO), marijuana in, 198
Seibert, Peter, 160
Shafroth, Gov. John F., 155
Sharpley, Dr. William H., 90,
    91–92, 94
sheepherders, 69–70
Sherman, Sen. John, 45
Sherman Silver Purchase Act, 24,
    45–46
Shooters Grill, 213–14
Shotgun Willie's, 223
silver mining, viii, 24–39, 41–44
    price of, 45–47
Silver Purchase Act, viii
*Silver Saga: The Story of Caribou,
    Colorado* (Smith), 30
Silverton (CO), 41–42
    gambling in, 101
    1918 pandemic in, 88, 97–98
Silverton Mountain, 228
Sing Lee, 183
ski industry, 158

impact of pandemic on, 228
Slanting Annie, 43
Smaldone, Clyde, 110, 111
Smiley, Jerome, 3
Smith, Duane A., 30
Smith, Jefferson Randolph, 36–37, 42, 43
Smith, Jefferson Randolph, II, 106–7, 109
Smith, Soapy, 42, 109
Smokey and the Bandit (film), 168
Smokin' Gun Apothecary, 196–97
Smuggler Mine, 39
Solly, Dr. Edwin, 142, 143
Southern Utes. *See* Utes
South Park (CO), 125–26
South Platte River, viii
Space Command Headquarters, 138
Speer, Mayor Robert W., 84–87, 88–89
Spring Restaurant Rebellion. *See* Shooters Grill
St. Anthony Hospital, 63
St. Cajetan's Church. *See* Mullen, John Kernan
St. Francis Hospital, 63
St. Joseph Hospital. *See* Mullen, John Kernan
St. Louis Cardinals, 168
St. Mary's Hospital, 63
St. Vincent Hospital, 63
stagecoaches, 120–22
Stanley, Freelan Oscar, 153, 155
Stanley Hotel, 153, 154

Stapleton, Mayor Benjamin, 135, 136
Stapleton International Airport, 135–36
State Historical Fund (SHF), 117–18
State Home for Dependent Children, 62
Stevens, William H., 31
Strater Hotel, 83
Stratton, Winfield Scott, 21
streetcars, 133
Student Army Training Corps, 89
sugar beet industry, 73, 75, 185
Sunday, Billy, 174
Sunnyside Music Festival, 223
Swank, George W., 71
Swan River Dredge No. 4, 18
Swan's Nest, 18
Swedish National Sanitarium, 145
Switzerland, international tourism in, 147
Switzerland of America (Bowles), 147
Symes, Judge J. Foster, 189

T
Tabor, Augusta, 16, 34–35, 50, 51
Tabor, Elizabeth McCourt "Baby Doe," 34, 35, 50–51
Tabor, Horace, 34–35, 50, 64–65
Tabor, Horace A. W., 16, 83
Tabor, Lillie, 50
Tabor, Maxcy, 51
Tabor, "Silver Dollar," 50

Tabor Grand Opera House, 83
Taos Lightning, 166
Tapper, Mark, 179
Telluride (CO), gambling in,
    105, 106
Templars, 173
Temple, Judy Nolte, 50–51
Tenth Mountain Division,
    159, 160
Tikas, Louis, 80
Tipton, Scott, 214
Tivoli Brewing Company, 163,
    166, 169, 171
Tivoli Club, 106–7
Tivoli-Union Brewery Company,
    161, 166
Tobin, Margaret. See Brown,
    Margaret "Molly"
tourism, 139–60
    automobile, 152–55
    health/medical, 142–45
    heritage, 160
    hot springs, 140–41
    impact of COVID-19 on,
        226–28
    Lincoln Hills, 150–52
    national and mountain parks,
        155–58
    sightseeing and train, 145–50
    skiing and winter sports, 158–60
transportation industry, impact of
    COVID-19 on, 225–26
Trinidad (CO), 230
    marijuana in, 198, 199
Truman, Pres. Harry S., vii

Tubbs, Poker Alice, 42
Twain, Mark, 1
Two Elks Lodge, 160

U
UMWA (United Mine Workers of
    America), 80, 81
Union Colony, 70, 171
    See also Greeley (CO)
Union Pacific Railroad (UP), 122,
    123, 124, 127
University of Colorado, 171
    marijuana at, 192
    student-army training corps
        at, 89
University of Colorado Health
    Sciences Center, 145
Unsinkable Molly Brown, The (play/
    movie), 60
U.S. Air Force Academy, 138
U.S. Mint, 86
Utah, and marijuana, 198
Ute City. See Aspen (CO)
Utes, 8–9, 101, 140, 160
    casinos of, 113
    treaty of, 41

V
Vail, Charles Davis, 132, 160
Vail (CO), 160
Vastine, Timberline Rose, 43
Vélez de Escalante, Father
    Silvestre, 3
Vendome Hotel, 83

Vesta (restaurant). *See* Wolken, Josh
Victor (CO), 20, 23
Viet Nam War, protests against, 192, 194

W
wagon trains, 120
Wahrer, Terry, 114
Waite, Gov. Davis H., 47, 49, 55, 107
Wallace, Dr. Mark, 216
Walnut Brewery, 175
Walsenburg World, on 1918 pandemic, 95
Walter, Lynne, 15
Walter, Martin, 170
Walter's Brewing Co., 170–71
Ware, Randolph "Stick," 174–75
Warman, Cyrus, 43–44
Warshauer Mansion. *See* Antonito (CO)
Washington State, marijuana in, 195
Weld County, COVID-19 in, 217
Western Federation of Miners (WFM), 49, 52, 54
See also Haywood, William Dudley
Western Packing Co. *See* Boettcher, Charles
West from a Car Window, The (Davis), 42
Wheeler, Jerome B., 39

Wheeler Opera House, 83
Wilde, Oscar, 33, 35–36, 172–73
Wildermiss (band), 223
Williams, Jerry, 175
Wilson, Pres. Woodrow, 81, 157
Windsor Hotel, 150
Winks Lodge, 152
Winter Park Ski Area, 158–59
Wolken, Josh, 212
Womack, "Crazy Bob," 19–20, 21
Women's Christian Temperance Union (WCTU), 173–74
Women's Literary Club. *See* Fassett, Mrs. Lillian
Wood, Alvinus B., 31
Woodmen of the World Sanatorium, 144
Working Boys' Home and School, 62
See also Byers, Elizabeth
Wynkoop Brewing Company, 175
Wyoming
cattle-sheep wars in, 70
mountain passes in, viii
women's suffrage in, 56–57

Y
Young, Richard D., 102

Z
Zang, Philip, 161–63
Zucchini-Fowler, Austin, 209
Zyback, Frank, 71

ABOUT THE AUTHORS

Thomas Jacob Noel is a Professor Emeritus of History and Director of Public History, Preservation & Colorado Studies at the University of Colorado Denver. Tom is the author or coauthor of fifty-three books. A longtime former Sunday columnist for the *Rocky Mountain News* and the *Denver Post*, he appears as "Dr. Colorado" on Channel 9's *Colorado & Company*. In 2018 he was appointed Colorado's official State Historian. Tom completed his BA at the University of Denver and his MA and PhD at CU-Boulder, where his mother (a psychiatrist) and grandmother (a teacher) also did their graduate work. Please check Tom's website, dr-colorado .com, for a full résumé and updated list of his books, tours, and talks where you are most welcome.

William J. Hansen is an attorney who, after obtaining a business degree from the University of Colorado in Boulder, graduated from the University of Colorado Law School in 1974. Bill has been extremely active in the Colorado Trial Lawyers Association and is a frequent writer and lecturer on the evolution of Colorado law. Since childhood, he has had a passion for history. After purchasing an old Victorian home in Denver's Montclair neighborhood, he researched and guided the restoration of the Molkery in Montclair Park and went on to coauthor with Professor Noel two local bestselling books for Historic Denver, Inc.: *The Montclair Neighborhood* and *The Park Hill Neighborhood*. Bill continues to collect, research, write, lecture, and provide periodic walking tours on Denver and Colorado history.